RELIGIOUS EDUCATION IN AUSTRALIAN CATHOLIC SCHOOLS

The authors offer a diverse and compelling analysis of religious education, addressing current trends and future challenges in curriculum, leadership, and pastoral practices. Teachers will find enriching ideas in Scripture, spirituality, ecology, early childhood, and social justice. Administrators will appreciate the thoughtful treatment and discussion of school families who do not attend Sunday Mass, the attrition and retention of school-level religious education leaders, and the ongoing need for enhancing Catholic identity.

RONALD NUZZI
Alliance for Catholic Education, University of Notre Dame, Sydney

The continuing role of Catholic education within secularizing, or by now laregely secularized, societies raises critical theological, political, and educational questions throughout the West. Catholic schools exist, indeed, at the very coalface of the New Evangelization. Rymarz and Belmonte's rich and wide-ranging collection of reflections on, and case-studies of, Catholic RE provision in Australia offers much for those in other contexts - myself included - to think about and learn from.

STEPHEN BULLIVANT
Professor of Theology and the Sociology of Religion, St Mary's University, UK

This book brings great insight, and opportunity for deep reflection on practice and purpose, to anyone working in the world of Catholic Religious Education.

COLIN MACLEOD

EDITED BY RICHARD RYMARZ AND ANGELO BELMONTE

RELIGIOUS EDUCATION IN AUSTRALIAN CATHOLIC SCHOOLS
Exploring the Landscape

Published in Australia by
Vaughan Publishing
32 Glenvale Crescent
Mulgrave VIC 3170
A joint imprint of BBI - The Australian Institute of
Theological Education and Garratt Publishing

Copyright © 2017 Richard Rymarz and Angelo Belmonte

All rights reserved. Except as provided by Australian copyright law, no part of this publication may be reproduced in any manner without prior permission in writing from the publisher.

Book design by Upside Creative
Edited by Greg Hill
Printed by Lightning Source

The author and publisher gratefully acknowledge the permission granted to reproduce the copyright material in this book. Every effort has been made to trace copyright holders and to obtain their permission for the use of copyright material.

The publisher apologises for any errors or omissions in the above list and would be grateful if notified of any corrections that should be incorporated in future reprints or editions of this book.

A Cataloguing-in-Publication entry is available from the National Library of Australia, www.nla.gov.au

Cover image: istock

Introduction

Angelo Belmonte and Richard Rymarz

Religious education has been a key part of the life of Catholic Schools in Australia since their inception. As we are well into the second century of this history, it is timely to reflect on our current practice and to begin to address, more explicitly, some of the issues that challenge religious educators going into the future.

The genesis of this book was in a conversation between us after many years of collaboration and writing. On this occasion, Richard mentioned that several times while at the University of Alberta, a number of Australians had approached him asking about where in North America they could encounter 'cutting edge' RE. After some reflection, his conclusion was that much of the best thinking and praxis about religious education in Catholic schools was to be found in Australia. This is not to demean the efforts of religious educators in Canada, the United States and other places. Rather it recognises the significant commitment in this country, over a considerable length of time, to provide quality religious education. In light of this a book that gathered some of the most prominent people working in religious education seemed a good way of capturing some of the commitment. It was also an opportunity to provide in one volume a type of a showcase of work done. Thus religious education in Australian Catholic schools was born!

This book then has two foci. Firstly, it presents religious education in an explicitly Australian context. It recognises that what is done in this country represents a significant and ongoing contribution that arises from a particular cultural context. The history of Catholic education in this country highlights the importance that the Australian church has given to providing a quality education that has as it foundation an explicit religious identity. In maintaining this identity religious education has a preeminent role. Think for a moment of the amount of time devoted to religious education in Australian Catholic schools. This is a marker of the quantity of effort in this endeavor. Hopefully this book highlights also the quality of some of the work. A second focus of the book is that it is on religious education in Catholic schools. Religious education in this context brings with it specific assumptions and a range of expectations. This is what gives it its particular style and emphasis. It is a reflection of the discipline as it is conveyed through the prism of Catholic beliefs, values and worldview. This is something we celebrate and it comes with recognition that the field is not static but develops in unison with the changing social context.

Even in our lifetime we can readily recall the movements in the field. Some of these changes have been structural where, for example, we witnessed the transition from religious education being taught by professed religious to lay teachers. Angelo recalls being taught in his early years through a question and answer approach by Sister Celsus. A Mercy nun dressed in a modified habit made popular following Vatican II, Sister Celsus would take students through the Green Catechism question by question with the view to successfully navigate to an external and very public examination by the diocesan school inspector. It is worth noting how prepared we were for an unexpected and unscheduled visit from Fr Delaney!

There were also changes in underlying theology and pedagogy. Richard recalls the halcyon days of experiential catechesis. Who can forget class after class entering the room and to be told time and time again that the lesson was devoted to class discussion of topics that were seen as being relevant to the development of our faith? Funny thing is he cannot remember what many of these topics were. If we now move forward to our professional lives, both of us have been heavily involved in developing religious education curriculum over several decades. These include being part of movements towards incorporated overarching guidelines to developing more content driven religious education with the aid of specially developed textbooks.

This book is a panorama of religious education in Australian Catholic schools. It seeks to be this through both a broad and narrow focus. The first part of the book looks at some key conceptual issues. The second part takes on a particular focus on the curriculum. There is no one approach to religious education in Australian Catholic schools, and in recognizing this diversity we have set out to provide a critical overview of the field.

We thank all the contributors and look forward to ongoing collaboration which has as its goal maintaining and improving the quality of religious education in Catholic schools. We are privileged to produce a book with chapters from such well credentialed figures. At the same time, we are both very aware that often the most significant voice in Catholic education is somewhat hidden. And that is the voice of the classroom RE teacher. She is the person who on a daily basis encounters students and is charged with the responsibility of delivery of religious education curriculum which in the context of Catholic schools in centred on a proclamation of the Kingdom of God and the person of Jesus Christ. Her contribution is invaluable. And it is to her that this book is dedicated.

Contents

Introduction *Angelo Belmonte and Richard Rymarz* 5

Part One - Setting the Framework

Chapter 1: A Personal, Critical Perspective on the Development of Australian Catholic School Religious Education: Where to From Here? *Graham Rossiter* 13

Chapter 2: Religious Education in a Changing Context: The Paradox of Catholic Schools *Richard Rymarz* 35

Chapter 3: Better Understanding the Context of Religious Education: The CECV Leuven Research *Paul Sharkey* 53

Chapter 4: Improving Leadership in Religious Education: Implications for Policy Reform *Michael Buchanan* .. 77

Chapter 5: Developing Religious Education Curriculum for Early Childhood in Australia *Jan Grajczonek* 99

Chapter 6: Between Desire and Reality: The Presentation of Scripture in Religious Education *Margaret Carswell* 119

Chapter 7: Missing in Theory and Praxis? – Teaching Spirituality in the Catholic Classroom and Beyond *Peter Mudge* 141

Chapter 8: Teaching Ecological Themes in Religious Education *Shane Lavery, Debra Sayce and Sandra Peterson* .. 161

Chapter 9: The Religious Education Curriculum in Australian Catholic Schools: An Overview *John McGrath* 181

Part Two: Curriculum: Overview and Focus

Chapter 10: *Curriculum Overview* The RE Curriculum in a Small Rural Diocese: Focus on Teacher Capacity and Formation *Angelo Belmonte*..................................203

Chapter 11: *Curriculum Overview* Religious Education Curriculum in Melbourne *Rina Madden* 223

Chapter 12: *Curriculum Overview* Religious Education in the Diocese of Rockhampton *Di-Anne Rowan and Gail Davis*......................................243

Chapter 13: *Curriculum Overview* 'The Truth will set you free': Religious Education in Western Australia *Chris Hackett, Debra Sayce and Diana Alteri*..........263

Chapter 14: *Curriculum Focus* Old Wine in New Wineskins? A Comparison of Approaches to Religious Education in Catholic schools in Four Australian Dioceses *Brendan Hyde*...285

Chapter 15: *Curriculum Focus* K-2 Religious Education in the Archdiocese of Sydney *Anthony Cleary and Sue Moffat*.....................................305

Chapter 16: *Curriculum Focus* Fostering Social Justice in Catholic Schools in Bathurst Diocese *Paul Devitt* 327

Chapter 17: *Curriculum Focus* Towards a New Integrated Approach to Religious Education: The Tasmanian Experience *Tony Brennan*..349

Chapter 18: *Curriculum Focus* Finding and Implementing Aboriginal and Torres Strait Islander Themes in Religious Education in Armidale Diocese: A Journey of Discovery and Reconciliation *Lee Herden*..........369

Part One: Setting the Framework

Chapter 1

A Personal, Critical Perspective on the Development of Australian Catholic School Religious Education: Where to From Here?

Graham Rossiter

CHAPTER 1

This chapter reflects on my decades of involvement with religious education in Australian Catholic schools. It does not reprise or summarise work already done that interpreted the historical development of Australian Catholic school religious education.[1] Rather the focus is on how two particular aspects have changed, and on some implications for the future. The two areas of change are:

1. How religion teachers managed their dual commitments to the church and to the personal development of their students.
2. Change in the key words used to explain the normative purposes of religious education (RE).

How religion teachers understood their dual commitments to the church and to the personal development of their students

The history noted above showed that in the 1960s, as a result of significant socio-cultural change, educational change and changes in the Catholic Church in the wake of the Second Vatican Council, there was a period of uncertainty and some confusion in Catholic school RE. The old ways of the green catechism, Bible history and apologetics were no longer felt to be relevant, but it was not clear just which new direction should be taken. But one thing was quite evident: religion teachers worked hard trying to make RE more relevant and meaningful for students. To this day, commitment to promoting the personal development of young people and to trying to continually improve the relevance of RE has never been lacking in Catholic school religion teachers.

In the 1960s, the RE teachers were almost all members of religious orders. They had committed their lives to the service of the church, so no one could question their commitment to its welfare or to the promotion of its mission. Nevertheless, these same teachers never saw RE as an exclusively ecclesiastical activity. They hoped that RE would educate students well in the Catholic faith tradition and hopefully too, this might leave them favourably disposed towards a long term engagement with the church; but these hopes were held in creative tension with efforts to help young people make sense of life, and to negotiate the perils of adolescence in what was becoming a more complex and challenging culture. These dual commitments were so strong, so embedded and held in creative tension, that they were often taken for granted and not articulated as they have been here. In my experience of that period, I never met a religion teacher who thought that getting the students to Sunday mass was the central aim of RE – even though there were some vocal groups like Catholics Concerned for the Faith who felt that faulty RE was responsible for declining mass attendance. Religion teachers thought that good RE would benefit young people whether or not they chose to be regular churchgoers.

At this same time, following new government funding arrangements for private schools and the gradual development of diocesan Catholic Education Offices, there was not a strong exercise of church control over the religion curricula in Catholic schools. There were Catholic doctrinal syllabuses, but the religious order schools were in effect free to develop their own religion curricula. This was also a vogue period for SBCD – School Based Curriculum Development – and this was often the only sort of religion curriculum in operation. So both schools and religion teachers had freedom to experiment. With this freedom and given the period of rapid change, there was much trial and error in RE. Also the religion teachers in the 1960s and 1970s often had little in the way of professional learning in scripture and theology. One significant development in Australian Catholic school RE at this stage was the Communitarian retreat (Rossiter, 2016).

A crucial lesson to be learned from this history is that healthy Catholic school RE needs to retain a creative tension between ecclesiastical concerns and teachers' views about the spiritual/moral needs of pupils. Where there is no creative tension, and where ecclesiastical purposes predominate, RE could more readily be perceived as if it were just 'telling students about Catholicism'. There is a tendency for ecclesiastical interests in RE to be concerned with promoting engagement with the church and regular mass attendance; and from the teachers and students' points of view, this focus appears somewhat unrealistic and not so relevant to young people's lives. Naturally, ecclesiastical expectations of RE will be conservative. In the sense of conserving and handing on the religious tradition, these are valuable, justified purposes. But if this perspective is so prominent to the extent of eclipsing other more personal-development and educational purposes, then RE runs the risk of being perceived increasingly as irrelevant.

By the 1990s, a general consensus emerged about what might be best described as a 'subject-oriented' approach in RE. This meant that religion was treated as a core learning area in the school curriculum, aspiring to be as challenging as any other learning area, with content and pedagogy that did not suffer by comparison with what was being done in other subjects. This included all the protocols and procedures of the established academic subjects/learning areas – with a normative curriculum, objectives, performance indicators, varied student-centred pedagogies and appropriate assessment and reporting. In many Catholic secondary schools, RE in Years 11-12 consisted of a state board-determined course in Religion Studies (or Studies of

Religion) which had the same academic status as subjects that counted towards tertiary entrance scores.

For many religion teachers, subject-oriented RE was about educating pupils religiously and spiritually – it was an educational exploration of religion and not necessarily a religious experience as such. There still remains, however, some variation in the views of teachers about how devotional and religious the activity should be. This ambiguity is also related to language problems in RE to be discussed later. At the same time RE was acquiring more academic status and respectability in the school curriculum, this development was being affected by an increasing tendency to regard it as more an ecclesiastical activity than an educational one. I believe that this tendency runs counter to the academic and core educational character of RE. Also, the more centralised and fixed the religion curriculum, the less freedom there was for adapting RE to meet contemporary needs.

My conclusion: There is an urgent need to restore the creative tension between educational and ecclesiastical concerns. This is needed above all to promote the relevance of RE as an academic subject for students – but also to promote research, creativity, and innovation in RE. It is pertinent to note that the academic study and research related to RE at tertiary level (in Catholic and other institutions) is a crucial reference point for maintaining a creative tension between educational and ecclesiastical concerns. Tertiary religious education has usually always had academic freedom giving it the independence needed to explore and appraise insights from education and the social sciences, as well as from theology and religious studies.

CHAPTER 1

The language for Australian Catholic school religious education

Within the discourse of Catholic schooling, the use of ecclesiastical words has tended to eclipse, and create ambiguity about, the fundamental term *religious education*. The frequent use of words like faith development, faith formation, Catholic identity, catechesis, new evangelisation, mission and ministry to encompass RE tends to make the unrealistic presumption that what happens to pupils psychologically during religion lessons will change their faith and religious practice. And what gets neglected is a realistic understanding of what it means to *educate* them spiritually and morally. This latter purpose is one that RE can actually achieve quite well – but efforts to enhance pupils' religious knowledge do not automatically generate personal faith. Also, a successful, meaningful, and relevant RE cannot adequately be appraised in terms of traditional religiosity performance indicators like Sunday mass attendance.

Through different metaphors and perspectives, the ecclesiastical terms noted above can nuance the understanding of RE from the church's point of view. But there is also a downside – too many normative constructs can constrain thinking and can stifle freedom and creativity, as well as create confusion about fundamental purposes. The problems for RE posed by ecclesiastical language were identified as early as 1970 by Gabriel Moran in the article *Catechetics RIP*. They are even more prominent today. Religion teachers readily recognise the problems when they are discussed in postgraduate RE programs, and the ambiguity both they and parents see in the ecclesiastical terms is evident in research findings (e.g. Finn, 2011). But this is an issue yet to be acknowledged and addressed in Australian Catholic schooling.

Attention will now be given to the evolution in the use of normative ecclesiastical terms in Catholic church documents. But it is important initially to note that the succession of Roman documents dating from the second Vatican Council have been more generally concerned with the church's broad Ministry of Catechesis and the Ministry of the Word. Religious education across age groups, and more specifically RE in schools, was only part of the wide scope of those documents. But they have often been read by educators as if everything applied to the school context. By contrast, the documents from the Congregation for Catholic Education – especially *The Catholic School* (1977) and *The Religious Dimension of Education in Catholic Schools* (1988) – were more focused on the Catholic school and RE.

This evolution is evident in the percentage frequencies of key words that have been used in a selection of authoritative documents that have been applied to religious education.

The Vatican II 1966 document *Gravissimum Educationis* (GE, Declaration on Christian Education) focused mainly on the word *education* (66%). This emphasis was both expansive and ecumenical in scope. It was naturally open to dialogue with other Christian denominations where 'Christian education' was prominent. This also articulated with the wider, international discourse of education, showing how education within a particular religious tradition and 'educating one's faith' could make a valuable contribution to people's spiritual and moral development, as well as to civic education.

Documents	Length in words	Faith	Education	Catechesis	Evangelisation	Development	Formation	Identity	Mission Ministry Witness
1966 Vatican II Declaration on Christian Education	5K	11%	66%	1%	0	8%	6%	0	8%
1970 Renewal of Education of Faith (Australian)	47K	40%	14%	23%	0	4%	2%	0	18%
1971 General Catechetical Directory	31K	30%	4%	40%	2%	2%	6%	0	15%
1988 Religious Dimension of Education in Catholic schools	19K	23%	36%	3%	4%	7%	13%	1%	14%
1997 General Directory of Catechesis	69K	25%	6%	49%	0	1%	9%	0.5%	11%
2007 Catholic Schools at a Crossroads (NSW/ACT Bishops)	4K	21%	29%	7%	12%	2%	8%	6%	15%

Key words that have been applied to religious education as % of total key words per document

Table 1. Analysis of the frequency of words that have been used to refer to religious education

In 1970, the Italian and Australian bishops in a sense 'jumped the gun' in publishing their post-Vatican II directories (*The Renewal of the Education of Faith*, REF) before the Roman *General Catechetical Directory* (GCD) was issued by the Congregation for the Clergy in 1971. The idea of educating people's faith was carried through from the Vatican document, while catechesis (23%) became more prominent – it was used only once in the Vatican II document.

A sharp decline in the use of the word 'education' was evident in the Roman GCD (1971). From roughly 70% prominence in the Vatican

II document, education was virtually replaced by a 70% usage of 'catechesis' and 'faith'. This naturally inhibited ecumenical links with those outside Catholicism who used the words 'education' and 'Christian education'. From then on, the discussion of RE from a normative Roman Catholic perspective tended to become 'in-house' and not as open to wider educational discourse because it was more or less locked in to a set of ecclesiastical constructs that had little currency outside the Catholic church. This also meant that the RE endeavour was understood and talked about more as if it were an ecclesiastical activity. The more ecclesiastical, and correspondingly the less educational, it was perceived to be, RE became increasingly insecure in the Catholic school curriculum. If it was not regarded primarily as education, in all likelihood this would eventually have negative consequences in terms of the perceptions of teachers, students and parents. However, to be fair to the GCD, it was never intended to be a document about RE, but rather the wider religious ministry of the Catholic church for faithful of all ages in a variety of contexts.

As might have been expected, the Roman Congregation for Catholic Education's 1988 document *The Religious Dimension of Education in a Catholic School* (RDECS), as also its earlier document *The Catholic School*, 1977, gave special attention to the word 'education' – consistent with the emphasis in the Vatican II document. These documents helped raise the status of RE in the Catholic school curriculum, noting that it was distinct from catechesis. From the church perspective, both catechesis and religious education were needed, and RE was 'at home' in the school.

The Roman document *The General Directory of Catechesis* (GDC) was a 1997 rewrite of the 1971 GCD. It too was concerned with the church's ministry of the Word and not just education in Catholic schools. The word frequencies for both documents were similar. While not as prominent as the other ecclesiastical constructs, the words 'mission', 'ministry' and 'witness' were used in all six documents. They showed a church mission perspective on activities. Religion/religious was common through the documents – used 200 times in the GDC and 10 times in GE. Theology/theological was less common – 21 and 18 times in REF and GCD, and not at all in GDC and CR – it was used twice in GE.

The 2007 Australian document (NSW & ACT) (CR) used education four times more frequently than catechesis. In addition, it is the first of the documents to use the specific words 'faith formation' and 'Catholic identity'. While 'forming/formation', 'develop/development' and 'identity' (to a lesser extent) were used in the earlier documents, the precise words 'Catholic identity' appeared only once (in the 1997 Roman document), and 'faith formation' not at all. Somewhat surprisingly, the term 'faith development' does not appear in any of the six documents; it did, however, come to have great prominence in Australian Catholic RE circles after the publication of John Westerhoff's *Will our Children have Faith?* (1976) and James Fowler's *Stages of faith: The psychology of human development and the quest for meaning* (1981). (See also Crawford & Rossiter, 2006, ch 18).

What is a feature of the 2007 *Crossroads* document, which contrasts with the focus on education in the Vatican II document, is the way that RE was treated primarily as an ecclesiastical process. Coupled with this assumption was a concern that, despite the high level of resources invested in Catholic schools, they were not successful in inclining young Catholics to become regular churchgoers. Because of low church participation rates amongst Australian Catholic youth, it was considered that there must be a crisis of Catholic identity in Catholic schools. New evangelisation and strengthening Catholic identity were proposed as principal strategies for 'reigniting' young people's spirituality and improving their engagement with the Church. Increased Sunday mass attendance was listed as a performance indicator for Catholic schools. This author contests these views, considering that there is no crisis of identity in Australian Catholic schools, and that there are no causal links between Catholic schooling/religious education and the ultimate mass attendance rates of Catholic school graduates. RE is about educating young people religiously in their own tradition as well as helping them find a more meaningful view of life in a complex and confusing culture. This is primarily an educational task and not an ecclesiastical one; and Catholic schools are capable of doing this well. But no matter what the quality of school RE, this cannot make the church more meaningful and attractive to young people – only the church itself can do this. While there is evidence of a widespread crisis in the Catholic church, this cannot be said of Catholic schools in Australia, which are thriving (Rossiter, 2010A, 2013). This chapter is ultimately about helping to make Catholic school RE more meaningful and relevant for pupils. Making the church more relevant is of great concern for Catholics, but it has a different and extensive agenda to be addressed, and school religious education has little if anything to do with that.

Special attention will now be given to the use of the term 'faith formation'. In 1987, one priest Diocesan Director of Catholic schools said 'What we need is faith formation and not religious education'. Then and subsequently I found that those who used the term rarely if ever defined what they meant. It appeared to be used with the connotation that somehow faith formation was more important and influential than religious education – as if the intention to *form* faith made the activity more effective in changing the quality of the individual's personal relationship with God. Education was apparently considered inferior to formation. No indication was given about how an observer could look at activities and clearly see why one was faith formation and others were 'merely' religious education. Also apparent in the connotation was its focus on recruitment to regular mass attendance; this seemed to be the criterion of faith formation that 'works'. This language trend devalues religious education and distracts from giving attention to what it means to educate young people religiously.

Faith formation has etymological roots in the use of the words 'houses of formation' in first half twentieth century religious order practice in Australia (and elsewhere). Formation was like a 'religious Marine boot camp'. The emphases were: conformity, 'marching in formation', uniformity, obedience, being moulded and changed personally according to a desired model. Faith formation tends to become something of an oxymoron when this connotation is associated with a comprehensive view of Christian faith as a committed personal relationship with God, and as a gift from God freely accepted. On the other hand, education today tends to connote being informed, critical thinking and personal autonomy. It may be that fear of such potential could foster a negative view of RE and a more positive valuation of faith formation because it seemed to better serve ecclesiastical purposes.

Faith formation tends to be used more with reference to voluntary religious ministry programs than with reference to formal RE. But its increasing prominence in schools is now eclipsing RE and this will in turn devalue its place in the school curriculum and its status as a challenging academic subject. A division between 'educational' and 'faith formation/faith development' aspects of the school's overall religious education can make a useful distinction but it uses the wrong language to do so. It makes long term outcomes, or more accurately 'hopes', take the place of the main process word. It gives an impression that the educational engagement with religion in the classroom does not contribute to the development of the individual's personal faith – and this is not the case. The classroom study of religion can make a vital contribution to the understanding and deepening of the individual's faith. This would be the one aspect of the overall development of an individual's faith that is most in tune with what schools do best – educate.

The points made above are also pertinent to interpreting problems with the use of the other ecclesiastical terms 'faith development' and 'Catholic identity', as discussed elsewhere (Crawford & Rossiter, 2006; Rossiter, 2013). What surprises me in the new focus on Catholic identity is an absence of substantial ideas about what it means to *educate young people in identity* – this is a topic that is in my opinion a crucial one for RE. A corollary to the problems considered above is the emergence of new religious leadership positions in Catholic schools. Originally there was the Religious Education Coordinator (REC) or Assistant Principal Religious Education (APRE). Now there is a variety of positions with names like: Director of Catholic Identity, Dean of Mission, Coordinator of Mission and Catholic identity, Director of Evangelisation, Faith Development Coordinator. Anecdotal evidence suggests that apart from changing the language patterns, this development has had no appreciable impact on the quality of RE and pastoral care in Catholic schools. This is an issue that merits investigation through research. It must be noted that these comments are about language and new leadership roles and not about any evaluation of the Enhancing Catholic Schools Identity Project that has been conducted in Catholic schools across the country, and especially in Victoria.

The same problems with ecclesiastical language for school RE have affected the academic discipline of RE in Catholic tertiary institutions. Where it has become more ecclesiastical, and less academic and research oriented, it is weakened as an academic discipline. And this in turn has negative repercussions within school RE. Religious education at tertiary level should be a 'lighthouse' for academic freedom and independence both for its scholars as well as for the educators who engage with scholarship in their professional development studies.

Conclusions and recommendations

In the light of discussions with Catholic school religion teachers in postgraduate programs over the years, I know that the conclusions and recommendations will be acknowledged as important and in need of further consideration and debate. I also know that not all will agree with the interpretation and some will find the conclusions challenging because they do not sit comfortably with the status quo or because they conflict with the views of authorities. My confidence in the views expressed here is based on practitioners' judgment that they are *realistic*, and as such they could be tested by research.

It appears to me that the biggest problem facing RE in Australian Catholic schools today is the perception that it is essentially an *ecclesiastical* rather than an *educational* activity. It needs to be thought of, talked about, appraised and developed more as *education* and not judged in terms of how it promotes pupils' church practice. This would hopefully restore the creative tension between the ecclesiastical and educational concerns that operated just after Vatican II – this does not mean returning to the same practice of those times. I consider that this will be the best trajectory for the students and also for the church.

Final comments are organised under 3 headings.

Building up the critical dimension in the RE curriculum: Trying to address the needs of contemporary young people to help them chart a constructive path through the maze of contemporary culture.

The complexities and ambiguities of culture today both promote human wellbeing as well as causing harm, leaving casualties in their wake. RE is well placed in the Catholic school curriculum to help young people look critically at the shaping influence of culture on people's beliefs and values. Also it can study the importance of religions in contemporary discourse and world affairs. It is no longer adequate or relevant to spend practically all the RE curriculum time studying Catholicism. Adding elements of a critical approach, especially from Year 9 onwards, dealing with a selection of contemporary life issues (personal, social, political, environmental etc.) can help young people 'interrogate' their cultural conditioning to discern both the healthy and unhealthy influences. A student-centred, research-oriented pedagogy can empower the students to develop critical skills in studying important issues in an academic way. Such an approach helps resource their basic human spirituality and can help them better negotiate the complexities of contemporary life and find a more meaningful and satisfying pathway – whether they are formally religious or not. This approach needs more prominence in the secondary RE curriculum, complementing the important need for young people to study their own religious tradition in an academic way – together with some reference to other religious traditions (Rossiter, 2010B).

Taking into account the religious disposition of the students and their perceptions of RE.

Religious educators need a good understanding of contemporary youth spirituality as a starting point for seeing how RE might enhance spirituality. In addition, the relatively secular spirituality of most students in Catholic schools needs to be acknowledged and addressed in other than a 'deficit' way (Rossiter, 2011). It helps to note recent statistics.

Data from the National Catholic Education Commission (2012) and from the National Church Life Surveys (Dixon, 2013) show that in 2012, there were 734 thousand students in 1706 Australian Catholic schools. 71% (522,000) were Catholic and 29% (212,000) were not Catholic. Of the Catholic students, the surveys suggest that by the time they reach their twenties less than 7% will be regular church goers – that is 37,000. This means that overall just under 700 of the 734 thousand pupils will not be Sunday mass attenders. While there was an overall increase in the total number of Catholic students by 1000 over the years 2006-2012, in the same period the numbers of non-Catholic students increased by 46,000.

In the light of this data, there is an apparent discontinuity between the assumptions within Catholic school RE (as if all students are or should be regular mass attenders) and the classroom reality. Catholic RE documentation showed little or no acknowledgement that most Catholic students are not (or will not be) churchgoing. If many of the pupils are not going to reference their personal spirituality to regular church attendance, then this makes it more relevant to attend to the proposal above that increased attention to a critical approach is needed to help resource their spirituality. Whether students have a religious or a secular spirituality, the crucial thing for Catholic schools is whether they are *well-educated spiritually and religiously*.

In tune with the general indifference to religion in secularised Western countries, most of the pupils in Catholic schools do not care much for RE. They do not see it as a subject that 'counts', and while not antagonistic, they do not engage in RE in the same way they do in subjects like English, Maths and Science (Crawford & Rossiter, 2006). There are no formulae that can change such perceptions significantly; but anything that increases the academic status, as well as perceived relevance, will help. I think that the inward-looking focus of asserting Catholic identity in RE exacerbates the problem; it is like 'RE through a *selfie*', where the constant reference to Catholic identity skews the perceptions. The emphasis should be more outward-looking – simply on developing the *education* dimension to RE. Having a rationale for RE in words that explain how it helps *educate* young people is more likely to win the approval and moral support of students and parents, as well as teachers, than does a rationale that appears to be just about replicating Catholicism.

Some may not want to acknowledge the reality here, but the more the word 'Catholic' is used the more the activity is perceived as irrelevant. This is a principal reason why I think that the current emphasis on Catholic identity is counterproductive – it is not the label that RE really needs. For example, there appears to be further decline in the academic status of Catholic school RE as evident in the perceptions of *Catholic Studies* in some NSW secondary schools. It is a Board-endorsed study but does not 'count' for tertiary entrance scores like regular subjects including *Studies of Religion*. *Catholic Studies* is often chosen by students (when religion is compulsory but there are options) who want the least interference in their secular studies. It may be taught with the understanding that there are no assignments or homework with a short open book exam at the end of the year, while the teachers may feel that they can do anything to keep the students reasonably occupied whether the syllabus is covered or not.

Simplifying the language of religious education and exercising leadership in Australian education

The confusing ecclesiastical terms noted above need to be phased out and only used where their meanings are clearly defined. In practice, they tend to carry ill-defined and unrealistic assumptions about religious starting points, goals and processes and this adds unwanted ambiguity and complications to the discussion. It would be more fruitful to redirect the discourse towards how best to educate young people theologically, in scripture, in personal identity development, and in critical interpretation and evaluation of the shaping influence of culture. In the long run I think this change of focus would also be more successful in disposing students towards the ecclesiastical hopes for Catholic schooling.

This change in focus and language is not only more meaningful and relevant for Catholics, it makes the RE discourse more accessible to the Australian educational community; it also readily articulates with educational and psychological research. Otherwise, the discourse remains narrowly and idiosyncratically Catholic. This change is also important because Australian Catholic schools are in effect semi-state schools funded by state and federal governments; they are therefore accountable to the civic community and need to show how they are contributing to the common good (Bryck et al. 1993; Conroy, 1999). Such a rationale is better suited to justifying continued state funding.

Educating young people spiritually and religiously from within a base of their own religious tradition makes a valuable contribution to the education of young Australians. This exercises a leadership role in Australian education showing that a well-rounded schooling needs a subject area that deals directly with the spiritual and moral dimensions to life. As the school system that maintains the largest commitment to religious education in terms of teachers, curriculum and teacher professional development, Catholic schools can demonstrate how a commitment to this dimension of education might take shape.

NOTES

1. See the 7 references: Buchanan, Hamilton, Ryan, Rossiter, 1981, 1999, Rummery, and Lovat.

REFERENCES

Bryk, A.S., Lee, V.E., Holland, P.B. (1993). *Catholic Schools and the Common Good*. Cambridge: Harvard University Press.

Buchanan, M. (2005). Pedagogical drift: The evolution of new approaches and paradigms in religious education. *Religious Education*, 100(1), 20-37.

Conroy, J.C. (Ed.) (1999) *Catholic Education, Inside Out, Outside In*. Dublin: Lindisfarne.

Crawford, M & Rossiter, G. (2006). *Reasons for living: Education and young people's search for meaning, identity and spirituality*. Melbourne: Australian Council for Educational Research.

Dixon, R., Reid, R.S. & Chee, N. (2013). *Mass Attendance in Australia: A Critical Moment*. Melbourne: Australian Catholic Bishops Conference.

Finn, A. (2011). *Parents, teachers and religious education: A study in a Catholic secondary school in rural Victoria*. Sydney: Catholic Schools Office, Diocese of Broken Bay.

Hamilton, A. (1981). *What's been happening in religious education in Australia?* Melbourne: Dove Communications.

Lovat, T. (2009). *What is this thing called religious education?* (3rd Edition) Terrigal: David Barlow.

Moran, G. (1970). Catechetics, R.I.P. *Commonweal*, December 18, 299-301.

NCEC – National Catholic Education Commission (2012). *NCEC 2012 Annual Report*. Canberra: NCEC.

Rossiter, G. (1981). *Religious education in Australian Schools*. Canberra: Curriculum Development Centre.

Rossiter, G. (1999). Historical perspective on the development of Catholic religious education in Australia: Some implications for the future. *Journal of Religious Education*, 47(1), 5-18.

Rossiter, G. (2010A). Perspective on contemporary spirituality: Implications for religious education in Catholic schools. *International Studies in Catholic Education*. 2(2), 129-147.

Rossiter, G. (2010B). A 'big picture' review of K-12 Australian Catholic School religious education in the light of contemporary spirituality. *Journal of Religious Education*. 58(3), 5-18.

Rossiter, G. (2011). Some perspectives on contemporary Youth Spirituality: A 'need to know' for church school religious education. *Religious Education Journal of Australia.* 27(1), 9-15

Rossiter, G. (2013). Perspective on the use of the construct 'Catholic identity' for Australian Catholic schooling: Part 1 The sociological background and the literature; Part 2 Areas in the discourse in need of more emphasis and further attention. *Journal of Religious Education.* 61(2), 4-29.

Rossiter, (2016). *Research on Retreats: A study of the views of teachers and students about retreats in Australian Catholic secondary schools.* Sydney: ACU NSW School of Education. http://203.10.46.163/grrossiter/retreats/index.html

Ryan, M. (2013). *A common search: The history and forms of religious education in Catholic schools* (Revised Edition), Brisbane: Lumino Press.

Rummery, R.M. (1975). *Catechesis and religious education in a pluralist society.* Sydney: EJ Dwyer.

Graham Rossiter is a Professor of Moral and Religious Education. After teaching in Catholic secondary schools in Sydney, he conducted research in Religious Education for the Federal Government and then completed doctoral research on comparative theory for school Religious Education. He specialised in teacher professional development, conducting seminars in Australia and the Pacific, Hong Kong, North America, Europe and South Africa. He has been working in religious education at university level for many years and has published widely – including *Reasons for living: Education and young people's search for meaning, identity and spirituality* (ACER, 2006) and *Research on retreats* (ACU, 2016).

Correspondence to:
BBI - The Australian Institute of Theological Education
Caroline Chisholm Centre, 423 Pennant Hills Road, Pennant Hills
Postal Address: PO Box 662, Pennant Hills NSW 1715
Ph: +61 2 9847 0030 Fax: +61 2 9847 0031
Email: grossiter@bbi.catholic.edu.au

Chapter 2

Religious Education in
a Changing Context:
The Paradox of
Catholic Schools

Richard Rymarz

Introduction

Religious education takes place within a particular social and cultural context. For those involved in the discipline, especially those in classroom teaching, an understanding of this context is critical for effective and engaging pedagogy. There are many ways though that contemporary culture can be conceptualised (Singleton, 2014). Some clarity is necessary, therefore, in order to establish a focus and framework for discussion. One useful way of proceeding is to begin with the presentation of a salient, suggestive issue and then to utilise this as a foundation for discussion and elaboration. This is the method that will be followed here. This chapter will be in two parts. The first explores a paradox in Catholic education and the second offers a discussion of some of the factors contributing to this paradox as well as drawing out implications for religious educators.

The Paradox

Those working in religious education in Australian Catholic schools are faced with a paradox that is indicative of significant cultural shifts in religious expression and identity in the wider culture. In many parts of the world Catholic schools are growing, attracting new enrolments and expanding their facilities (Belmonte and Cranston, 2009; Franchi, 2014). From a contemporary cultural perspective what makes this paradoxical is that this is taking place at a time when the institutional strength of the Church, in conventional measures, is declining (Dobbelaere, 2002; Smith and Snell, 2009; Eagle, 2011; Singleton, 2014). The observation that Catholic schools are flourishing in an era of generalised institutional religious decline is not new. Greeley and Rossi (2002), for example, observed that the same paradox was evident in the United States. In 1966 they confidentially predicted that the Catholic school system in the US would continue to expand making the contrast with the wider Church community even starker. In fact, 1966 marked the high water mark for American Catholic schools. From that date onward enrolments in Catholic schools have been in steady, relentless decline. From a peak enrolment of 5.2 million in the mid-1960s, enrolment in 2014 has declined to 1.9 million. And this trend, too, seems to be escalating. Between 2004 and 2014, the number of students in Catholic schools in the USA declined by 578,699 or 23% (NCEA, 2014).

In the United States the predicted bright future has not been realised (Greeley et al., 1984). This is not the case in many other countries such as Australia. In general, Australians are relatively strong supporters of private education (Windle, 2009). Mussart (2012, 9) has noted the comparatively high level of private school enrolment in Australia, a trait shared with countries such as the Netherlands, Belgium, Great Britain and Sweden. In 2014, 35% of all Australian school students attended a private school (ISCA, 2015). Of this figure over 90% of all Australian private schools are affiliated with Christian Churches (Buckingham 2010).

By far the largest private school provider in Australia is the Catholic Church and this sector is expanding. Comparing enrolments between 1985 and 2012 reveals an increase in that time of 21%. This trend seems to be escalating. Comparing enrolment figures for 2011 and 2012 shows an increase of 11,931 or 1.6%. In 2012 there were 735,403 students enrolled in Australian Catholic schools. Of that number, 522,190 were Catholic and 212,237 (29%) were non-Catholic (NCEC, 2013). The growth in enrolments is anticipated to continue to increase into the next decade. By 2025 the number of students enrolled in Australian Catholic schools is projected to rise to 950,000.

In choosing a Catholic school, parents are making a considered choice that helps them realise their hopes for their children and one aspect of their decision is taking into account religious considerations. Part of what is offered by Catholic schools is a religious dimension. This is not incidental to the nature of Catholic education and parents are prepared to accept this as part of their children's education. This dynamic can be illustrated by consideration of the following micro-narrative (Higgins, 2007). This is not intended as an empirical argument but rather as a brief story that is both dense and illustrative and which introduces a range of themes that will be explored in more detail later.

Last year I attended a Confirmation liturgy. The very clear majority of children being confirmed were enrolled in the Catholic school adjacent to the church where the Confirmation was being held. It was held on a Friday evening on a cold and rainy winter's night. The end of a busy work week with a vacation not even in sight! I miscalculated how long it would take me to drive to the church from the nearby railway station. As a result I was almost half an hour early. This was a good thing for even at this stage the church was already filling. In fifteen or so minutes there was not a spare space on any pew. Those who arrived after this had to stand at the back or in the foyer of the building.

It was a very well conducted, vibrant service. You could see that the teachers had put a good deal of effort into planning and preparation. The children sang beautifully and offered reflections at various times. The bishop was a warm and inviting presence and seemed very much at ease. He gave an appropriate homily that addressed the challenges of following Christ, especially in a world where so much stands in the way of this. The overwhelming feature of the evening, though, was the human element.

As mentioned earlier the church was packed. There were grandparents, other relatives, friends as well as a host of very excited candidates, sponsors and parents. At the end of the liturgy large numbers of people waited around for photographs with the bishop and to mingle with others.

The above narrative captures a number of aspects of the changing cultural context in which Catholic schools operate in Australia today. The statistics on Church attendance are well known (Dixon et al, 2013). The majority of families who are involved in Catholic schools do not regularly attend Church services (Pollefeyt and Bouwens, 2014). This is true for Catholic and non-Catholic families (Rymarz, 2016). At the same time there seems to be no great desire to completely severe any connection to the worshipping community. For an important rite of passage such as a Confirmation parents, family and friends will eagerly take part in a long church ceremony as this is effectively mediated through the school.

For many Catholics the 'thick culture' that helped sustain religious allegiance is now a thing of the past (Smith et al, 2014, 36). The triad of school, family and parish working toward similar religious goals has been supplemented by a model where the school has become the preeminent association that many Catholics have with the Church (McQuillan, 2011; Gray, 2015). This is turn is a reflection of a changed cultural contest where religious affiliation has become more fluid and reflective of a broader cultural assimilation. The second part of this chapter will be directed toward an overview of these cultural changes as a way of better understanding the paradox of Catholic schools. In addition, engaging with these cultural changes gives a clearer perspective of the challenges facing religious educators.

Catholic schools in a changed cultural context

A critical question becomes, what implications does the increase in enrolments have for the assumptions that religious educators make about the students and families now involved in Catholic schools? In addressing this question it is imperative to recognise the changed religious and cultural context. This change allows much more readily for multiple and transitory expressions of religious identity. In addition, these expressions can co-exist with a range of other factors which are often considered to be more important. This is well illustrated in the seminal work of Marcellin Flynn (Flynn, 1995; Flynn and Mok, 2002). Over several decades Flynn's longitudinal studies investigated what he called the culture of Catholic schools. As part of this extensive study he surveyed key stakeholders in Catholic education, including parents and students. He found that parents sent their children to Catholic schools for many reasons, but religious formation was not the primary one. Flynn has shown that in a five point forced response, parents consistently placed religious considerations last as their reason for choosing Catholic schools (Flynn 1993, 171). Students' religious expectations were similar. Of the 12 lowest priorities for Catholic schools, 11 listed by students were of a religious nature, (Flynn 1993, 164). The top five expectations in rank order of parents who sent their children to Catholic schools are as follows: prepare students for the HSC as well as possible; respect each student individually; assist students to achieve a high standard; develop students' intellectual abilities; help students to prepare for their future careers (Flynn, 1993, 169). A range of studies, both local and international, confirm Flynn's analysis of the multi-dimensional motivation of parents for sending their children to religiously affiliated schools (Levitt, 1996; Branff, 2007; Campbell et al., 2009; Heft, 2011; McCarthy, 2016).

A key characteristic of contemporary religiosity is that many find a place for religion but it is not the only or the most important aspect of personal identity (Crawford and Rossiter, 2006). In Flynn's list of expectations of parents who enroll their children in Catholic schools it is not that religious expectations, such as providing an atmosphere of Christian community, are not valued. They are just not ranked as highly as other expectations. What is important is not so much the number of expectations but how they are arranged into a total package. The ordering of salient features of personal identity is a fluid process and is heavily influenced by dominant cultural forces. There was a time, for example, when a much higher prominence was given to religious factors. This can be seen in the generational contrast between Catholics. The religious experience and expression of post-conciliar Catholics is different from previous generations (D'Antonio et al., 2013). Catholics who were born after the Second Vatican Council and subsequent generations, have far more in common with each other than with those whose formation was shaped by the pre-conciliar era or the immediate period of transition after the Second Vatican Council (D'Antonio et al., 2007).

The demise of the salience of religion in personal identity leads to many Catholics lacking an identity that makes them different or distinctive from others in the general culture (Greeley, 2004). Significant life decisions are not made on the basis of deeply held religious convictions. Rather they are arrived at after a wide range of considerations, the most influential being the norms of the culture (Rymarz 2015). Religious educators must be mindful of assumptions that they make about the impact of these normative views on students. Bouma (2006) speaks of a new normal in the way in which young people engage with significant life questions. In these considerations the dominant influences are hegemonic cultural norms that are often not clearly articulated or understood, much less critiqued, by students.

Younger Catholics today have many more options before them, including holding multiple or no allegiances (Stoltz, et al., 2015). This allows for individuals to negotiate a place for themselves within a religious community. Without a strong socialised sense of religious belonging many may make a choice to retain some allegiance to a religious community without ever taking this to a personal or transformative level (Edgell, 2012). The rituals, symbols and language of a religious tradition may have some familiarity to many younger Catholics but this may be only be a superficial understanding.

Davie (2015), writing from a British perspective, describes well the negotiated dimension of religious affiliation in contemporary culture. In broad terms she describes the new religious societal pattern as having moved from obligation to consumption. As such, a simple dichotomy between those who are religious and those who are not is no longer an accurate description of what can be called the religious marketplace. Despite the rise in the number of 'nones', that is, those with no expressed religious affiliation there is a substantial group that can take part in religious activities if the conditions surrounding this meet their needs. Church affiliated schools thrive because they offer a very good example of a desired religious option. This is illustrated by, for example, an openness to take part in religious, school based activities under certain circumstances. Think of the people at the Confirmation Liturgy mentioned earlier. This was well attended but there were also clear limits. A Confirmation service is a relatively rare occurrence in most families. There is no sense that this is an ongoing commitment to attend other services or to become involved in the parish. More importantly, it is a communal marker of an important life event, namely, a ritualization of the movement into adulthood. As such it is a significant occasion. There are, therefore, several good reasons for parents to take part in this service which is very much seen as part of the school based education of the child and not involvement with the worshipping community.

The idea of negotiated religion can be extended to a generalised argument about the nature of religious belief and practice in contemporary culture. The attitude of many Catholics to the Church is not hostile and the typical pattern of contemporary religious socialization has had little lasting impact. Many, though, feel in some way part of the Church, albeit, in a loose sense. Having the Church there makes people feel comfortable; it is reassuring to know that there are committed religious believers as long as there is no expectation that one must join them. This vicarious attitude to religion gives further clues as to the enduring appeal of religious schools in contemporary culture (Davie, 2000). Religious education in schools is acceptable as long as what is being offered is seen to be as not being restrictive of other aspirations. The wider expectations of parents are clear. The religious aspirations of Catholic schools are valid but cannot be seen to be overriding these primary concerns. This is an example of the competition between religious and secular institutions in contemporary culture. Stoltz (2009) uses this idea of competition as the basis for a new understanding of the place in religion in society. Religion remains viable only as long as it can offer something that places it in an advantageous position over what is generally available. This is often seen in the competition between allegiances to either religious or secular institutions. School choice is a good illustration of this dynamic. In many places both secular and religious agencies offer educational options. Which one is chosen depends on a range of factors and these can change over time.

We can extend the ideas of negotiated religion by drawing parallels between it and what is referred to as lived religion (McGuire, 2008). Ammerman (2013) points out that for most people religious choices are not binary ones, the choice to be religious or non-religious or the choice to belong to one particular faith community. Hard distinctions between Catholic and non-Catholic, for instance, may not be reflected in the lived reality of those involved in Catholic schools. Rymarz (2016) notes that when examining religious beliefs and practices amongst students in Catholic schools there are often more similarities between Catholic and non-Catholic students then there are differences. In a similar way people do not chose religion over spirituality. In fact, the nature of their religious expression is far more complex. Ammerman, (2013B) points out that lived religion is not a uniform phenomenon and that it can be expressed in a range of cultural packages. The exact nature of these packages is only seen within the context of a lived experience, what the person believes and what the person does. Closer attention needs to be paid to the phenomenon of lived religion in relation to seemingly unconventional choices such as those without strong religious beliefs or overt practice deciding to send their children to schools with strong institutional religious affiliation. Ammerman (2013, 7-8) writes:

> There are, in other words, interesting things still to learn about religion, but in a time of significant change, we cannot assume we will find religion in the predictable places or in the predictable forms. And if we do not find as much of it in those predictable places as we did before,

we cannot assume that it is disappearing. Religion is not an insignificant force in the social world today, but discovering its presence and impact may require asking our questions in new ways.

A feature of Catholic schools now and in the past has been the considerable effort put into establishing a religious identity (Martin, 1983; Mulligan, 2005; Sharkey, 2015). This is shown in many ways such as; the compulsory teaching of religious education, marking of significant events such as opening of the school year with liturgical celebrations and filling schools with a range of religious symbols (Cook, 2002). This is not an exhaustive list. The point here is that parents, even if they are not strongly affiliated, chose to send their children into this environment so it is a decision that tells us something about their deeper motivations. In terms of Ammerman's analysis, education of children could be a good indication of lived religion in a very practical context. If we return to Flynn's research on the expectations of parents of Catholic schools, religious ones are not top ranked. But religious expectations are still reported as being important: 76% of parents rated 'teach students to be guided by the Church in moral issues' as being very important; 74% rated 'help students to come to know Jesus Christ' as very important; 70% found 'provide an example of life based on the values of Christ and the gospel' as very important (Flynn 1993, 170).

Results such as these suggest that if the religious aspects of the school were not on offer then the demand for Catholic schools may lessen. This is because they would not be meeting a desire on the part of most parents for some overtly religious dimension to the school. This can be seen as part of a negotiated identity but it also speaks to a deeper sense of lived religion that is very much a part of the demand for Catholic schools. This is confirmed if we consider once again the Confirmation liturgy. From the bishop and priest in full regalia, to the scriptural readings, to the large cross over the altar and the countless symbolic liturgical actions it is hard to imagine seeing this as some type of secular celebration of moving into a more adult stage of life. In this analysis parents are doing much more than 'ticking a box' by participating in a ceremony that is part of the school's life. They are willing to allow their children and by extension their families to enter the sacred space that lived religion recognises as a key to understanding transcendence in everyday life. This is not a passive acceptance but also involves a reciprocity where involvement with the school helps frame religious expression. This may not be in conventional categories but it can have an impact on supporting one key lived religion cultural package, namely, that of theistic discourse (Ammerman, 2013B). This is an aspect of lived religion where religious institutions, like Catholic schools, could play an unrecognised role in giving expression to an often inchoate need to express a religious affiliation. In a similar fashion religious education may also be able to address a sense that religion, at least in some lived form, is a part of the life of many parents and students in Catholic school communities.

Conclusion

The discussion in this chapter on the paradoxical nature of Catholic schools in Australia has several implications for religious education. Many of these revolve around how religious education responds to the changed cultural context in which schools operate and the nature of the choice that many parents make to send their children to Catholic schools. Further work is needed that seeks to ascertain the interplay between factors such as lived religion and how this is negotiated and the manner in which religious education is approached in the classroom. The demise of thick Catholic cultures and the subsequent loss of a common religious language and sensibility has been well reported on for several decades. Students are no longer socialised into a world where traditional religious meaning, language and symbols are clearly articulated. The dominant influences on students come from the wider culture and are exerted across religious and social boundaries. The students in catholic schools today irrespective of family background are more likely to have been influenced by this pervasive social culture than by any overtly religious formation. It is important for the religious educator to be aware of this and recognise that students bring with them a range of beliefs and assumptions, often uncritical, that are reflective of the dominant culture.

Even though enrolments in Catholic schools are rising more and more students come from homes where religion is not dismissed but where it lacks salience and vibrancy. A negotiated sense of religion allows a place for religious discourse but it is not a preferential or privileged one. The links between a sense of lived religion and explicit classroom religious education are often not obvious and need some effort to be cultivated. All of this places considerable pressure on the discipline of religious education. This is summarised in a comment made to me by a senior teacher; 'In RE we can't take things for granted, the students are listening, it's just that they are not listening that hard!'

In addition many parents and students in Catholic schools may be challenged by a well supported and rigorous school based religious education program. This is evident if we consider that for many there is a place for religious education in schools but this cannot be seen as detracting from the other aspects of education. Religion is seen as part of the mix but it can easily become too onerous and demanding. How many religious education coordinators working in Catholic schools, for example, have been confronted by parents who ask that their children be excused from religious education, especially in the senior years, because it is distracting them from what they see as more important studies? As one exasperated parent memorably once remarked to me many years ago, 'Isn't 10 years of RE enough?' In addressing these questions the Catholic school is in a vulnerable situation if it cannot match the expectation on parents to support the RE curriculum with a serious, systematic and scholarly program that welcomes comparison with other subject offerings.

The challenge for religious educators then is to respond to this changed context in a fashion that recognises the pedagogical challenges ahead by focusing more on what is being offered in the classroom. To return to the earlier analogy, if students are prepared to listen – to give the school a chance to articulate its message - but to do so in a guarded and limited way, a renewed emphasis on religious education is needed. A critical aspect of this response is the quality of the religious education program that is being offered. In what has been described here as a religious marketplace schools must offer a thoughtful and resourced curriculum that is well taught and engaging. If this is done then the school can legitimately insist that the religious education is a vital part of the package of Catholic education.

REFERENCES

Ammerman, N. (2013). *Sacred stories, spiritual tribes: Finding religion in everyday life.* New York: Oxford University Press.

Ammerman, N. (2013B) Spiritual but not religious? Beyond binary choices in the study of religion. *Journal for the Scientific Study of Religion*, 52(2), 258-278.

Belmonte, A and Cranston, N. (2009). The religious dimension of lay leadership in Catholic schools: Preserving Catholic culture in an era of change. *Catholic Education: A Journal of Enquiry and Practice*, 2009, 12(3), 1-21.

Bouma, G. (2006). *Australian soul: Religion and spirituality in the 21st Century.* Sydney: Cambridge University Press.

Braniff, J. (2007). Charism and the concept of a Catholic education. *The Australasian Catholic Record*, 2007, 84(1).

Buckingham, J. (2010). *The rise of religious schools.* Centre for Independent Studies, Melbourne. Retrieved from http://www.cis.org.au/images/stories/policy-monographs/pm-111.pdf

Campbell, C., Proctor, H., and Sherrington, G. (2009). *School choice: How parents negotiate the new school market in Australia.* Sydney: Allen & Unwin.

Cook, T. (2002). *Architects of Catholic culture: Designing and building Catholic culture in schools.* Washington DC: National Catholic Education Association.

Crawford, M and Rossiter, G. (2006). *Reasons for living: Education and young people's search for meaning, identity and spirituality – A handbook.* Camberwell, Vic: ACER.

D'Antonio, W., Davidson, J., Hoge D and Mary Gautier, (2007). *American Catholics today: New realities of their faith and their Church.* New York: Rowman and Littlefield.

D'Antonio, W., Dillon, M and Gautier, M. (2013). *American Catholics in transition.* Lanham: Rowman & Littlefield.

Davie, G. (2000). *Religion in modern Europe: A memory mutates.* Oxford: Oxford University Press, 2000.

Davie, G. (2013). *The sociology of religion: A critical agenda.* London: Sage.

Davie, G. (2015). *Religion in Britain: A persistent paradox.* Oxford: Wiley Blackwell.

Dixon, R., Reid, S and Chee, M. (2013). *Mass attendance in Australia: A critical moment. A report based on the National Count of Attendance, the National*

Church Life Survey and the Australian Census. Melbourne: Australian Catholic Bishops Conference Pastoral Research Office.

Dobbelaere, K. (2002). *Secularization: An analysis at three levels*. Brussels: Peter Lang.

Eagle, D. (2011). Changing patterns of Church attendance at religious services in Canada, 1986-2008. *Journal for the Scientific Study of Religion*, 50(1), 187-2000.

Edgell, P. (2012). A cultural sociology of religion: New directions. *Annual Review of Sociology,* 384, 247-259.

Flynn, M. (1993). *The culture of Catholic Schools: A study of Catholic schools, 1972-1993*. Homebush, NSW: St. Paul's Publications, 171.

Flynn, M and Mok, M. (2002). *Catholic Schools 2000: A Longitudinal Study of Year 12, Students in Catholic Schools*. Sydney: Catholic Education Commission, 2002.

Franchi, L. (2014). The Catholic School as a Courtyard of the Gentiles. *Journal of Catholic Education*, 17 (2), 57-76.

Gray, M. (2015). *The Catholic family: 21st century challenges in the United States*. Washington DC: CARA.

Greeley, A. (2004). *The Catholic revolution: New wine, old wineskins and the Second Vatican Council*. Los Angles: University of California Press.

Greeley, A., McCreay, W. and McCourt, K. (1984). *Catholic Schools in a Declining Church*. Kansas City: Sheed and Ward.

Greeley, A and Rossi, P. (2002). *The education of Catholic Americans*. New Jersey: Transaction Publishers.

Heft, J. (2011). *Catholic High Schools: Facing New Realities*. New York: Oxford University Press.

Higgins, s. (2007). The value of anecdotal evidence', in Lorne Tepperman and Harley Dickinson, (Eds), *Reading Sociology: Canadian Perspectives*. New York: Oxford University Press.

ISCA. (2015). *Independent schooling in Australia: Snapshot*. Retrieved from http://isca.edu.au/wp-content/uploads/2011/07/ISCA-Snapshot-2015.pdf

Levitt, M. (1996). *Nice when they are young: Contemporary Christianity in families and schools*. Aldershot: Avebury.

Mason, M., Singleton, A. and Webber, R. (2007). *The spirit of Generation Y: Young people's Spirituality in a changing Australia*. Melbourne: John Garrett Publishing.

Martin, F (1983). Catholic Education in Victoria 1963-1980. In *Catholic Education in Victoria Yesterday Today and Tomorrow*. Melbourne: Catholic Education Office.

McCarthy, M. (2016). Parental choice of school by rural and remote parents. Issues in Educational Research, 26(1), 29-44.

McGuire, M. (2008). *Lived religion: Faith and practice in everyday life*. New York: Oxford University Press.

McQuillan, P. (2011). Who's coming to school today?' How might it affect tomorrow? *St Mark's Review*, (217), Aug 2011: 50-69.

Mulligan, J. (2005). *Catholic education: ensuring a future*. Ottawa: Novalis.

NCEA (2014) National Catholic Education Association, https://www.ncea.org/data-information/Catholic-school-data

NCEC (2013). *Australian Catholic Schools 2012*. Sydney: National Catholic Education Commission.

Musset, P. (2012). School choice and equity: Current policies in OECD countries and a literature review. *OECD Education Working Papers*, No. 66, OECD Publishing. http://dx.doi.org/10.1787/5k9fq23507vc-en

Pollefeyt, D and Bouwens, J. (2014). *Identity in dialogue: Assessing and enhancing Catholic school identity. Research methodology and research results in Catholic Schools in Victoria, Australia*. Berlin: Lit Verlag.

Rymarz, R. (2002). When I was at School. *British Journal of Religious Education*, 24(1), 20-32.

Rymarz, R. (2015). *Authentic Catholic schools*. Toronto: Novalis.

Rymarz, R. (2016). Comparing Catholic and non-Catholic Students in Catholic Schools: Some Implications for Understanding of Secularization. *Compass*, 50, 9-16.

Sharkey, P. (2015). *Educators guide to Catholic identity*. Mulgrave, Vic: John Garratt Publishing.

Singleton, A. (2014). *Religion, culture and society: A global approach*. Los Angeles: Sage.

Smith, C and Snell, P. (2009). *Souls in transition: The religious & spiritual lives of emerging adults*. New York: Oxford University Press.

Smith, C., Longest, K., Hill, J. and Christoffersen, K. (2014). *Young Catholic America: Emerging adults in, out of, and gone from the Church*. New York: Oxford University Press.

Stoltz, J. (2009). Explaining religiosity: Towards a unified theoretical model. *British Journal of Sociology* 60: 345-376.

Stoltz, J., Purdie, S., Englberger, T., Konemann, J and Kruggeler, M. (2015). *(Un)Believing in Modern Society: Religion, Spirituality, and Religious-Secular Competition*. London: Ashgate.

Windle, J. (2009). The limits of school choice: some implications for accountability of selective practices and positional competition in Australian education. *Critical Studies in Education*, 50(3), 231-246.

CHAPTER 2

Professor Richard Rymarz is Head of Religious Education and Director of Research at BBI – The Australian Institute of Theological Education. Prior to this, after many years working in Australia, he took up the Peter and Doris Kule Chair in Catholic Religious Education, St Joseph's College, University of Alberta. Richard has a long history of research, teaching and writing in religious education and related fields. Some of his most recent work has focussed on young people and religion and teacher formation. His most recent book explored the concept of authentic Catholic education.

Correspondence to:
BBI – The Australian Institute of Theological Education
PO Box 662, Pennant Hills NSW 1715
Email: rrymarz@bbi.catholic.edu.au

Chapter 3

Better Understanding the Context of Religious Education: The CECV Leuven Research

Paul Sharkey

CHAPTER 3

Introduction

The Enhancing Catholic School Identity (ECSI) research has unfolded over the past decade in a partnership between the Catholic Education Commission of Victoria (CECV) and the Catholic University of Leuven (KU Leuven) in Belgium. The research builds on the capacity of school leaders to enhance the Catholic identity of their schools by understanding what is happening culturally within their community and the profile of the religious responses being made by community members, given that cultural context.

Professor Didier Pollefeyt from KU Leuven is the 'Promoter' of the research and Drs. Jan Bouwens is the chief researcher. The research began in 2006 initially in the Archdiocese of Melbourne and soon thereafter in the other Victorian dioceses. It has since been taken up in other places within and beyond Australia. Pollefeyt and Bouwens developed multivariate attitude scales and surveys on the basis of the theoretical models of Catholic identity described in this chapter. Books could be written on the sophisticated theological, sociological and statistical analysis associated with this research. There is however space within this chapter to focus on the three scales which lie at the heart of the research: the Post-Critical Belief Scale, the Melbourne Scale and the Victoria Scale. These scales are described in some detail in (Pollefeyt & Bouwens, 2010) and in a major report from the research called *Identity in Dialogue* which presented the findings of data collected from 96 Victorian schools and approximately 17,000 research participants (Pollefeyt & Bouwens, 2014). Although these reflections are based on the published data from the 2012 round, the total data collected to date is from 479 schools and more than 95,000 students, 25,000 staff and 15,000 parents. The strategy in this chapter is to describe each scale briefly and then reflect on a finding from *Identity in Dialogue* to illustrate how the ECSI research might be used by school and system leaders to enhance the Catholic identity of their schools.

The Post-Critical belief scale

What is the Post-Critical belief scale?

Whilst some people experience the world as being absolutely charged with the presence of God, others are convinced atheists and of course there are all manner of faith and non-faith positions in between. For example, the phenomenon of 'somethingism': 'I know there is something out there, but I am not sure what it is.' This sense of God being present or absent is one of the dimensions of the Post-Critical Belief (PCB) Scale and the other dimension concerns the extent to which religious truths are interpreted literally or symbolically. The PCB scale was developed in the 1990s by Dirk Hutsebaut (1996) on the basis of a religious engagement typology David Wulff (1991).

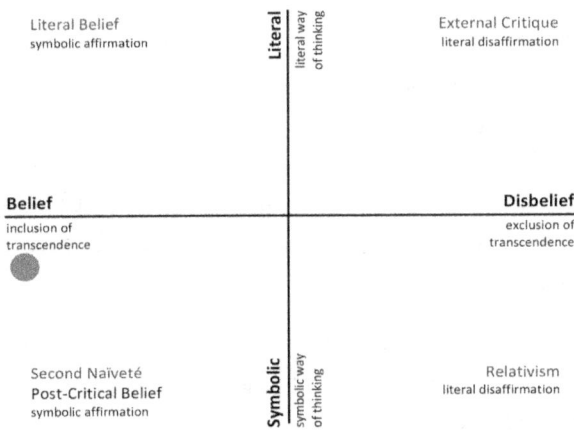

Figure 1: Diagram of the Post-Critical Belief Scale (Pollefeyt and Bouwens, 2014)

The four quadrants of the PCB Scale are derived from combinations of the two dimensions of transcendence and literalism. The upper left quadrant is high in belief and literalism and so people exercising this option hold their religious beliefs strongly and literally. Those who operate in the upper right quadrant also understand religious beliefs in literal terms but are strong in rejecting religion (high literal, strong disbelief). Those in the lower right quadrant are called relativists because whilst they do not hold a personal belief in God themselves, they are open to the beliefs of others – their understanding is that belief (or non-belief) is always a personal interpretation so there is no 'one way' to truth. Those in the lower right quadrant also recognise that truth is mediated (rather than being directly grasped) but in this quadrant there is a sense of the God who lies beyond the human interpretations and therefore an understanding that notwithstanding the mediated nature of truth, religious belief has a foundation and an anchor that prevents beliefs from slipping down a slippery slope into relativism.

Within the PCB Scale, school communities can be profiled on the basis of their responses to the PCB questionnaire which has 33 items for adults and 20 for students. It is important to note that individuals have elements of each quadrant in the way they engage with religious beliefs and there is no suggestion that people are placed exclusively in any one of the quadrants. Having made this point, clear preferences are often evident in the way individuals engage with religious expressions such as sacred text, doctrine and code.

Each of the scales in the ECSI research has a 'preferred position'. This is the position that the promoter of the research believes is most appropriate or 'normative' on theological grounds. This preferred (or theologically normative) position is represented in each scale as an orange dot. As can be seen in Figure 1, the dot is placed at the extreme right side of the belief scale and therefore the research advocates for the strongest experience of the transcendent. The dot is also placed in the symbolic quadrant, indicating that God is never 'grasped' literally but always known through mediations such as scripture, prayer, sacraments and doctrine as well as being discerned in daily life through experiences of beauty, loving relationships and truth as it is disclosed in its many rich and varied manifestations. The dot is placed close to the horizontal axis in the symbolic quadrant because whilst God is neither grasped literally nor directly, God is nonetheless eminently knowable because God reaches out to humanity in love. A lower placement of the dot might imply an esoteric and figurative God whose revelation lies beyond us.

How do the results from the PCB Scale help us to enhance the Catholic identity of our schools?

Table 1 represents the percentage of students who Agreed or Strongly Agreed with questions in each of the four categories of the Post-Critical Belief Scale. Primary school (Year 5/6) students are represented by the upper bar in each pair and secondary students by the lower bar. As has been noted, the preferred position in the PCB Scale is Post-Critical Belief and it is encouraging that roughly two thirds of students identify with post-critical belief in their secondary years of schooling. One challenge that the data above offers though is that instead of remaining or increasing in Post-Critical Belief as they move from childhood into adolescence, some students are moving into External Critique and Relativism. This movement is not surprising given the cultural context that is described below when considering the Melbourne Scale where the effects of pluralising, detraditionalising and individualising cultural currents are discussed. The PCB Scale gives system and school leaders a language and a framework for profiling what is developing in their communities and then taking action in the light of these profiles.

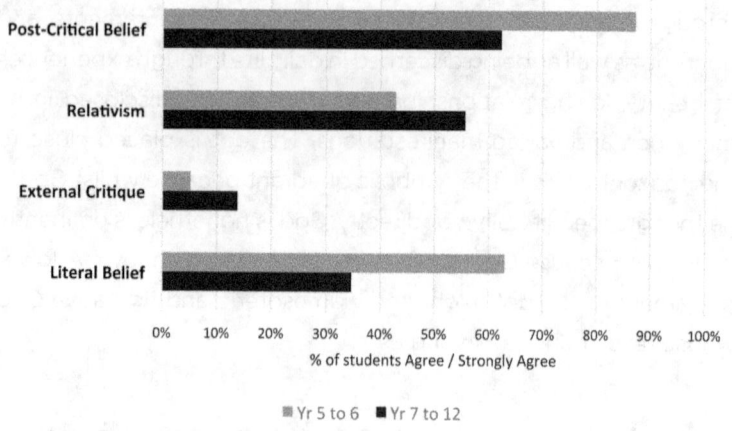

■ Yr 5 to 6 ■ Yr 7 to 12

Table 1: PCB comparison Primary to Secondary. Source: Figure II-45 and Figure II-50 for Primary and Secondary student data respectively in Pollefeyt and Bouwens (2014).

It is clear from the research that Literal Belief is not sustainable in the longer term for students as approximately half of them drift away from that literal believing style as they move from their primary school years into adolescence. As indicated, the preferred believing style is Post-Critical Belief and yet there is a drift into External Critique and Relativism. The ECSI research therefore leads us to ask: How do we develop curriculum and pedagogical strategies which support a movement into Post-Critical Belief? Space does not permit an exploration of this question here but I have drawn from the philosophy of Paul Ricoeur (1965/1970) to consider it elsewhere (Sharkey, 2015). Ricoeur's analysis applies not only to religious belief but to understandings that we have in any area of significance in our lives – for example, what it means to be a parent, an Australian, a Catholic, a teacher etc. In any of these areas we have an initial understanding (First Naïveté) and from time to time this initial understanding is challenged by some experience that we have. We either turn away from the challenge or we face it and critically evaluate the understanding that we have. When we critically evaluate the understanding, we step back and deconstruct it to some extent. Depending on what unfolds in this critical engagement, we can either develop a new understanding or we can step away from the belief or conviction altogether. The new understanding that we have after the critical engagement always differs from the initial understanding as we can never return to the first naïveté once we have entered the critical space. The new post-critical understanding is named Second Naïveté in Paul Ricoeur's analysis and Post-Critical belief in the ECSI research. Teachers can play an important role in helping their students negotiate their way through critical engagement into post-critical belief. The ECSI research provides a rich framework for clarifying the curriculum and pedagogical approaches which are most effective in this regard.

The findings from the Post-Critical Belief Scale lead educators to ask questions like: Why do some students move from literal belief into post-critical belief whereas others do not? Is a 12 year old student capable of Post-Critical Belief? or What does Post-Critical Belief look like in a Primary School? (These are three questions that have been asked rather rigorously and fruitfully in recent times.) How does one accompany students into their critical spaces, even as one clearly conveys that what is learned in the critical space can become a foundation for a post-critical belief and commitment that is richer and more mature than one's pre-critical understanding?

There are no easy answers to questions such as these and Catholic educators have been addressing them for years in their professional deliberation and action. One of the frameworks used in Belgium is for the teacher to be a Witness, a Specialist and a Moderator (Pollefeyt, 2008). Teachers are witnesses when they are able to give a credible account of what Catholic faith means from their perspective. They are moderators when they support and challenge their students in critical spaces to consider new possibilities beyond the attitudes and outlooks they currently hold. And teachers are specialists when they can draw effectively from the Catholic tradition and other sources to support their students' religious formation.

The Melbourne scale

What is the Melbourne scale?

The Congregation for Catholic Education stated that the duty of the Catholic school was to find a meeting place between faith, culture and life (The Catholic School, 1977). With this in mind, those who lead Catholic schools need to be grounded in Catholic faith and they also need to understand how to link faith, culture and the lives of the people who comprise their school community. The research literature on culture is vast but these reflections draw on the writings of Lieven Boeve, a theologian associated with KU Leuven. Boeve's analysis provides the foundation for the Melbourne Scale and he describes three important cultural phenomena which need to be recognised and appreciated by those seeking to understand the religious identity options being taken up by individuals and communities at this time.

Boeve refers to individualisation, detraditionalisation and pluralisation and he makes an important distinction between these cultural phenomena and the various ideologies which might be developed in response to them. For example, there is a distinction between individualisation (the cultural phenomenon) and individualism (an ideology formed in response to individualisation). Individualisation occurs when individuals are seen as creating their own identities, rather than having their identity assigned to them by the society or culture in which they live. In a culture shaped by individualisation, elements of identity such as gender, religion, marriage or ethnicity are seen as being shaped by personal choice, rather than by culture, religion or biology. Individualism is a specific strategy that one uses to deal with the process of individualisation – namely that 'the individual's preference constitutes the all-determining norm' (Boeve, 2016).

I find Boeve's distinction between cultural phenomena and ideologies empowering. If the analysis begins with the cultural phenomenon, rather than with ideologies formed in response to it, then there is the opportunity to recognise new possibilities for culture going forward. Rather than beginning with a negative stance towards culture, we can begin by understanding what is happening, then we can identify new opportunities for proclaiming the Gospel at the same time as we critique ideologies which run counter to it. Having understood what is happening culturally, having critiqued ideologies and strategies which run contrary to our faith, it becomes possible to propose new strategies which are culturally plausible, rather than proposing strategies which tilt at cultural windmills. This does not mean bending Catholic identities out of shape to fit within the constraints of culture, it means growing new Catholic identities out of cultural soil in ways that are faithful to the tradition at the same time as they are accessible and credible for current and future generations.

As well as discussing individualisation, Boeve also reflects on pluralisation and detraditionalisation in his analysis. In a detraditionalised context, cultural traditions (including religious traditions) no longer naturally transfer from one generation to the next. In a pluralised culture a variety of religious and ideological traditions sit visibly and legitimately in the public space so that individuals are forced to confront the reality that one's own tradition is but one among many alternatives. Instead of understanding secularisation simply as a movement from a religious stance to a non-religious one, Boeve understands secularisation as a sociocultural context shaped by detraditionalisation and individualisation. Boeve's analysis sits comfortably alongside other elements of the research literature on culture and faith – for example, Charles Taylor's ethic of authenticity (Taylor, 1991) and the findings from the Spirituality of Generation Y research project where young people prefer to put life together themselves, rather than accepting traditional beliefs and values (Hughes, 2007). Those who teach religious education know that many of their students can be cynical about religion or are very diverse in their beliefs and attitudes. As the context shifts, so must our pedagogy and curriculum if we are to remain connected and engaged with our students.

Pollefeyt and Bouwens used Boeve's typology to develop the Melbourne Scale which represents responses that Catholic institutions typically make at this time. The first thing to note about the Melbourne Scale is the ever-widening gap between Christianity and culture, represented by the sloping lines of the diagram in Figure 2 which widen as each decade passes by – see timeline on right hand side of the diagram. The gap between culture and Christianity widens because of the effects of cultural currents such as detraditionalisation, individualisation and pluralisation.

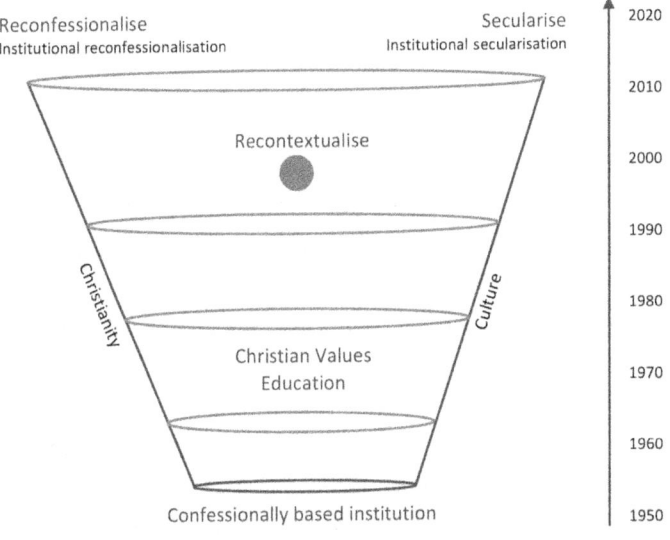

Figure 2: Diagram of the Melbourne Scale (Pollefeyt and Bouwens, 2014).

At the bottom of the diagram is the 'Confessionally-based institution'. Those who lead these institutions do not see that their school faces a Catholic identity problem. They believe that the prevalence of traditional identity markers in their school (such as liturgy, religious imagery, R.E. curriculum and prayer) provide clear evidence of the health of their school's Catholic identity. The presence of these markers has been likened to petrol in the tank (Pollefeyt & Bouwens, 2014, p. 284). Each year that passes by drains the tank further still when the surrounding culture does not support the school's Catholic identity. The ECSI research challenges Catholic educators to develop new identity strategies with students that are culturally plausible in our time.

On the top right side of the figure is the option of institutional secularisation. Those who take this option have abandoned the school's Catholic identity, either because they are not committed to the Catholic project or because they believe that secularisation is inevitable given the magnitude of cultural currents which shape the life of the school. On the top left side of the figure is the reconfessionalising option. Here, those responsible for the school actively reassert its Catholic identity through such strategies as raising the profile of prayer and liturgy, installing religious symbols, increasing the profile and active involvement of priests, tightening the ties with the local parish and taking other steps to present a more explicit and public rendering of the school's Catholic identity and life (Pollefeyt & Bouwens, 2014, p. 54). Strategies such as these may also be enacted in the recontextualising approach which is the preferred stance within the ECSI research but the difference is that in the recontextualising approach, cultural realities such as pluralisation, detraditionalisation and individualisation are recognised as the cultural soil out of which Catholic identity grows whereas the reconfessionalising approach seeks to grow Catholic identity in a soil where these realities have been leached out. Reconfessionalisation may well work as a strategy with subpopulations that, for one reason or another, are not greatly affected by the cultural dynamics identified in Boeve's analysis. The strategy is likely to fail however when dealing with the broader, mainstream Catholic population.

In the lower-middle section of the figure is the strategy of Christian Values Education (CVE). The CVE strategy is to link a Catholic belief with a culturally accepted value on the basis that students will deepen their Catholic faith because of their appreciation of the cultural value. For example, cultural values such as forgiveness, reconciliation and love are presented to the students in the belief that the students will link the value with some element of Catholic faith and will grow in faith as a consequence. Boeve's hypothesis is that Christian Values Education strategies may have been effective in the past when the gap between culture and faith was narrower but are ineffective and counterproductive in our current context. The ECSI research confirms this hypothesis. The pluralised context means that students understand all too well that culturally accepted values have many sources besides Christianity and the detraditionalised context means that they will not commit themselves to a belief behind a value simply because some religious authority urges them to do so. The individualised context means that individuals will want to actively create their own worlds of meaning and so those seeking to proclaim the Gospel in our time need to be more explicit in their approach and create spaces where the students are actively involved in appreciating what Catholic faith can mean in our time. It is to that explicit and active strategy that we now turn – the strategy of recontextualisation.

Recontextualisation is a religious identity option which actively responds to pluralisation, detraditionalisation and individualisation. Recontextualisation responds to the pluralised context by expecting and respecting the plural views and voices that will be present in any typical school community. Rather than seeking an easy or superficial consensus, the recontextualising strategy strongly respects not only the diversity of worldviews of community members but also the integrity and cogency of Catholic faith. In recontextualisation it is not a matter of being responsive to pluralism OR being faithful to the Tradition, it is a matter of developing culturally plausible expressions of Catholic faith within an explicitly appreciated pluralised context. This is a BOTH/AND approach that appreciates that in a detraditionalised and individualised cultural setting, faith commitment only becomes feasible when religious expressions are personally meaningful, rather than seeing religious commitment as a response to religious authority or simply the culture in which one was raised. Recontextualisation also challenges those who lead Catholic systems and schools to become more *explicit* in their engagement with Catholic faith. In contrast to the Christian Values Education approach where traditional elements (such as doctrine, ritual and sacred text) are reduced down to culturally comfortable values, forms or themes, recontextualisation opens up a more explicit engagement with the tradition. It is not simply a matter of understanding and respecting diversity within the school community, it is also a matter of respecting the integrity of the faith and the claim it makes when it is encountered on its own terms, rather than being heavily translated, thematised or accommodated to provide a comfortable cultural fit for students.

Recontextualisation also responds to the reality that school leaders can no longer assume that faith is formed for students within their families who participate actively in parish communities. The family was described as the 'domestic Church' at the Second Vatican Council (Lumen Gentium, 11) and parents were recognised as the 'primary and principal educators' of their children (Gravissimum Educationis, 3). Many still share these ideals but most would recognise that the ideals are frequently not the lived experience of students in our schools when it comes to their formation in Catholic faith. Recontextualisation is a strategy which seeks to create the conditions where faith is able to germinate and grow roots to mature as an authentic Catholic lived commitment in the pluralised, detraditionalised and individualised context in which our schools operate. An orange dot has been placed against Recontextualise to represent this identity option as being the preferred stance within the research.

The Melbourne Scale uses a 46 item questionnaire for adults and a simpler version for students. The Questionnaire not only asks respondents to identify where their school is now but also where they would like it to be in relation to the various aspects of Catholic identity being explored. These two levels are called the 'factual' and 'normative' levels respectively and the differences between them can lead to very valuable insights for those with leadership responsibilities at system and school levels.

How do the results from the Melbourne Scale help us to enhance the Catholic identity of our schools?

The results from the 2012 ECSI data shows that as students move from being children to adolescents, they reject reconfessionalising strategies and become more open to secularisation. They remain very open to Christian Values Education and continue to support recontextualising approaches but at a slightly reduced level. These results are what one would expect if the cultural analysis discussed above was accurate. The good news from Table 2 below is that only a very small percentage of adults support the secularisation of the schools' Catholic identity and close to 80% affirm the presence of Catholic identity markers in their school such as the celebration of the Eucharist, crucifixes on the wall, etc.

The Melbourne Scale recognises that individuals do not belong exclusively in one identity category, thus it is possible for respondents to support a Recontextualising approach as well as a Values Education approach. The challenge from this data is that whilst well over 80% of adults support the preferred stance of Recontextualisation, almost as many also support Values Education and therefore, if the research analysis is correct, a significant change process needs to be initiated to shift staff from a Values Education approach into the more explicit strategies of engaging with the tradition associated with recontextualisation.

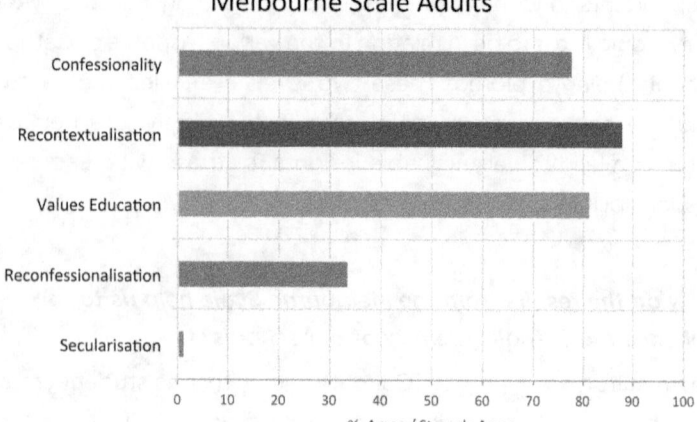

Table 2: Melbourne Scale, adults Agree/Strongly Agree. Source: mean scores for adults in Primary and Secondary schools in Figures II-60 and II-66 respectively of Pollefeyt and Bouwens (2014).

This data is valuable because it is opening up new conversations among those who lead our Catholic systems and schools. Are the adults who are taking a Values Education approach doing so in the belief that it leads students into a deeper appreciation of Catholic faith? Is the analysis correct that such approaches are misguided in the current context shaped by individualisation, detraditionalisation and pluralisation? How might staff be led to understand why the assumptions underneath the CVE approach no longer hold? How do recontextualising approaches differ from the Christian Values Education approach? How can those who are committed to a reconfessionalising approach make their unique contribution to the religious formation of students? How might staff be motivated and equipped to make the shift from the CVE approach into recontextualising pedagogical strategies which are preferred in this research?

The Victoria scale

What is the Victoria scale?

In a pluralising context it will be expected that students, staff and families will bring a rich variety of outlooks and worldviews into the life of the school. Some of these attitudes and outlooks will support the school's Catholic identity and others will not. Those who lead Catholic schools must decide how they are going to respond to the many and varied worldviews of its members. The Victoria Scale was developed on the basis of a typology devised by the Dutch researchers Wim ter Horst and Chris Hermans. The typology is similar to the PCB Scale in the sense that it is built around two dimensions. These two dimensions – solidarity and Christianity – are depicted below in the diagram of the Victoria Scale.

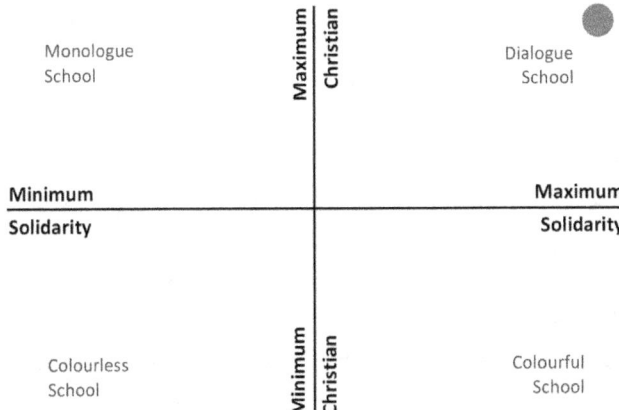

Figure 3: Diagram of the Victoria Scale. Source: Pollefeyt and Bouwens, 2014.

In the ECSI research the vertical axis is understood in Catholic terms so that the two strongly Catholic options are represented higher in the diagram whereas the two options at the bottom of the diagram are weak in their Catholic identity. The 'solidarity' dimension represented along the horizontal axis signifies the extent to which community members wish to draw views that differ from their own out into the public forum of the school. Those who are represented on the left hand side of the diagram are not interested in engaging in a dialogue with community members whose views differ from their own. As we move from left to right there is an increasing interest in opening up a public dialogue with community members in all their diversity about questions of faith and meaning.

Beginning on the upper left hand side of Figure 3, the Monologue School places a strong emphasis on its Catholic identity and has little interest in engaging with non-Catholic beliefs and outlooks. There is only one voice allowed to sound in the public space of the Monologue School and it is the Catholic voice. The Colourless School is like the Monologue School in the sense that the diverse beliefs and worldviews of students are not brought into the public forum of the school. Unlike the Monologue School though, the Colourless school is low in Catholic identity and so questions of meaning and belief – even Catholic beliefs – are not encouraged in the school's public spaces and discourses. In the Colourless School, religion is seen as being a private matter lying outside of the school's essentially secular educational mission. The Colourful School is also low in Catholic identity and so there is no sustained intentional engagement with Catholic beliefs, symbols and practices in the life of the school. Unlike the Colourless School though, questions of meaning, belief and value are encouraged and difference and diversity are celebrated. The Colourful School typically has a strong commitment to social justice, pastoral care and other ethical concerns such as sustainability but does not engage these concerns explicitly or systematically with Catholic doctrine. The religious traditions of the diverse members of the

Colourful School are celebrated equally and the Catholic liturgical seasons and feasts would be no more prominent than the key moments of other religious and non-religious traditions.

The Dialogue School is like the Monologue School with its strong commitment to Catholic beliefs, practices and symbols but it differs from the Monologue School by welcoming diversity as a means to building a contemporary Catholic identity. Instead of amplifying the Catholic voice so that it is the only one that sounds in the school, the Dialogue School creates the conditions where all voices are respected and invited to join a conversation that is systematically and intentionally engaged with Catholic beliefs. This is a BOTH/AND approach to Catholic identity. It is not a matter of choosing between diversity OR strong Catholic identity, it is a matter of growing a strong Catholic identity out of the soil of religious and cultural plurality. Catholic beliefs are never imposed on members of the school community but they are systematically proposed to them in ways that respect the diversity of community members and their right to respond freely to what is being proposed to them. An orange dot has been placed in the Dialogue School quadrant to represent this option as being preferred within the research.

We have noted above that Pollefeyt and Bouwens operationalised Boeve's typology into the Melbourne Scale and they did likewise with the Hermans/ter Horst typology that forms the basis of the Victoria Scale. The Victoria Scale uses a 40 item questionnaire for adults and a simpler version for students. The questionnaire has a similar structure to the Melbourne Scale in the sense that it not only asks respondents to identify where their school is now but also where they would like it to be in relation to the various aspects of Catholic identity being explored.

How do the results from the Victoria Scale help us to enhance the Catholic identity of our schools?

One of the first things to notice in the Victoria Scale data represented in Table 3 is that support for the Monologue School drops away dramatically as students move from childhood into adolescence. The older students are not interested in belonging to a school where the Catholic voice is the only one allowed to sound. The fact that more than half of the students support the preferred stance in the research – the Dialogue School – is encouraging for those who accept the ECSI analysis.

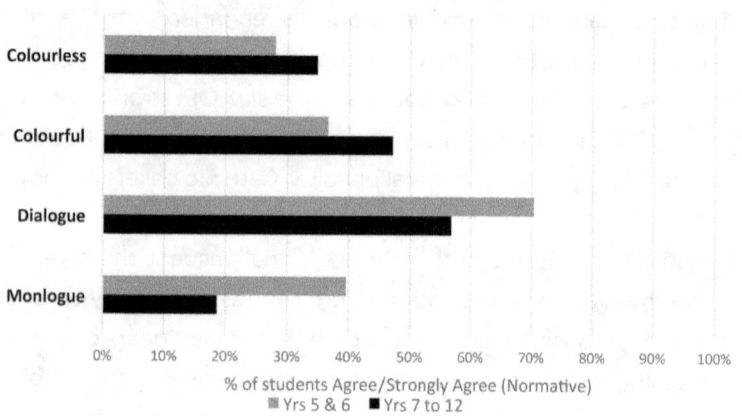

Table 3: Victoria Scale, Primary and Secondary students Agree / Strongly Agree. Source: Figure II-80 and Figure II-86 for Primary and Secondary student data respectively in Pollefeyt and Bouwens (2014).

The challenge in the data is that whilst support for the Dialogue School remains relatively high, some of the older students are moving away from this preferred option into the Colourless and Colourful school options. Catholic educators who accept the ECSI analysis are finding ways to remain inclusive in their approach by welcoming diversity without watering down their school's Catholic identity. Whilst the Colourful School welcomes diversity, it does not engage students systematically and explicitly with the Catholic beliefs and practices. The Dialogue school not only welcomes diversity, it presents a strong and sustained engagement with Catholic beliefs, rituals, stories and symbols. Teachers in a Dialogue School open up spaces where the diversity of voices that one would expect in a pluralised cultural context are allowed to sound and they engage the dialogue explicitly and systematically with Catholic perspectives, without seeking to impose those perspectives on the students. The data in Table 3 shows that adolescent students reject Catholic beliefs and symbols when they are imposed on them – see the halving of support for the Monologue School from Primary to Secondary. The steps involved in Dialogical pedagogies can be perceived as being a sophisticated dance where missteps easily occur but when the right expertise and formation is provided, teachers understand the issues and enact strategies which invite students into faith even as their freedom and diversity is respected. It is neither a matter of imposing Catholic beliefs nor being silent about them, it is a matter of witnessing to the power and meaning of the Gospel confidently in the midst of plurality without seeking to deny or suppress the diversity that is expected in a pluralised, detraditionalised and individualised cultural context.

Future directions and challenges

As system and school leaders in Victoria have familiarised themselves with the conceptual basis for the ECSI research, they have learned to interpret the data and the reports that they have received. As this knowledge is acquired, there is an increasing capacity to take action to enhance the Catholic identity of the schools on the basis of findings such as those mentioned in these reflections. Certainly in my own diocese our Archbishop and our Executive Director have been very clear in their expectations that the next phase of the research needs to focus on improved outcomes for students. Those of us engaged in this work are learning from our shared action and this learning is being distributed broadly across the network of Catholic education.

Those who exercise leadership in the broader Church are also engaging with this research and their insights are helping us to deepen our understanding of the implications of the research for parish life and the wider Church. The deliberations of a recent clergy conference in Melbourne provide a case in point in this regard as has the development of a scale for parishes which draws on the Leuven research (Reed, 2015). The research has already grown well beyond its Victorian roots with a number of Catholic institutions of higher education engaging with the research. One dimension of this engagement is to ensure that teachers understand the ECSI language as they engage in pre-service teacher education and also postgraduate programs of study. As this academic engagement deepens, it is to be expected that key elements of the research will be scrutinised and tested. I am aware for example of questions which are being asked about the capacity of primary-aged children to engage in post-critical belief. As we pursue questions such as these our understanding of students will deepen and our capacity to respond effectively to their formation needs will be improved. Considerable research is required to develop resources and strategies which respond to insights and findings from the research and the momentum for this development is currently building.

Dioceses beyond Victoria are also participating in the research and we are learning together as we move forward in our respective contexts. It is clear already that teachers need to have at least a basic theological literacy if they are to respond effectively to the challenges which are being identified in this research. They also need to understand what is happening culturally and the implications of the cultural context for the pedagogies they enact and the curricula they devise. Some of these issues are considered at greater depth in the chapter of this book written by Rina Madden.

I have sometimes been bemused by those who confuse the ECSI research with Catholic identity per se. Catholic identity is never reducible to a project and always transcends any attempt to package it or systematise it into surveys or reports. There is no such thing as an ECSI diocese or an ECSI school even though there are many schools and dioceses that have been helped greatly by the light that the ECSI project has thrown onto the Catholic identity options being taken up in their schools. Those who lead the ECSI research are clear that it was never intended to be an end in itself, rather it provides another strand in a continual effort to provide quality and effective religious formation for the students who have been entrusted to us.

REFERENCES

Boeve, L. (2016). *Theology at the crossroads of university, Church and society: Dialogue, difference and Catholic identity*. London: Bloomsbury.

Congregation for Catholic Education. (1977). *The Catholic School*. Retrieved from http://www.vatican.va/roman_curia/congregations/ccatheduc/documents/rc_con_ccatheduc_doc_19770319_catholic-school_en.html

Hughes, P. (2007). *Putting life together: Findings from Australian Youth Spirituality Research*. Fairfield: Fairfield Press.

Hutsebaut, D. (1996). Post-Critical Belief: A new approach to the religious attitude problem. *Journal of Empirical Theology, 9*(2), 48-66.

Pollefeyt, D. (2008). The difference of alterity: A religious pedagogy for an interreligious and interideological world. In J. D. al. (Ed.), *Responsibility, God and*

Society: Festschrift Roger Burggraeve (pp. 305-330). Leuven: Peeters.

Pollefeyt, D., & Bouwens, J. (2010). Framing the identity of Catholic schools: empirical methodology for quantitative research on the Catholic identity of an education institute. *International Studies in Catholic Education, 2*(2), 193-211.

Pollefeyt, D., & Bouwens, J. (2014). *Identity in dialogue: Assessing and enhancing Catholic school identity.* Zurich: Lit Verlag.

Reed, B. (2015). Engaging with the Hopes of Parishes: A Systematic, Empirical and Practical Search for a Parish Engagement Scale (SPES). KU Leuven, Faculty of Theology and Religious Studies: unpublished Doctoral Dissertation.

Ricoeur, P. (1965/1970). *Freud and philosophy: An essay on interpretation.* (D. Savage, Trans.). New Haven: Yale University Press.

Sharkey, P. (2015). *Educator's Guide to Catholic Identity.* Mulgrave: Vaughan Publishing.

Taylor, C. (1991). *The ethics of authenticity.* Cambridge: Harvard.

Wulff, D. (1991). *Psychology of religion: Classic and contemporary views.* New York: Wiley.

Dr Paul Sharkey is the Director of Catholic Educational Services at the Catholic Education Office, Melbourne. Prior to this role he was State Director of Catholic Education in South Australia. Paul is interested in exploring issues of identity and culture in the Catholic sector as they have a particular significance for schools at this time. He has recently written a book which explores how the Enhancing Catholic Identity research might be used to illuminate mission and identity endeavours in Catholic schools. He lectures on this topic at Catholic Theological College (Melbourne) and is currently documenting exemplary practice with a view towards publication in 2018.

Correspondence to:
Email: psharkey@cem.edu.au

Chapter 4

Improving Leadership in Religious Education: Implications for Policy Reform

Michael T. Buchanan

Introduction

This chapter considers some problematic issues regarding the role and responsibilities of religious education leaders in light of recent policy recommendations in Australia. A key finding from the research described here is that, while the policies maintain that religious education leaders should promote the religious identity of the school as well as foster a sense of connectedness through building school community, those very leaders are at times the ones who feel the least connected to the school community. They are also more likely than other leaders to resign from the position prior to completing their full term.

One of the things school principals fear most is the resignation of the religious education leader in their school (Crotty, 2005). There is at the same time a high turnover rate of these leaders and a dearth of applicants to fulfil this role; consequently the combination of these two elements has resulted in less experienced personnel being appointed to senior positions, often with disastrous results. The lack of suitable successors willing to take on the role gives reasons for concern to religious education leaders themselves as well as principals, who want experienced successors who are capable of senior leadership. Over the past decade, the diocesan-based centralised authorities for Catholic education across Australia have attempted to address these concerns by putting in place specific policy reforms and initiatives to enhance the experience of religious education leadership and plan for its systematic succession. The chapter draws on insights from a recent study into the kinds of support religious education leaders need to do their job effectively. It also explores the general limitations of these policies and proposes some recommendations for policy reform.

The position of religious education leader is relatively new in Australia. It began to emerge countrywide in Catholic schools across many dioceses immediately following the Second Vatican Council (1962-1965) (Crotty, 1998; see also Buchanan, 2005). Since the time of its conception there has been a lack of clarity about what the role actually entails which has served to generate feelings of isolation and disconnectedness amongst many religious education leaders (Fleming, 2002). This has been evidenced by a history of rapid religious education leadership turnover (Blahut & Bezzina, 1998; Engebretson, 2006). In fact, for some Catholic schooling systems the average employment span of a religious education leader has been approximately two years (Engebretson, 1998; Rymarz, 1998). The swift turnover of these leaders hinders a school's ability to promote and deliver consistently high quality religious education (Crotty, 2005; see also Blahut & Bezzina, 1998). There has been a range of policy reforms and initiatives across many dioceses oriented towards highlighting the importance of the role of the religious education leader. However, a recent study regarding the kinds of support these leaders perceived they needed to do their jobs effectively suggested that the policy initiatives might be counterproductive to enhancing a sense of connectedness for religious education leaders which is vital to minimising high turnover rates.

This chapter will provide an overview of some of the complexities associated with the position of the religious education leader and posit that this has led to a lack of clarity about the role within schools as well as feelings of disconnectedness for many leaders. It will proceed to explore some recent policy initiatives designed to engender recognition for the status of the role within Catholic education schooling systems and discuss these initiatives in the light of the perspectives of the religious education leaders involved in a study which sought to identify the kinds of support they needed to do their job effectively.

Complexities associated with the role of the religious education leader

Each diocese in Australia is responsible for Catholic education and religious education within its defined geographical region. Therefore it is inaccurate to refer to Catholic schools in Australia as one Catholic schooling system. Each diocese has the jurisdiction to make up its own policies including education and religious education policies so long as they comply with (or do not breach) federal and state laws. After the Second Vatican Council (1962-1965) a range of policies emerged establishing the position of religious education leader across various dioceses throughout Australia. No two policies were exactly the same as they were designed to cater for schooling systems at the local diocesan level. However, regardless of the differences Engebretson (2006) noted an emphasis on certain ministerial aspects associated with the role. Some of the ministerial tasks required religious education leaders to take responsibility for developing and fostering the liturgical and prayer life of the school community as well as sacramental programs and encourage the faith development of staff and students by facilitating activities such as retreat programmes and reflection days. These ministerial tasks, while catechetical in nature, were traditionally regarded as integral to parish life and the Catholic school (Buchanan, 2011; Grajczonek, 2006). Throughout the latter part of the twentieth century the religious education policies from various dioceses differed in terms of whether the religious education leader role served a ministerial function or an educational purpose. The following table adapted from Buchanan, (2010: 47) shows the variance across a range of early diocesan policies regarding where the religious education leadership emphasis was placed.

Diocese	Employment centralised	Emphasis	Educational Emphasis	Ministerial Emphasis
Sydney	Yes	Educational	Implementation and administration of the religious education curriculum; the professional development of religious education teachers.	Mission of the Church; Catholic ethos; liturgical and faith life; positive relationships.
Hobart	Yes	Ministerial	Implementation and administration of the RE curriculum including resources.	Teacher formation; commitment to the Catholic tradition and Catholic education; prayer, liturgy and retreats; pastoral care and personal development; Catholic ethos.
Canberra Goulburn	Yes	Ministerial	Implementation and administration of the RE curriculum including resources.	Mission of the Church; commitment to Catholic tradition and Catholic education; witness; Catholic ethos; inspire faith; share vision; build community; spiritual leadership.
Darwin	Yes	Ministerial	Approved tertiary qualifications in religious education; member of the school executive; coordination of religious education curriculum.	Active member of the Catholic Church; role model; prayer and liturgy; develop the school as a faith community.

Diocese	Employment centralised	Emphasis	Educational Emphasis	Ministerial Emphasis
Brisbane	Yes	Educational	Educational leadership of the religious education curriculum; member of the school executive.	Contributes to the Catholic ethos and the religious life of the school.
Western Australia	Yes	Educational	Religious education curriculum leadership.	
Parramatta	Yes	Educational	Learning programs; resources; professional development; quality of teaching and learning.	Mission of the Church.
Melbourne	No	Ministerial	RE curriculum leadership and administration.	Witness; models and teachers of faith.

Table 1: Religious education leadership role emphasis across certain dioceses between the 1980s - 1995.

The variance in emphasis on tasks illustrates the lack of clarity across the dioceses regarding the role. Furthermore recent studies indicated that there is also a lack of clarity within a given diocese regarding how the role should be exercised (Buchanan, 2010; Crotty, 2002; Fleming, 2002). This was regardless of whether the appointment of the religious education leader was determined at the school or at a centralised diocesan level. There were certain factors that were perceived to have an influence on where the emphasis would be placed. The personality of the religious education leader was regarded as having a significant influence upon shaping the position within a school (Liddy 1998). The professional knowledge of the teacher was found to be another significant factor (Rymarz, 1998).

Two major studies in the early part of the twenty-first century explored inconsistencies in the way in which the role was carried out within a diocese. An investigation into the role of the religious education leader in Sydney by Crotty (2002) conceptualised the role as one containing a bi-dimensional nature in that it was perceived as a position both within the *Church* and within *education.* In the same diocese Johnson's (1998) research discovered that even in times when the classroom curriculum was in need of attention many religious education leaders tended to ignore these concerns and focus on the Church or ministerial aspects of the role. This tendency to make the ecclesial and ministerial dimensions of the role the main focus was also prevalent at the turn to the twenty-first century (Crotty, 2005). From one perspective the emphasis placed on the ministerial aspects of the role by the religious education leaders appeared to contradict the emphasis reflected in Table 1, which showed that in Sydney the policy orientated towards and educational bias with a focus on the implementation and administration of the religious education curriculum. Clearly there was a lack of clarity pertaining to where the emphasis should lie. Another major study in the Melbourne diocese also highlighted the lack of clarity pertaining to the role. Fleming (2002) sought to articulate the role of the religious education leader in Catholic schools in Melbourne and found that there was an inconsistent interpretation of how the role should be carried out. For some religious education leaders the role was perceived as educational with the key responsibility being to lead the development and implementation of the classroom religious education curriculum. However many of the religious education leaders who participated in Fleming's (2002) study were confused about whether the emphasis should be placed on the educational or ministerial dimensions of the role. Fleming

(2002) noted that several religious education leaders recall that at the time of their interview for the position they were asked many questions regarding their ability to carry out the ministerial aspects of the role. This was despite the advertised position emphasising skills and expertise in the curriculum and educational dimensions of the role. They were seldom, if ever, asked questions about their expertise in developing and designing the classroom religious education curriculum. They were mainly asked questions regarding whether they could prepare a school Eucharistic service, or a retreat programme, or foster the faith development of staff and students. Their recollections of their interviews also alluded to an exclusive bias amongst principals towards the ministerial dimensions of the role.

A question that has never been fully examined is whether a religious education leader is a ministerial role or an educational role. The leaders themselves are not necessarily clear on this. Engebretson (2006) noted that in a study on the management of curriculum change in religious education a leader expressed a preference for a *practising* Catholic over a Catholic with qualifications in the discipline of religious education. While ideally a religious education teacher who is both practicing and qualified to teach is more likely to be the preferred choice, the point that Engebretson (2006) was stressing alluded to a level of confusion about the perceived nature and purpose of religious education in schools. This confusion was prevalent amongst a number of religious education leaders despite the emphasis on the academic aspects of classroom religious education being conveyed by the Congregation for the Clergy (CC) being that:

> It is necessary, therefore, that religious instruction in schools appears as a scholastic discipline with the same systematic

demands and the same rigour as other disciplines. It must present the Christian event with the same seriousness and the same depth with which other disciplines present their knowledge. (CC, 1998: para. 73)

The line of questioning at the interview stage suggested a bias from many principals in terms of perceiving the role of religious education leader as ministerial (Fleming, 2002). For some religious education leaders this perception alienated them from representation on school leadership teams and for some leaders, who were included as a member of a school's leadership team, they felt disconnected from the decision-making process. They believed that they were not valued for their educational experiences and expertise because they were perceived as the *religious* person carrying out ministerial functions (Fleming, 2002; see also Buchanan, 2006).

During the twenty-first century a wave of religious education leadership policy reforms set out to confirm the role of a senior leadership position in Catholic schools. However, these reforms did very little to bring clarity to the role or to overcome feelings of disconnectedness experienced by many religious education leaders. Prior to exploring two policies and critiquing them against the insights gained from the research into the kinds of support religious education leaders perceived they needed to do their jobs effectively, a brief overview of the research design informing this study is presented. It provides a context for considering the discussion and potential for policy reforms.

Research design that informed this study

The participants were religious education leaders in Catholic primary and secondary schools across Australia and they were enrolled in a postgraduate study unit that was generally undertaken by students in the final stages of a Master of Religious Education degree at Australian Catholic University, Australia. The unit focused on various leadership dimensions which have been associated with the distinctive nature of leadership in Catholic schools (but not exclusive to leadership in such schools). These dimensions include educational leadership, curriculum leadership, faith leadership, spiritual leadership, ministerial leadership, and religious leadership (Buchanan, 2013a). The unit was offered in a fully online mode and those enrolled in the unit had access to their lecturer and their peers via online discussions, email and telephone communication. There were regular online discussion forums for students to interact with each other as a means to stimulate peer learning and feedback. These participants were suitable for this study because they were religious education leaders committed to professional growth in their discipline.

There were a total of twenty-one people enrolled in the unit and at the completion of the unit a letter was sent to each person. The letter invited them to participate in the study. If they agreed to participate they were asked to download a survey/questionnaire from an online learning environment website, type their responses to the survey/questionnaire and return it via post in a stamped self-addressed envelope which was provided. The surveys were completed anonymously in that participants were asked not to disclose their name or any information that would reveal their identity. Twenty responses were received out of a potential of twenty-one participants.

The survey/questionnaire asked four broad questions about the type of support participants perceived they needed to do their job effectively. They were asked what type of support they felt they needed in general and what type of support they felt they needed from the school in which they were employed, the centralised authority to which their school belonged (the Catholic Education Office in their respective diocese) and the university in which they were undertaking their course (in this case Australian Catholic University).

The conceptualisation of the participants' responses to the questionnaire was guided by the principles underpinning the original approach of Glaser and Strauss (1967) to grounded theory. By intensive engagement with the participants' responses particular categories of findings began to emerge. According to Glaser (1998; 1992) the categories of findings should emerge from the data. Categorising the data in this way allows for the data to tell its own story (Goulding, 2002). This approach was appropriate because little is known about the kind of support religious education leaders in Catholic schools perceive that they need. As indicated by the number of participants, this was a small scale study. Glaser (1998; 1992) has emphasised that it is only necessary to stay in the field of data collection until the categories have reached saturation point. This is not determined by the quantity of participants but rather the quality of data, for saturation occurs when no new information or categories emerge from the data. Category saturation is an important factor that contributes to the plausibility of the study (Glaser, 1998).

An associated category of findings, which is the focus of this study, indicated religious education leadership policies did very little to help the participants overcome the feelings of alienation and disconnectedness they encountered in carrying out their role. These findings are explored in the following section in the light of two recent policy reforms pertaining to religious education leadership.

Examining the policies in light of the perspectives of the religious education leaders

There are 28 dioceses throughout Australia and all have the jurisdiction to generate their own policies pertaining to Catholic education and religious education. It is not possible to explore all policies pertaining to religious education leadership that have emerged in the twenty-first century within the scope of this chapter. Therefore the policies pertaining to two different regions within Australia are explored in this section. The two chosen tend to illustrate the policy trends in religious leadership in the past decade. The policies from Brisbane (Catholic Education Office Archdiocese of Brisbane, 2012) and South Australia (South Australian Commission for Catholic Education, 2004) confirm religious education leadership as a senior leadership position in Catholic schools. In Brisbane the religious education leader is referred to as Assistant Principal – Religious Education and the South Australian policy refers to the religious education leader as a Religious Leader. Both policies give recognition to the role as a senior leadership position requiring representation on a school's senior leadership team. This level of recognition is intended to highlight the importance of the role within Catholic education. However it comes at a cost as it also places another demand on religious education leaders who have already been identified as holding a position that is already too big for one person to manage (Crotty, 2005; Liddy, 1998). When positions become overloaded with too many responsibilities there is a greater risk of leaders becoming overwhelmed and a less likely chance of them being able to successfully fulfil all their leadership responsibilities and achieve all their goals. A sense of underachievement can spiral into a feeling of despair and disconnection from the role as one participant alluded to:

> I need support to get on top of all the duties I have to fulfil [as a religious education leader]. Sometimes I wake up in the night thinking about all the things I have to do before the end of the next day. By the time I get to work I am already tired and then I discover that I have a leadership meeting which will take another two hours out of the day. My colleagues on the leadership team seem to be coping yet I feel like I am drowning. It should not be like this. I need an assistant. (Participant D)

For this participant a sense of being overwhelmed has contributed to a feeling of being lost and disconnected in the work place.

The policy expectations for eligibility to undertake the role are comparatively more demanding than for other senior positions in Catholic schools. For example, the religious education leader must be a committed, practicing Catholic with professional qualifications in not only education but also in religious education. In larger schools the religious education qualification must be at a Masters Degree level. Five years of experience as a successful teacher, together with five years of experience teaching religious education in a Catholic school is also required. To take on the position of religious education leader in a larger primary or secondary school the incumbent must have previous experience as an Assistant Principal – Religious Education. The religious education leader must also demonstrate an ability to provide *religious leadership* and foster the religious life of the school. In the areas of *educative leadership,* the ability to develop and implement high quality religious education programmes and infuse a religious dimension across the entire curriculum is required. They must also demonstrate competencies to exercise appropriate *staff and community leadership*, *strategic leadership* and *organisational leadership* (Catholic Education Office Archdiocese of Brisbane 2012). In the South Australian context the policy requires religious education leaders to have qualifications in religious education or be working towards obtaining such qualifications. They must be appropriately involved in the senior leadership structures of the school and are also required to commit themselves to ongoing formation and appropriate forms of staff appraisal. They are also required to demonstrate the ability to animate the religious dimension of the Catholic school by fostering partnerships with families, parishes, dioceses and the universal Catholic Church. Furthermore, they must demonstrate the ability to enable their contribution to the school to include building up its religious ethos. They must be able to ensure that the religious education curriculum and entire school curriculum assume a religious character. They are required to show leadership in animating the religious life of the school through liturgical celebrations, faith formation experiences and enliven the school community to strive towards the kind of justice that is geared towards the improvement of social structures (South Australian Commission for Catholic Education, 2004).

The policies allude to the important and demanding role religious education leaders fulfil within the school and their wider Church community. The policies emphasise the position as one of senior leadership, however some religious education leaders felt unsupported in their role. This lack of support fostered a sense of alienation and inadequacy. The participants involved in this research were all working towards obtaining a qualification in religious education at master's degree level while working full-time as religious education leaders. Many felt overwhelmed and unable to do justice to both their role and their studies.

Working full-time in a leadership position and studying at master's degree level is undoubtedly challenging for many participants and a commitment to both would make a huge demand on one's time. Participant L's testimony reflects this and also shows the loneliness that arises in the demanding schedule of the religious education leader. This seems to result from the perception that they don't have the support from staff members in activating religious education related initiatives. Such feelings can contribute to a sense of disconnectedness for religious education leaders.

The religious education leadership policies focus strongly on confirming the status of this position as a senior leadership position within schools (Catholic Education Office Archdiocese of Brisbane, 2012; South Australian Commission for Catholic Education, 2004). However there remains a lack of clarity about what the role actually entails. The bi-dimensional nature of the role that Crotty (2005; 2002) referred to remains a prominent feature of the policies pertaining to the religious education leader. However, where the emphasis should be placed is not made clear in these policies, and the responsibilities of the religious education leaders become duties and tasks that the leader ultimately carries out.

The insights shared by this religious education leader suggest that without structured followership a leadership title carries very little significance for leaders eager to fulfil their role effectively and foster the religious dimensions that are integral to the Catholic school. Participant S provides examples of structured followership for curriculum leaders and wellbeing leaders, yet is at a loss to identify structures within the domain of religious education. The religious education leadership policies stop short of articulating a structured followership and it is not clear who in fact the leader is actually leading.

Without structured followership it would be difficult for religious education leaders to do their job effectively. Their role is too complex and demanding for one person to take on every responsibility individually (Dowling, 2012; Healy, 2011; Liddy, 1998). Furthermore without provision for a structured followership it becomes difficult to plan for appropriate leadership succession (Buchanan, 2013b). Given the high turnover rates and the average expectancy of remaining in the position averaging around two years (Engebretson, 1998; Rymarz, 1998), policy reforms that provide for structured followership might support opportunities for suitable succession as well as contribute to enabling religious education leaders to do their jobs effectively. One way to promote leadership succession is through creating opportunities to build leadership capacity in schools (Elmore, 2000). The following table adapted from Buchanan (in press) provides an example of possible ways to build leadership capacity pertaining to religious education leadership.

The column titled Middle Leader highlights a range of key portfolios a religious educator is responsible for. Each of these is a demanding role in itself. The participants in this study indicated that they tended to work alone attending to each of these areas. In so doing other staff members do not have the opportunity to share in exercising religious education leadership. Each of the portfolios could be assigned to a range of staff members and promote opportunities for middle leadership. The middle leaders in turn could work in small teams to develop and maintain these areas of religious education. Such an initiative would distribute the workload amongst staff members and enable them to develop leadership skills relevant to (but not exclusive to) religious education leadership. The capacity for religious education leadership would be spread more broadly amongst staff members.

Senior Leadership	Middle Leader	Teacher Leader	Teachers
Leader in Religious Education	RE Curriculum Leader	Year level curriculum team conveners	Classroom religious education teachers
	Retreat Programme Leader	Retreat Team	Teachers and Students
	Prayer & Liturgy Leader	Prayer & Liturgy Team	Teachers and Students
	Mission & Engagement Leader	Mission & Engagement Team	Teachers and Students
	Social Justice Leader	Social Justice Team	Teachers and Students
	Staff Faith Development Leader	Staff Faith Development Team	Teacher and other Staff members
	Sacrament Programme Leader	Sacramental Team	Teachers and Students

Table 2: Building Leadership Capacity in Schools.

This is vitally important in an area such as religious education where there is a problem with attracting educators to apply for positions as religious education leaders (Crotty, 2002). It is a leadership position that many educators have shied away from because they are not clear on what the role entails (Crotty, 2005; Fleming, 2002). Providing opportunities for middle leadership in religious education through policy development will help staff members to gain insights and into what religious education leadership entails. It will inspire confidence in middle leaders to take on religious education leadership. The policies pertaining to religious education leaders that have emerged across Australian dioceses in the twenty-first century have confirmed the role as a senior leadership position with representation on school leadership teams. However, these policy initiatives have done very little to clarify what the role actually entails. It is still debateable where the emphasis should be oriented. Should the leadership emphasis be pointed towards the ministerial or education dimensions of the role (Crotty, 2005). The policies have done very little to address the concern that the position is too big for one person to manage (Liddy, 1998). Given the turnover rate for religious education leaders is approximately two years (Engebretson, 1998; Rymarz, 1998), it is concerning that policies have not addressed this by making provision for succession planning. The religious education leaders who participated in this study perceived that the recent policies had not alleviated their experiences of alienation and disconnectedness.

Drawing on the insights gleaned from the religious education leaders who participated in this study, it is recommended that policy makers consider the following recommendations. It is recommended that in order to bring clarity to the role policy developments outline a clear distinction between the ministerial and educational responsibilities pertaining to religious education leadership. A clear indication as to where emphasises should be placed would undoubtedly be helpful in shaping a leader's professional practice. It could act as a point of reference for appraising the goals achieved by the leader in a given period of time. The participants perceived that commitment to postgraduate studies, while fulfilling their responsibilities as a religious education leader, sometimes disconnected them from their work and other commitments. Consideration could be given to negotiating monthly study leave blocks from their schools to enable them to fully concentrate on their classes and completing the assessment requirements. The participants also felt that in many situations they relied on staff members to volunteer to support some of the initiatives associated with religious education. They indicated that volunteers were generally reluctant to come forward and that they found themselves fulfilling all the tasks rather than leading educators to contribute to the religious dimension of the Catholic school. Experiences of working in isolation contributed to feeling disconnected from the school community. These concerns, when also considered in the light of aforementioned problems with religious education leadership succession, could be addressed in a policy by establishing a structure of followership through the creation of middle leader positions. Middle leaders undertaking responsibilities for religious education would directly report to the Religious Education Leader and enhance the leadership capacity for religious education. It would help staff members in these role to gain an insight as well as experience in religious education leadership. It may foster a generation of aspiring religious education leaders. Moving in this direction contributes to increasing the potential for competent leadership succession in religious education.

REFERENCES

Blahut, L. and Bezzina, M. (1998). The primary religious education coordinator: Role demands and job turnover in the diocese of Parramatta. *Journal of Religious Education, 46*(2), 2-7.

Buchanan, M.T. (2005). The religious education coordinator: Perspectives on a complex role within Catholic education. *Journal of Religious Education, 53*(4), 68-74.

Buchanan, M. T. (2006). Curriculum management: Influencing school outlook towards religious education. *Journal of Religious Education, 54* (2), pp. 71-78.

Buchanan, M. T. (2010). *Managing curriculum change in religious education: An inside perspective from school leaders in religious education.* Germany: Lambert Academic Publishing.

Buchanan, M. T. (2011) Ministerial leadership: A dimension of leadership in religious education. *Religious Education Journal of Australia, 27*(2), 34-38.

Buchanan, M. T. (2013a). *Leadership dimensions associated with leadership roles in faith-based schools.* M. T. Buchanan. (Ed.). *Leadership and religious schools: International perspectives and challenges* (pp. 127-144). New York, USA: Bloomsbury Academic.

Buchanan, M. T. (2013b). Learning for leadership in religious education in schools through continuing education. *International Journal of Continuing Education and Lifelong Learning, 6*(1), 119-136.

Buchanan, M. T. (in press). Supporting Learners Learning for Leadership in Religious Education. *Journal of Religious Education.*

Catholic Education Archdiocese of Brisbane. (2012). *Role description: Assistant Principal Religious Education.* Catholic Education Archdiocese of Brisbane: Brisbane, Australia.

Congregation for the Clergy (1998). *General directory for catechesis.* Australia: St Paul's.

Crotty, L. (1998). The religious education coordinator: Evolution and evolving agendas. *Journal of Religious Education, 42*(2), 8-14.

Crotty, L. (2002). *Religious leadership in the Catholic school: The position of the religious education coordinator.* Unpublished doctoral dissertation, The University of Sydney, Australia.

Crotty, L. (2005). The REC and religious leadership. *Journal of Religious Education, 53* (1), 48-59.

Dowling, E. (2012). An investment in our future: Reimaging professional learning or religious education. *Religious Education Journal of Australia, 28*(1), 23-29.

Elmore, R. F. (2000). *Building a new structure for school leadership.* Washington DC: Albert Shanker Institute.

Engebretson, K. (1998). Structural arrangements for the role of religious education coordinator in Australian dioceses. *Word in Life, 46*(2), 23-26.

Engebretson, K. (2006). A framework for effective religious education leadership in the Catholic secondary school. In R. Rymarz (Ed.). *Leadership in religious education* (pp. 135-151). Australia: St Pauls Publications.

Fleming, G. P. (2002). *An analysis of religious education coordinators perceptions of their role in catholic secondary schools in the archdiocese of Melbourne.* Unpublished doctoral dissertation, Australian Catholic University, Australia.

Glaser, B. (1992). *Basics of grounded theory analysis: Emergence v forcing.* Mill Valley, CA: Sociology Press.

Glaser, B. (1998). *Doing grounded theory: Issues and discussions.* Mill Valley, CA: Sociology Press.

Glaser, B., & Strauss, A. (1967). *The discovery of grounded theory: Strategies for qualitative research.* New York: Adeline.

Goulding, C. (2002). *Grounded theory: A practical guide for management, business and market researchers.* Great Britain: Sage Publications Ltd.

Grajczonek, J. (2006). School leadership and sacramental education in the Catholic school. In R. Rymarz (Ed.). *Leadership in religious education* (pp. 115-134). Australia: St Pauls Publications.

Healy, H. (2011). *Implementing curriculum change in religious education: A study of the perceptions of primary school religious educators in the Archdiocese of Hobart.* Unpublished doctoral dissertation, Australian Catholic University, Australia.

Liddy, S. (1998). Key issues for the REC. *Journal of Religious Education 46*(2) 27.

Rymarz, R. (1998). The religious education coordinator (REC): A four-fold approach. *Journal of Religious Education, 42*(2), 28-32.

South Australian Commission for Catholic Schools. (2004). *Religious leadership in a Catholic School policy.* South Australian Commission for Catholic Schools: South Australia.

Michael T Buchanan PhD is an Associate Professor in Religious Education at Australian Catholic University and is the Course Leader of the Master of Leadership. His research interests include religious education and leadership in faith based schools. He has published widely in national and international journals and is the immediate past editor of *Religious Education Journal of Australia*. Michael's latest publication is *Global Perspectives on Catholic Religious Education in Schools*. He is an affiliated Associate Professor in the Faculty of Education at the University of Malta and a Research Fellow at York St John University, UK.

Correspondence to:
Associate Professor Michael T Buchanan
Email: michael.buchanan@acu.edu.au

Chapter 5

Developing Religious Education Curricula for Early Childhood in Australia

Jan Grajczonek

It is only since the 1990s, that Australian Catholic education has prioritised early childhood education becoming more intentional in developing religious education curricula for the early years. This does not imply however, that there had been no religious education in early childhood in previous times but it certainly had not received the same attention as did primary and secondary religious education during the 19th and 20th centuries and the first eighty years of the 21st century. Indeed, it is only in the last three decades that early childhood education and care (hereafter ECEC) has become a major agenda item for governments around the world (Siraj-Blatchford & Mayo, 2012). Catholic education has not been immune to such increased interest in, and development of, ECEC as it deliberates on its own distinct space and place in the ECEC sector. This in turn has led to the development of religious education curricula for both Catholic prior-to-school settings and school early years classrooms. This chapter explores curriculum development in early childhood religious education in Australia. First, it traces the contexts that prompted such interest by diocesan Catholic education offices and agencies in curriculum development of early childhood religious education in Australia. Second, it examines the actual phenomena of curriculum development in early childhood religious education in terms of educational theories, approaches and elements that influence, shape and guide effective religious education curriculum for early childhood.

Contexts that prompted religious education curriculum development for early childhood

In the late 1980s, the Australian federal government recognised children's early formative years as a critical and decisive factor in their development, wellbeing and learning. In the following years,

ECEC became a key agenda item for the government which led to the publication in 2009 of the nation's first early childhood learning document, *Belonging, Being Becoming: The Early Years Learning Framework for Australia* (hereafter EYLF) (Australian Government Department of Education, Employment and Workforce (DEEWR), 2009). It would not be wrong to claim that the EYLF document was a watershed publication for ECEC as for the first time, young children's development and learning between the ages of birth and five years had been mandated nationally. Certainly prior to 2009, some states had published their own kindergarten/preparatory/preschool guidelines/frameworks for children but these were for the immediate year prior to schooling; for example, the Queensland Government's *Early Years Curriculum Guidelines* (Queensland Studies Authority, 2006) for the introduction of the preparatory year in 2007. EYLF signalled young children's learning from birth as a matter of importance for Australia. A second significant characteristic of the EYLF document was that it explicitly required educators to consider the spiritual aspects of young children's lives and learning (DEEWR, 2009, p. 14); the first Australian government learning framework to do so. Australian Catholic diocesan education offices and agencies embraced the nation's increased emphasis on ECEC and all Catholic prior-to-school settings implemented their state/territory EYLF along with other mandated quality assurance regulations.

Before the development of religious education curriculum for religious education in early childhood can be traced, it is first important to distinguish the various levels of Catholic ECEC. Early childhood is the term given to any form of care and education provided for children from birth to the age of eight years. Within this age range there are four main forms of education and care:

1. Non-compulsory long day care is offered to children from birth to five years. Some diocesan Catholic education offices have established and administer long day care centres (for example the Diocese of Perth in Western Australia and the Dioceses of Rockhampton and Townsville in Queensland). In other dioceses, other Catholic agencies offer long day care (for example, Centacare's Child Care Services in the Dioceses of Brisbane and Toowoomba). All day long day centres are required to implement the EYLF (DEEWR, 2009).

2. A non-compulsory one-year prior-to-school kindergarten or preschool program is another form of early childhood education offered to children aged 4-5 years in the year immediately before formal schooling. This program can operate within long day care centres, in off-school-site or on-school site centres. Again, in some dioceses, Catholic Education Offices have established and administered these centres in their schools (such as in the Townsville diocese). In other dioceses such as in Brisbane and Toowoomba, Centacare's Child Care Services offers kindergarten programs both within their long day care centres and in centres on Catholic school sites. Other independent Catholic groups also offer prior-to-school programs (such as the Order of the Canossian Daughters of Charity Servants of the Poor who established and administer the Canossa Kindergartens in the Archdiocese of Brisbane). All one-year prior-to-school settings are required to implement either the EYLF (DEEWR, 2009) and/or their local state or territory learning guidelines.

3. A preparatory/preschool/kindergarten year (assigned different names in different states and territories) which

is part of primary school education is available on all school sites, including Catholic schools, for all children between 5 and 6 years. These classrooms are required to implement the curriculum as specified in the Foundation level of the Australian Curriculum (Australian Curriculum Assessment and Reporting Authority (ACARA), 2013).

4. The first three years of formal primary education for children aged between 6 and 8 years is considered to be part of early childhood education. Ideally their educational programs should be underpinned by early childhood education theory and practice.

While religious education programs in various formats had been integrated into Catholic early years in school settings before the 1990s, it is only since then that more formal curriculum development in religious education had been initiated. One example of this was in the Archdiocese of Brisbane Catholic Education which published its *Religious Education: Curriculum Guidelines for the Early Years* (Barry, Brennan, Lavercombe & Rush, (eds.)) in 2007 in preparation for the introduction of the preparatory year for all schools in Queensland. Such curricula were to complement existing religious education curriculum implemented in the Catholic school. These curriculum documents were underpinned by ECEC theory and practice and generally sought to reflect the government mandated curriculum documents for other key learning areas.

In terms of the Catholic prior-to-school settings, more formal religious education curriculum development has been in response to the publication of the EYLF (DEEWR, 2009) document. The Catholic Education Office of Western Australia was one of the first dioceses to commence this formal journey into religious education curriculum development in prior-to-school ECEC settings. It completed its draft document, *Raising Religious Awareness* in 2010 and in 2014, the final curriculum, *Let the Little Children Come to Me: A Resource for Raising the Religious Awareness of Children in the Early Years* (Catholic Education Office of Western Australia) was published. This curriculum which was five years in the making, is underpinned by the EYLF principles to which examples for the Catholic prior-to-school setting have been described, for example:

- Secure, respectful and reciprocal relationships including such examples as:
  - Modelling Jesus' love for everyone.
  - Making connections between how students relate to one another and Jesus and his teachings.
- Respect for diversity including such examples as:
  - Acknowledging students of different cultures and their celebrations.
  - Discussing different cultural traditions for special religious celebrations (e.g. Christmas/Easter) (p. 7).

In similar ways, this document makes several explicit links to pedagogical practices as outlined in EYLF (see pages 7-11).

In 2010, the Queensland Catholic Education Commission's (henceforth QCEC) Pre-Prep Taskforce was created to assist all Queensland Catholic diocesan prior-to-school settings introduce and implement the various new ECEC quality assurance regulations. In response to the publication of EYLF (DEEWR, 2009) particularly with its references to young children's spirituality, the QCEC Pre-Prep Taskforce commissioned a literature review of children's spiritual and religious development (Grajczonek, 2010a) which then led to the publication of the *Framework for Early Years Spiritual Development in the Catholic Tradition* (Grajczonek in collaboration with QCEC Pre-Prep Taskforce, 2010b). The framework specifically focused on nurturing young children's spiritual development in Catholic long day care and early learning centres such as kindergartens. This document is not a curriculum but rather a framework from which diocesan early childhood settings can develop their own spiritual/religious education curricula.

One of the first Queensland dioceses to use the *Framework for Early Years Spiritual Development in the Catholic Tradition* to shape their early years religious education curriculum was Catholic Education Diocese of Rockhampton which in 2012 published its draft early years prior-to-school curriculum document, *Spirituality in the Early Years*. The format of the Rockhampton document reflects EYLF identifying: (i) learning outcomes; (ii) key learning components; (iii) examples of evidence; and (iv) examples of teaching practice. To the five outcomes specified in the EYLF document, the Rockhampton framework specifies an additional outcome, 'Children have a strong sense of their innate spirituality' (p. 8) which includes three key components of learning:

- Children have a sense of wonder about their identity.
- Children have a sense of wonder about the present moment – of people, events, experiences and surroundings.
- Children have a sense of wondering at the big questions about life and the divine as they respond with a sense of awe and wonder to the intangible, an event, an experience or natural phenomena (p. 8).

The outcome and key learning components are complemented with examples of evidence educators might observe in children as well as examples of teaching practice. For example, for the key learning component 'Children have a sense of wonder of the present moment – of people, events, experiences and surroundings' (p. 11) suggested examples of observations of children and teaching practice include:

This is evident, for example, when children

- Investigate and communicate the social, religious and cultural practices of people with respect and dignity.

Educators promote this learning, for example, when they:

- Explore prayers from other religious traditions, in particular those represented in the centre/class (p. 11).

Spirituality in the Early Years (Catholic Education Diocese of Rockhampton, 2012) also draws from the Queensland Studies Authority (2006) document, *Queensland Kindergarten Learning Guideline* which nominates intentional teaching practices through the contexts for learning including:

- Play – e.g. role play ways to be a good friend.
- Real-life engagements – e.g. look at Mary's role as mother of Jesus.
- Routines and transitions – start each day with a prayer experience either through spontaneous prayers, music or meditation (p. 15).

In addition to the influences of government early years learning frameworks, various Catholic early childhood religious education programs and curricula have also been influenced by specific religious early childhood programs, such as Cavalletti's (1983) Catechesis of the Good Shepherd and Berryman's (1991) Godly Play. Cavalletti, a student of Montessori developed Catechesis of the Good Shepherd which incorporates the use of three-dimensional materials to teach children about the symbols of the Church, sacraments, Bible stories and so on. Berryman who studied with Cavalletti, adapted his program from hers but it is set within an Anglican/Episcopalian perspective. The early years spiritual/religious education frameworks in both the Catholic Education Office of Western Australian (2014) and the Catholic Education Diocese of Rockhampton (2012) have drawn on Godly Play techniques in the specific area of scripture.

Intentional curriculum development in religious education for early childhood in comparison with primary and secondary religious education curriculum development, is a relatively recent phenomenon responding to the emphasis on early childhood in Australia over the last three decades. Those dioceses that have developed their early childhood religious education curriculum documents have been significantly influenced by their various state and territory government early years guideline and framework documents, such as the *Early Years Curriculum Guidelines* (Queensland Studies Authority, 2006) as well as the Australian Government's publication of *Belonging, Being Becoming: The Early Years Learning Framework for Australia* (DEEWR, 2009). Curriculum development for religious education in early childhood is ongoing in Australia, as other dioceses continue to plan and implement their own curriculum documents (such as the Department of Early Childhood Education and Care, Townsville Catholic Education Office). We now turn to the second section of this chapter examining what effective development of religious education curriculum for early childhood in Australian Catholic settings should consider and include.

Core elements to be considered in curriculum development of religious education for early childhood

As in all areas of education, the understanding and articulation of what ECEC curriculum actually is and encompasses, remains a contentious matter (Wood & Hedges, 2016) reflecting multiple understandings and perspectives (McLachlan, Fleer & Edwards,

2013; Arthur, Beecher, Death, Dockett & Farmer, 2015). Notwithstanding, the Australian stated position on what ECEC curriculum encompasses is adapted from New Zealand's ECEC curriculum document, *Te Whariki* (as cited in DEEWR, 2009),

> Curriculum encompasses all the interactions, experiences, routines and events, planned and unplanned, that occur in an environment designed to foster children's learning and development (p. 9).

At the heart of the aims and goals for ECEC curriculum is each child's successful learning and development. However, in terms of what that learning entails, the specified content, the method in which that content is delivered, and how it is assessed and evaluated are all determined by what image of the child is held by curriculum designers, teachers and educators. Contemporary early childhood education theory and practice advocate children as capable learners who bring diverse experiences and cultural perspectives to the early years setting/classroom. Previously held images, including of the universal child (that is, the *one* child representing *all* children), of children as deficient adults on their way to becoming or of children as empty vessels to be filled with knowledge, no longer inform ECEC curriculum development. The contemporary image of the child influencing ECEC curriculum development is that of a rich, capable and strong enacting agency and of a voice which participates in his/her own learning (DEEWR, 2009, p. 7; QSA, 2006, p. 10).

> Children actively construct their own understandings and contribute to others' learning. They recognise their agency, their capacity to initiate and lead learning, and their rights to participate in decisions that affect them including their learning (DEEWR, 2009, p. 9).

The contemporary image of the child underpins and determines both curriculum development and implementation in ECEC. Religious education curriculum in early childhood cannot stand apart from or beyond contemporary ECEC theory and practice. The contemporary image of the child must also be at the heart of, and underpin, curriculum development in religious education. It is important that both disciplines, early childhood education *and* religious education inform, shape and guide curriculum development in religious education for early childhood. Although curriculum development in the two contexts of early childhood, prior-to-school and school settings, is separated, the underpinning principles and practices of ECEC remain relevant and essential in curriculum development and delivery in both contexts. This is equally as necessary for religious education curriculum development and delivery.

What then is deemed important in curriculum development of religious education for early childhood? This section of the chapter examines those elements considered by contemporary research and scholarship in both early childhood and religious education literature as key in informing, guiding and shaping curriculum development and delivery in religious education in the early years. The first step in any curriculum design and development is to know and articulate what particular perspective, viewpoint or position underpins that curriculum. In other words, what philosophical position underpins the document? Arthur, et al., (2015) explain,

> A philosophy interprets the theoretical perspectives, beliefs and values that underpin practices. It may be called a philosophy, but often terms such as 'beliefs' or 'values' will be used as alternatives (p. 146).

The role of philosophy or beliefs and values in curriculum development and delivery, is an important one to understand, as a philosophical stance or perspective directs teachers' pedagogies (Arthur, et al., 2015, p. 209), use of time, space and learning resources (MacNaughton, 2003, pp. 128, 165, 192-193). MacNaughton (2003) uses the term 'position' which is determined by educators' beliefs and ideas about educating young children categorising these positions according to how any one position views the role of education in society (p. 113). She suggests that there are three such positions: conforming, reforming and transforming. In the conforming position, also referred to as a transmission or technical position (Smith & Lovat, 2003), predetermined content is the central consideration. In this position, the child is viewed as an empty vessel to be filled with 'the knowledge, skills and dominant cultural values' which are 'already determined, socially sanctioned and ready to administer' for children 'to be trained and conformed to the fixed demands of compulsory schooling' (Dahlberg, Moss & Pence, 1999, p. 44). Content is valued over process, as well as over individual children's learning styles, dispositions and sociocultural contexts. The second position is described by MacNaughton (2003) as the reforming position, also referred to as a transactional or procedural position (Smith & Lovat, 2003), which places more emphasis on process rather than content having a greater focus on each child's role in the teaching and learning process. A transactional or technical position is a more of a child-centred position than a procedural or transmission one.

However, contemporary ECEC curriculum development increasingly favours the third position, a transforming position that seeks to 'contribute to the creation of a more just and wise society that offers diverse possibilities for who one can become' (MacNaughton, 2003, p. 188). A transformational position in curriculum is underpinned by critical theory (MacNaughton, 2003; Smith & Lovat, 2003) and is informed by sociocultural, postmodern and poststructuralist theories. It aims to transform children from within, that is, gives children respectful power in the world, listens to their voices and sees them through multiple lenses (MacNaughton, 2003, pp. 189-194). MacNaughton maintains that this position recognises and acknowledges knowledge as being socially constructed, that is, generated in interaction with children. Further, meaningful content should enable children to think and act, assisting them to transform their world (MacNaughton, 2003, pp. 195-196).

Given its underpinning emphases on justice and transformation, on valuing and empowering children's agency and voice and in seeking to create a transformed society, a transformational position to curriculum development aligns to and reflects Catholic social teaching, concerns and priorities. It follows then, that curriculum development in religious education for a contemporary world might be influenced considerably by such a position.

In addition to these three underpinning curriculum positions, there are two further positions unique to religious education curriculum: the catechetical and educational positions. Teachers of religion need to pay attention to the particular position, catechetical or educational, which underpins their diocesan religious education curriculum and understand how such positions determine their curriculum approaches and pedagogies. A catechetical position presumes that all children in the setting or classroom are Catholic and aims to develop their faith. An educational position acknowledges the diverse nature of children's sociocultural and religiously diverse contexts and does not presume all children are Catholic. An educational position distinguishes religious education as comprising two dimensions or processes: (i) the classroom religion program aiming to develop children's knowledge and understanding of religion; and (ii) the religious or liturgical life of the school which involves children in liturgy, prayer and social justice activities.

In seeking to articulate the distinction between catechetical and educational positions, the Congregation for Catholic Education (1988) defined each approach, catechesis (the catechetical approach) and religious instruction (the educational approach), in terms of each one's aims.

> The aim of catechesis, or handing on the Gospel message, is maturity: spiritual, liturgical, sacramental and apostolic; this happens most especially in a local Church community. The aim of the school however, is knowledge. While it uses the same elements of the Gospel message, it tries to convey a sense of the nature of Christianity, and of how Christians are trying to live their lives. It is evident, of course, that religious instruction cannot help but strengthen the faith of a believing student, just as catechesis cannot help but increase one's knowledge of the Christian message (para. 69).

Increasingly, since the early 1990s Australian Catholic dioceses are adopting a more educational position to religious education albeit at varying points along a continuum between these two positions. Those prior-to-school settings and school classrooms that take a catechetical position in their religious education curriculum, have been criticised for constructing children in particular ways that do not recognise their diversity, for not attending to children's rights as articulated in the *Convention on the Rights of the Child* (United Nations, 1989), as well as impeding children's equal rights to participate fully and actively in the curriculum (Grajczonek, 2015). When all children are constructed in a particular way such as being presumed to be Catholic and taught as such, their diverse backgrounds are disregarded, their agency is dismissed and their voices silenced (Grajczonek, 2015). Children's sociocultural contexts, that is, their diverse backgrounds, are required to be recognised, acknowledged and valued (DEEWR, 2009; ACARA, 2013).

Young children's diverse backgrounds with regards to religious diversity, is an especially important consideration in religious education curriculum development and pedagogical decision-making. As the number of young children who are not Catholic or who have limited or no prior religious experiences increases in Catholic prior-to-school and school settings, early years educators are challenged to find a starting point in the religious education curriculum. In this matter, curriculum development in religious education for the early years can draw on the discipline of children's spirituality which offers insights and practical ways for finding relevant starting points for religious education. Research in the area of children's spirituality informs us spirituality is innate to children and exhibited in such characteristics as their relationships, connectedness, awareness sensing, value sensing and mystery sensing which includes the capacity to wonder about the meaning and purpose of life (Coles, 1990; Eaude, 2003; Hay & Nye, 2006). Such research also suggests that religious education for young children should begin with, and seek to develop, their spirituality ahead of a more formal religious education (Liddy, 2007; Nye & Hay, 1996). Bradford (1999) argues that intentionally nurturing 'human spirituality' can lead to the development of 'devout spirituality', that is, religiosity (pp. 3-4). For example, when children's sense of wonder is nurtured, Bradford suggests they can then develop a framework for worship and a focus for contemplation (p. 4). These insights are relevant for early years religion teachers as it provides them with relevant starting points for their religion lessons.

Within any one specific underpinning position, teachers can take a number of approaches (Arthur, et al., 2015) in their curriculum planning which in turn determines their pedagogy, use of time, space and learning resources. It is important though that the approaches and pedagogies enacted align with the curriculum position. For example, a curriculum document underpinned by a transformational position would have teachers view and respect children as individuals, understanding that they are shaped and influenced by their sociocultural contexts, all of which are valued equally in the setting. Children would be empowered to shape those contexts (including the setting) to be more equitable and just. Each child would be understood as bringing rich and diverse ways of being into the setting all of which would be acknowledged and validated. Teachers would implement a wide assortment of teaching and learning approaches and strategies that would respond to and activate children's learning in a variety of ways including, but not limited to:

- Involving children in the decision-making process of the setting by seeking, listening to and valuing their voices.
- Enacting play-based learning (which is equally as important in school early years classrooms as in prior-to-school settings).
- Advocating and enacting children as active participants (rather than as passive recipients of content) fully engaged in their learning.
- Implementing intentional teaching strategies (DEEWR, 2009) that include scaffolding, prompting, affirming, confirming, provoking, questioning, challenging and supporting children.
- Communicating with children in ways that advocate and promote sustained shared thinking (Siraj-Blatchford & Sylva, 2004) and dialogical interaction (Vygotsky, 1967).

Such teaching and learning approaches and strategies would occur in different contexts such as through play, focused teaching, real-life engagement, routines and transitions, and would incorporate different physical environments such outdoor areas, school libraries, community and parish places, various excursions and so on. They would also consider the temporal environment, that is how time could be used most effectively to support children's learning, as well as social environments including how children could be paired and/or grouped and supported in their social interactions. These core curriculum elements are central to ECEC curriculum development and delivery. They are therefore also central, relevant and essential to curriculum development of religious education for early childhood.

At the heart of all curriculum decision-making is the child and it is each child's successful learning and development that is the central goal in all ECEC curricula. Curriculum development in religious education for early childhood, if it is to be relevant, effective and authentic, must reside within an early childhood educational perspective, that is, it cannot be developed or delivered without reference to early childhood theory and practice. Young children's successful learning and development depends on the type of education they receive; an education that is enacted by curricula that not only acknowledge them as active participants in their learning, but also recognises and validates each child's sense of being, belonging and becoming.

Conclusion

This chapter has specifically focused on curriculum development in religious education for early childhood in Australia. Early childhood education has become a priority for governments around the world including the Australian government as they recognise its pivotal role in the development and wellbeing of each child. Catholic diocesan education offices and agencies have responded to the federal government's emphasis on early childhood education by expanding and intensifying their involvement in the sector. This intensified response has prompted them to consider in more intentional ways their distinct space and place in ECEC. To this end, Catholic education offices and agencies are engaged at varying levels, according to each diocese's needs and priorities, in curriculum development in religious education for early childhood. In comparison with the development of Catholic primary and secondary school religious education in Australia, religious education in early childhood may be a relative newcomer, but that by no means lessens its critical and distinct place and influence within Catholic education.

REFERENCES

Arthur, L., Beecher, B., Death, E., Dockett, S. & Farmer, S. (2015). *Programming and planning in early childhood settings* (6th ed.). South Melbourne: Cengage Learning Australia.

Australian Curriculum, Reporting and Assessment Authority. (2013). *Australian curriculum: Foundation Content for Foundation – Learning area content descriptions*. Retrieved from http://www.acara.edu.au/_resources/Content_for_Foundation_-_Learning_area_content_descriptions.pdf

Australian Government Department of Education, Employment and Workforce (DEEWR) (2009). *Belonging, being & becoming: The early years learning framework for Australia*. Retrieved from https://docs.education.gov.au/system/files/doc/other/belonging_being_and_becoming_the_early_years_learning_framework_for_australia.pdf

Barry, G., Brennan, D., Lavercombe, P. & Rush, K. (Eds.). (2007). *Religious education: Curriculum guidelines for the early years*. Brisbane: Catholic Education.

Berryman, J. (1991). *Godly play: An imaginative approach to religious education*. Minneapolis, MN: Ausburg.

Bradford, J. (1999). The spiritual needs and potential of the child and young person: A rationale for discussion. *Muslim Education Quarterly, 16*(4), 3-14.

Catholic Education: Diocese of Rockhampton (2012). *Spirituality in the early years*. Draft document. Retrieved from http://rokreligiouseducation.com/wp-content/uploads/2015/10/draft_spirituality_in_the_early_years_2012.pdf

Catholic Education Office of Western Australia (2014). *Let the little children come to me: A resource for raising the religious awareness of children in the early years*. Leederville, WA: Author.

Cavalletti, S. (1983). *The religious potential of the child.* (P.M. Coulter & J.M. Coulter, Trans.) New York: Paulist Press.

Coles, R. (1990). *The spiritual life of children*. London: HarperCollins.

Congregation for Catholic Education (1988). *The religious dimension of education in a Catholic school*. Homebush: St Paul Publications.

Dahlberg, G., Moss, P., & Pence, A. (1999). Beyond quality in early childhood and care. London: RoutledgeFalmer.

Eaude, T. (2003). Shining lights in unexpected corners: New angles on young children's spiritual development. *International Journal of Children's Spirituality, 8*(2), 151-162.

Hay, D. & Nye, R. (2006). *The spirit of the child* (Rev. ed.). London: Jessica Kingsley Publishers.

Grajczonek, J. (2010a). *Spiritual development and religious education in the early years: A review of the literature.* Retrieved from http://qcec.catholic.edu.au/wp-content/uploads/2015/12/Final_Spiritual-Development-Religious-Education-in-the-Early-Years_A-Review-of-the-Literature.pdf

Grajczonek, J. (in collaboration with Queensland Catholic Education Commission Pre-Prep Taskforce) (2010b). *Framework for early years spiritual development in the Catholic tradition*. Retrieved from http://qcec.catholic.edu.au/wp-content/uploads/2015/12/Framework-for-Early-Years-Spiritual-Development-in-the-Catholic-Tradition.pdf

Grajczonek, J. (2012). Acknowledging religious diversity and empowering young children's agency and voice in the religion classroom. In S. Parker, R. Freathy & L.J. Francis (Eds.), *Religious education and freedom of religion and belief* (pp.235-252). Oxford: Peter Lang.

Liddy, S. (2007). Spirituality and the young child. In J. Grajczonek & M. Ryan (Eds.), *Religious education in early childhood: A reader* (pp. 5-17). Brisbane: Lumino Press.

MacLachlan, C., Fleer, M. & Edwards, S. (2013). *Early childhood curriculum: Planning, assessment and implementation* (2nd5.). Melbourne: Cambridge University Press http://dx.doi.org.ezproxy2.acu.edu.au/10.1017/CBO9781107282193

MacNaughton, G. (2003). *Shaping early childhood: Learners, curriculum and contexts*. Berkshire: Open University Press. McGraw-Hill Education.

Nye, R. & Hay, D. (1996). Identifying children's spirituality: How do you start without a starting point? *British Journal of Religious Education, 18*(3), 144-154.

Queensland Studies Authority. (2006). *Early years curriculum guidelines*. Retrieved form https://www.qcaa.qld.edu.au/downloads/p_10/ey_cg_06.pdf

Ryan, M. (2007). Theorists informing early years religious education. In J. Grajczonek & M. Ryan (Eds.), *Religious education in early childhood: A reader* (pp. 32-43). Brisbane: Lumino Press.

Siraj-Blatchford, I. & Mayo. (2012). Editors' introduction: 'Advances in early childhood education'. In I. Siraj-Blatchford, & A. Mayo (Eds.). *Early childhood education: Volume 1: Foundational and contemporary thought on young children, home and society* (pp. xxxiii-xlvi). London: SAGE.

Siraj-Blatchford, I. & Sylva, K. (2004). Researching pedagogy in English pre-schools. *British Educational Research Journal, 30*(5), 713-730.

Smith, L. & Lovat, T. (2003). *Curriculum: Action on reflection* (4th ed.). Tuggerah: Social Science Press.

United Nations (1989). *Convention on the Rights of the Child*. Retrieved from http://www.ohchr.org/EN/ProfessionalInterest/Pages/CRC.aspx

Vygotsky, L. (1967). *Mind in society: The development of higher psychological processes*. Cambridge: HUP.

Wood, E. & Hedges, H. (2016). Curriculum in early childhood education: Curriculum questions about content, coherence, and control. *The Curriculum Journal, 27*(3), 387-405. http://dx.doi.org/10.1080/09585176.2015.1129981

Dr Jan Grajczonek is Adjunct Professor, University of Notre Dame, Fremantle. Her research interests are religious education in early childhood and young children's spirituality. She has authored several books and written academic papers in journals including the *British Journal of Religious Education*, *Religious Education Journal of Australia*, *Journal of Religious Education* and the *Australasian Journal of Early Childhood*. She has presented at conferences including at the *International Seminar on Religious Education and Values*, *International Association for Children's Spirituality Conference* and the *National Symposium on Religious Education and Ministry*. Her current work includes developing early childhood spiritual and religious education curricula.

Correspondence to:
Dr Jan Grajczonek
Email: jangrajczonek@bigpond.com

Chapter 6

Between Desire and Reality: The Presentation of Scripture in Religious Education.

Margaret Carswell

From research to the classroom

In 1994 Sr. Barbara Stead RSM, a lecturer in Theology at Australian Catholic University, submitted her Doctoral thesis for examination. Titled *The Use of Scripture in Catholic Primary Schools in Victoria* the thesis surveyed teachers about their understanding of Scripture and, in response, what they felt they needed to improve their teaching. Stead's thesis represented a watershed moment in Catholic Education in Australia; it was the first to bring the world of biblical scholarship to the Australian Catholic primary school classroom. The finding, that teachers in Catholic Schools were yearning for support to tackle a task that many felt was beyond them, drew much local attention. Stead herself developed the K.I.T.E. method and published *A Time of Jubilee* (1994), a resource for teachers that combined exegesis of commonly taught Lukan passages, together with a K.I.T.E. exemplar for teaching.

Immediately following the completion of Stead's thesis I conducted my own examination of the presentation of scripture in religious education. *Educating into Discipleship* examined the manner in which discipleship, as presented in Mark's Gospel, was taught in the 1984 iteration of the Melbourne *Guidelines for Religious Education*. The thesis again brought the demands of biblical scholarship into the Catholic classroom but this time the focus was different: rather than asking teachers what they needed the curriculum documents they were using were now under examination. The overall finding was clear: one of the major reasons why teachers were not teaching Scripture effectively was the manner in which it was presented in units of work. Poor curriculum design relegated Scripture to an instrument of the writers whose primary intent appeared to be promoting the topic or theme of the unit.

The issue is easy to summarise. Once the decision to produce a religious education programme is made the first task of writers is to determine what to include. The content of the programme is identified and arranged into workable units with desired learning expressed as outcomes or descriptor learning statements. While this formula represents a fairly standard writing pattern across most areas of the curriculum, in religious education it is inherently problematic in that it immediately limits interpretation of Scripture passages to the parameters of the topic. Students learning through topic based religious education know exactly what any Scripture passage, cited in the unit, means before it is even read. As a result, the critical engagement of students with Scripture is completely unnecessary. It is, therefore, neither planned for nor taught within the body of the unit. Indeed, such engagement would be redundant; placed within a defined topic, Scripture serves its purpose by validating its content; nothing more than its inclusion is necessary. This practice, commonly called 'proof texting', is rightly critiqued when found in arguments that cite Scripture passages completely out of context to validate a particular view. What is less common is recognition that the placement of passages within predefined religious education topics is equally a type of proof texting. Scripture passages are cited, with no reference to their literary or historical context, to legitimise or validate the topic experience or doctrine. Study of passages, as part of the teaching sequence or as background for teachers is, therefore, overwhelmingly ignored.

One example serves to model the point. In the 1984 *Guidelines* Luke 19:1-10, the story of Zacchaeus, is cited 11 times in topics called *Choosing, Forgiveness, Penance, Honesty, Growth, Change, This is me, Belonging, Decision Making, Jesus* and *We have a story.* In each instance the text is manipulated to fit the topic: not once is the passage presented in a manner congruent with the interpretations of biblical scholars using critical methods.

Educating into Discipleship concluded that while the presentation of texts associated with discipleship was flawed, poor curriculum design was at the root of the problem. By making the topics in the *Guidelines* their priority curriculum writers completely failed to engage in 'serious and orderly study of the message of Christ' (John Paul, Catechesis Tradendae, 22). Having found a significant issue the thesis moved to model an alternative approach for the teaching of Scripture. Named the Composite Model, as it drew on the work of a number of scholars, the model proposed that Scripture should be taught through three sequential steps: Prepare to Hear the Word, Hear and Encounter the Word, and Respond to the Word.

In asking that students be prepared prior to hearing a passage, the model reminded teachers of the historical and literary context of passages. It argued that before students came into contact with a passage they needed to know something about it. Questions such as who wrote it, when, why and how might be considered during preparation, as might any historical features of the passage: places mentioned might be found on a map; cultural or religious rituals might be examined and taught. In inviting students to Hear and Encounter the Word, teachers were asked to present the passage, preferably to tell it, and then to actively teach it. Encountering the Word meant, in shorthand, study it. This represented the strong educational focus of the model, one which was intended to highlight the need for learning about Scripture as well as from it. Finally, Respond to the Word proposed that Scripture could be transformative. New insights could be expressed in art, music or drama or become the focus of personal prayer.

Perhaps as important as the process itself the Composite Model followed Stead's own K.I.T.E. method in that it insisted that teachers articulate clear outcomes for learning about Scripture. Scripture could no longer be cited simply to support the theme of the curriculum writers: what students were expected to learn about it should be explicit, deliberate and planned for. In 2001 I published *Teaching Scripture: The Gospel of Mark,* a work which, like Stead's, brought together exegesis of passages from Mark's Gospel and exemplars of its teaching through the Composite Model.

Coming so soon after Stead's work, the Composite Model strengthened interest in the presentation of Scripture. Publication of *A Time of Jubilee* had placed the fruits of biblical scholarship into the hands of teachers. *Teaching Scripture* now did so again. In Dioceses in the south-east of Australia interest in Scripture flourished. Both K.I.T.E. and Composite Models were included within existing RE programmes. The Dioceses of Sandhurst, Sale and Ballarat included them in their teaching strategies resource book: https://stmaryswholeschoolreview.wikispaces.com/file/view/Teaching+and+Learning+Strategies+Book.pdf

The Composite Model was mandated and planned for in the Diocese of Sale and Ballarat. With K.I.T.E. it was adopted by the Diocese of Tasmania (http://catholic.tas.edu.au/our-schools/curriculum/religious-education-resource-banks/level-3-years-3_4-scripture). In the north of Australia in the Diocese of Darwin the principles of biblical scholarship if not the language were used for the presentation of passages in their religious education programme *Journey in Faith*. Both K.I.T.E. and Composite models became part of undergraduate and postgraduate courses at Australian Catholic University. Stead published her findings in *Exploring the Religious Classroom* (Ryan and Malone, 1996) and more recently Hyde and

Rymarz (2009, 2013) have included descriptions of both models in publications intended for training teachers. And, recognising the importance of teacher knowledge, diocesan staff in every diocese in Victoria and Tasmania developed inservice days to tackle poor teacher knowledge. 'Scripture in the classroom' became the flavour of the month.

Continuing an interest in the nexus between biblical scholarship and religious education curriculum documents in 2007 I submitted my own Doctoral thesis, *Biblical Metaphors for God in the Primary Level of the Religious Education Series 'To Know Worship and Love'*. Replicating the basic structure of *Educating into Discipleship*, both the student texts and the teaching companions of the primary level (prep to 6) of *TKWL* were examined for the way in which they presented biblical metaphors for God. The conclusion, while disturbing, was not surprising: the presentation of biblical metaphors was so poor that it was likely to lead students to develop a limited, if not distorted, understanding of God. The broader question of why this was the case was equally predictable. The reason that biblical metaphors were presented badly in the series was that all Scripture was presented badly. This finding affirmed what had been uncovered previously. What was new, however, was a much more precise description of the problem. By placing the curriculum against a set of 'best practice' principles drawn from Church documents concerning Scripture, the thesis provided a catalogue of specific errors. Beginning with poor curriculum design which continued to seriously compromise texts; the fragmentation of passages, the use of single verses, the amalgamation of multiple authors works, the creation of 'scripture stories' from different versions of passages, the simple failure to identify literary form, ignorance about historical contexts or cultural practices, and lack of exegetical information for teachers all contributed to a misleading and often erroneous presentation of Scripture. This new research added significantly to the discussion: with a comprehensive understanding of what was wrong, what was required to avoid these errors was possible.

International influences

In 2009 insights from Australian research and experience were brought to the international scene. Asked to undertake a 'health check' on the presentation of Scripture in *Here I Am* (1994), the programme which dominated religious education in England and Wales, I found the same raft of poor practices found in primary levels of *TKWL*.

With the support of successive Directors of the Education Service of the Diocese of Westminster, the Composite Model was used to develop exemplar resources to show what was possible. The framework for learning was the Liturgical Year: the 'topic' the life of Jesus as celebrated by the Church; the Gospel of the Year the primary source. Links to the Bishop's *Religious Education Curriculum Directory* (2012), to the rituals, beliefs and practices of the Church, would emerge from the study of Scripture not the other way around. Scripture would be presented as the source of belief not its proof. Websites were made to educate teachers about the underpinning research; Teach Scripture explained the theoretical background of the model (www.teachscripture.com) and the Bible Doctor provided an online Bible dictionary for students and other resources with material being refined and updated each cycle from Australia (www.thebibledoctor.com), (www.kipandfriends.com).

CHAPTER 6

New insights: Curriculum design

A number of unintended but important outcomes of this project have brought new understanding about how good curriculum design can eliminate the poor teaching of Scripture.

1. Have all teachers teach the same passage or passages.

Typically, topic based religious education means that at a single point in time different themes or content areas, each containing different Scripture passages, are being taught across the school. Individual teachers are, therefore, isolated from one another. When all teachers are teaching the same Scripture passage professional learning about the Bible is made significantly easier. Staff can be in-serviced together and can share questions, insights and understandings. Conversations, on pin boards and displays, and between students in cross age activities, are enabled. Liturgies and assemblies can speak to all students.

In addition, the use of the Gospel of the Year as the primary source means that both teachers and students work with one author's work for an entire year in keeping with its proclamation in the Church. Insights about an author and their community can be developed and connections between passages can be observed. Real biblical literacy is thus developed while skills in analysis and interpretation are practiced. In addition, with a three year cycle, what students learn in their junior years is only repeated in their senior years. Planning across year groups is both enabled and encouraged: differentiation becomes a shared responsibility. The development and sharing of resources is enabled.

2. Allow individual passages to come together to build the bigger story.

While topic based religious education jumps from idea to idea and passage to passage, structuring the resources on the liturgical year means that the 'story' develops as a continuous whole. At Advent we learn of the authors belief that Jesus is the messiah: at Lent we hear the Passion and learn of how the death and resurrection of the Christ found relevance to one author's community; at Pentecost we learn about the Spirit who came and remains with us. In the block of ordinary time in July we learn about the Gospel writer's particular interests: in Matthew, the Kingdom of God; in Mark, Discipleship, and in Luke, inclusion of the marginalised. Just as it does when students hear a novel over time, so the Christian story develops and a fuller, richer picture is revealed.

3. Develop a clear sequential plan for learning about Scripture.

The Bishop's *Levels of Attainment* (2007) offer significant insight into what can be achieved through clarity and consistency in outcomes. By making actual retelling of a passage the first step, engagement with the author's actual words is required. The expectation of textual criticism, which demands that those working with Scripture use a biblical text as close to the original as possible, is met. Further, learning the elements of a passage (its characters, events and settings) provides a prelude to interpretation and to the discovery of the beliefs a passage has given rise to. How these beliefs are lived and expressed in the Church now is a third step. The flow is natural and real; it places Scripture at the forefront of belief, as the springboard into practices and people within the Church.

CHAPTER 6

New insights: the Composite Model

Prepare to hear the Word

Prepare to Hear the Word was intended to make clear that Scripture was a window into a world that was beyond the experience of students. It was based on the notion that information about the passage *prior to hearing it* would mean that students were more likely to understand what they heard. However, when the process was placed with existing programmes, teachers grappled with the kind of information that should comprise 'preparation'. As a result in early use of the Composite Model students were often prepared by focusing on their own life experiences, anticipated in the text. This led to the kind of pre-interpretation that the process was trying to avoid. Two analytical approaches have now been identified as having particular relevance in preparing students to hear Scripture.

- Genre criticism which ascertains the literary form of a passage.
- Literary or source criticism which determines where an individual passage begins and ends.

a. Teachers must ascertain, then teach, the literary form of the passage

Dei Verbum (Vatican Council II, 1975) makes very clear that the observation of the literary form of Scripture is not just an academic exercise. Rather, it is critical for understanding a passage as it reveals the kind of truth a passage contains and, therefore, how it is to be interpreted. Moreover, demanding observation of literary form alerts to, and resolves, a problem rife in curriculum documents: the fragmentation of Scripture passages. Literary or source criticism determines where an individual passage begins and ends. Such a sense is vital as the most fundamental of all the contexts of a passage is its literary one. Placed into a wider work, sentences, phrases, pericopes and chapters all find their meaning as part of the much bigger whole that surrounds them. The most disturbing aspect of poor citation, then, is one that removes parts of literary forms and cites them as stand alone units. This practice was found repeatedly in *TKWL*: sixty (23%) of the 265 Scripture passages cited for use in the series are single verses. Most of these are individual verses taken from the Gospels. The dangers of citing fragments of passages are obvious. Removed from their 'whole' the literary form of a passage is almost impossible to determine; interpretation, therefore, defaults to a literalist, fundamentalist one explicitly censured by the Biblical Commission. *Dei Verbum* put it succinctly. Truth is deeply connected to literary form. Determining literary form, indeed making sure you are working with a whole literary form is the first step to ascertaining what the author was trying to convey, the truths they were trying to share. (Vatican Council II 1979), By insisting that teachers establish the literary form of a passage prior to sharing it, students are provided with the best foundation for meaning: a whole passage and a sense of the kind of message it is going to convey.

b. For effective teaching of Scripture teachers must ensure that they, and their students, understand the terminology found with a passage.

My own contribution to the Composite Model came in the conviction that teachers assumed that their students had knowledge of Scripture that they did not. Although Stead had found that knowledge about texts was their primary need, few teachers sought it out. Indeed, those who did soon came to the conclusion that while biblical commentaries were available most assumed a level of knowledge well beyond them. The many cultural or historical elements of the passage were, therefore, largely ignored.

While the area of teacher knowledge remains a significant limiting factor for the teaching of Scripture some movement in this area is evident. Australian theologians and publishing companies now recognise a new audience and are actively producing more accessible works. Garratt Publishing have published a series accurately named as *The Friendly Guide* which presents, in accessible ways, contemporary understanding of Scripture, and the children's literary project, *Start with the Heart,* includes a selection of books which teach biblical scholarship to junior children through their reading programme. Moreover, the internet has brought 1st century Judaism to our door. Online resources such as Nazareth Village let us see Jesus' world (www.nazarethvilliage.com), what the people wore and how they lived. Sites such as The Temple Institute in Jerusalem (https://www.templeinstitute.org/) allow us to see what a High Priest wore and did while sites offering a virtual tour of the Temple (http://jerusalem.com/tour/jewish_temple_3D/web) enable us to walk through Herod's Temple. Google Earth allows you to hover over Lake Galilee and see what the towns that Jesus visited look like now. With information more readily available, ensuring that students know the terminology found in the passage they are studying is not only desirable it is achievable.

Hear and encounter the Word.
Hear ...

From its inception, the Composite Model argued a strong preference for telling stories rather than reading them. This remains. However, *honesty* and *integrity* in any telling of Scripture is now mandated. Recognising that religious education occurs within a range of settings, the Church is quite comfortable with the view that Scripture passages might need to be adapted. The differing needs of the faithful; their circumstances, age levels, social conditions or culture of people, must be taken into consideration in the presentation of passages. However, clear boundaries are placed around both the manner of adaptation and the resultant texts. Texts should never be mutilated, falsified or rendered corrupt by adaptation. The *Renewal of the Education in Faith* (1970) puts it brutally: fidelity to the Word of God is 'the ultimate criterion by which catechists must appraise their work as educators' (Australian Episcopal Conference, 1970, 160).

In learning passages for retelling, teachers must refer to the actual Bible; in presenting it to students teachers must ensure that the author's story is told and not an erroneous version of it. While adaptation is allowed for, it must proceed from a sound understanding of the actual passage as written by the original author. The most fundamental knowledge of Scripture is knowledge of what passages actually say. Without any sense of *what* happens, *why* it might have happened or indeed why an author might have recorded it as they have, is lost. The practice of teaching inaccurate versions of passages must be considered completely unacceptable.

... Encounter the Word

Initially Encountering the Word asked teachers to study passages with their students so that genuine learning about a passage would enable students to understand it more fully; to draw meaning from it more authentically. Commitment to the need to study Scripture, before its interpretation, has been confirmed. It is without question.

Comment is needed on this point. Of all the difficulties found in the inclusion of the Composite Model within an existing Religious education programme, the genuine study of Scripture is the hardest to achieve. If curriculum writers have not indicated what students are to learn about and through the placement of a particular passage in a unit it is almost impossible for teachers to determine it retrospectively.

The inclusion of a clear purpose for Scripture *at the level of planning* is critical if it is to be taught effectively in keeping with the desires of the Church. The brilliance of the Bishop's *Attainment Levels* (2007) is again evident. Once foundational knowledge of a passage is established then interpretation is the next step. Study of the passage then becomes the activity 'in between' retelling and interpretation. Who are the characters? Does their role in society tell us something about them, about our expectations for them? Do they speak? What do they say? Are there geographical and/or time settings? What happens? How many 'scenes' compromise the single passage? What are the people doing? How would their actions have challenged society? How does it end? Increasing attention; to author, audience, writing style, literary form, geography, social and cultural inclusions, using a range of the critical approaches across primary and secondary sectors, will develop a deepening sense of what was, and is, being conveyed.

Respond to the Word

Respond to the Word was intended to make the point that Scripture could be transformative. Drawn very much from *Dei Verbum*, both K.I.T.E. and the Composite Model had a catechetical tone which supposed that learning about Scripture would deepen the learner's relationship with God. In light of the changing nature of Catholic Education and, in particular, the increasing educational nature of religious education, clarification of what constitutes an appropriate response to learning about Scripture is necessary. Three responses are now proposed.

1. Learn more.

Learning about Scripture often leads to further questions. Are there other passages that explore this idea? How does another writer record this event? Is there evidence of this outside the biblical text? How did the community that first heard this respond? How did this ritual or practice develop? What happened after this event? How are the beliefs expressed in this passage manifest in the Church today? Religious education in Catholic schools in Australia still extends to the two ends of the one continuum: some dioceses utilise Tom Groome's Shared Christian Praxis explicitly asking for integration of learning while others prefer a strong educational focus with little, if any, emphasis on personal adherence or faith acquisition. In either situation questions that prompt further learning are a gift, one that provides for a deepening of knowledge, understanding and, perhaps, even faith.

2. Act Differently.

For believers Scripture invites us to become the people of faith that the writers imagined their original audiences could be. For non-believers it provides the rationale for much of what the Church and its members do. While the original audiences of the passages they study may not have had laptops or mobile phones they still grappled with what God was like, with what it meant to be human, and how we – God and humanity – should live together. These truths are still evident in passages today; they continue to challenge and to redeem a believing community. An appropriate response to what students have learned might be either the implementation of actions that bring the beliefs expressed in Scripture to life, or a clear recognition that for believers Scripture provides the reason why social action is not just an option.

3. Pray.

A Catholic identity is recognised in its practice of prayer. Taking the insights gleaned from the study and interpretation of passages and incorporating them into the prayer life of the classroom or school is a way of bringing the intellect and the heart together. It is most appropriate in settings where learning is intended to touch the very soul of the learner.

Conclusion

The Composite Model was drawn from the clear realization that something needed to be done to teach Scripture better. Neither it nor K.I.T.E. were imagined as a silver bullet able to overcome all the problems that the research had uncovered. They were, however, intended to focus attention on a serious issue within religious education. While there is ample evidence that much has been done there is a scatter-gun feel to the response. In Australia individual dioceses are responsible for the development of their own religious education programmes. This means that commitment to the sound presentation of Scripture varies: poor practice is still apparent in many programmes used in Australian Catholic schools. Of all the issues identified, poor curriculum design still overwhelmingly prioritises the topic or theme over the authentic presentation of Scripture; passages are still being presented in a way that often renders their meaning lost. The student text of *TKWL* is still the mandated text in the two largest dioceses in Australia: Melbourne and Sydney.

It is clear that we have much to do. At present the Enhancing Catholic Identity project, a joint project by the University of Leuven and Diocese' in South Australia, Victoria and Queensland is providing significant evidence that many of the students in our schools have a fundamentalist approach to belief. I am convinced that the teaching of Scripture is both part of the problem and the answer. We must continue to act to ensure that Scripture is presented as it should be; authentically and validly. It is also clear that Australia is well positioned to do something. We have a strong, well-funded, highly respected, system of education. It more than holds its own in the education sector internationally. At tertiary level Australian Catholic University, Broken Bay Institute and the University of Notre Dame stand well positioned to offer academic support and critique. We also have Diocese' and Education Offices set up and capable of offering support second to none. Moreover, Catholic Education is a growing market. The production of high quality material for teachers and schools make the publication of resources worthwhile. So we have the structures and personnel capable of making this work.

In October 2008 the Twelfth Ordinary Synod of Bishops met in Rome under the theme 'The Word of God in the Life and Mission of the Church.' In *Verbum Domini*, the post-synodal exhortation, Pope Benedict said that he wanted to ensure that Scripture was not 'simply a word from the past, but a living and timely word' (Benedict XVI, 2008, 5). In affirming the 'positive fruit' yielded by the use of the Historical-Critical method which he claimed was both 'required' and 'undeniable' Pope Benedict warns about the dangers of separating exegesis from theology (Benedict XVI, 2008, 5). Exegesis undertaken outside a hermeneutic of faith risks becoming secularised and any presence of the divine being explained away or reduced to a human element. The historicity of the presence of God is, therefore, lost. Conversely, any theological reading of Scripture outside the principles of sound exegesis runs the risk of leading to fundamentalism. 'In a word, where exegesis is not theology, Scripture cannot be the soul of theology, and conversely, where theology is not essentially the interpretation of the Church's Scripture, such a theology no longer has any foundation' (Benedict XVI, 2008, 35).

As I write this, I look across the fields outside my window. Four big carriage horses are grazing, undisturbed by a man walking past them with two small black cats as his company. A woman is walking towards him, head collar in hand. I am reminded of the walk to Emmaus, where Christ came to the disciples to walk with them as they struggled to understand their lives. As they walked, he spoke with them, with a deep sense of the ancient and contemporary stories of his people as well as a deep understanding of his own vocation. And somehow, the stories made sense; in the space between teller and listener, connections were made, understandings were forged. What had been clouded, became clear.

The Emmaus story is often proposed as a model of religious education. We know that the current presentation of Scripture is flawed in much religious education, we know what the problems are and we know the hurdles that need to be cleared. What is required is a deep commitment of mind and heart to our story so that our conversations on the road might become transformative. Anyone fancy a walk?

REFERENCES

Archdiocese of Melbourne (1979). *Guidelines for Religious Education for Primary Students in the Archdiocese of Melbourne*. Melbourne. The Advocate Press.
Archdiocese of Melbourne (1984). *Guidelines for Religious Education for Primary Students in the Archdiocese of Melbourne*. Melbourne. The Advocate Press.

Archdiocese of Melbourne (1995). *Guidelines for Religious Education for Primary students in the Archdiocese of Melbourne.* Melbourne: The Advocate Press.

Australian Episcopal Conference (1970). *The Renewal of the Education of Faith: a translation of the original document from the Italian Episcopal Conference.* Sydney. E.J. Dwyer.

Benedict XV (1920). *Spiritus Paraclitus.* Encyclical of Benedict XV on St Jerome. September 15. https://w2.vatican.va/content/benedict-xv/en/encyclicals/documents/hf_ben-xv_enc_15091920_spiritus-paraclitus.html

Benedict XVI (2008). *Verbum Domini.* http://w2.vatican.va/content/benedict-xvi/en/apost_exhortations/documents/hf_ben-xvi_exh_20100930_verbum-domini.html

Carswell, M.F. (1996). *Educating into Discipleship.* Carswell, M.F. (1996). *Educating into Discipleship.* (Unpublished Masters thesis). Australian Catholic University: Melbourne, Australia.

Carswell, M.F. (2006). *Biblical Metaphors for God in the Primary Level of the Religious Education Series To Know Worship and Love* (unpublished thesis).

Carswell, M.F. (2001). *Teaching Scripture: The Gospel of Mark.* Pymble: Harper Collins.

Catholic Bishops Conference of England and Wales (2012). Religious Education Curriculum Directory http://www.catholiceducation.org.uk/schools/religious-education/item/1000034-religious-education-curriculum-directory

Catholic Bishops Conference of England and Wales (1994). *Here I Am.* London: Harper Collins.

Catholic Bishops Conference of England and Wales, Department of Catholic Education and Formation (2007). *Levels of Attainment in Religious Education in Catholic Schools and Colleges.* http://edurcdhn.org.uk/downloads/oldkeep/secmarch2010/Attainment%20Levels.pdf

Congregation for the Clergy (1998). *The General Directory for Catechesis.* Strathfield: St Paul's Publications.

Elliot, P. J. (Ed) (2000). *To Know Worship and Love. Student Text Level 1.* Melbourne: James Goold House Publications.

Elliot, P. J. (Ed) (2000). *To Know Worship and Love. Student Text Level 2a.* Melbourne: James Goold House Publications.

Elliot, P. J. (Ed) (2001). *To Know Worship and Love. Student Text Level 2b.* Melbourne: James Goold House Publications.

Elliot, Peter, J. (Ed) (2003). *To Know Worship and Love. Student Text Year 3.* Melbourne: James Goold House Publications.

Elliot, Peter, J. (Ed) (2001). *To Know Worship and Love. Student Text Year 4.* Melbourne: James Goold House Publications.

Elliot, Peter, J. (Ed) (2000). *To Know Worship and Love. Student Text Year 5*. Melbourne: James Goold House Publications.

Elliot, Peter, J. (Ed) (2002). *To Know Worship and Love. Student Text Year 6*. Melbourne: James Goold House Publications.

Hyde, B. and Rymarz, R. (2009). *First steps in religious education*. Ballan: Connor Court Publishing.

Hyde, B. and Rymarz, R. (2013). *Taking the Next Step*. Macksville, David: Barlow Publishing.

John Paul II (1979). *Catechesis Tradendae*. Homebush: Saint Paul Publications.

John Paul II (1994). *Catechism of the Catholic Church*. Homebush: St Pauls.

Leo XII *(1893)*. *Providentissimus Deus*. http://w2.vatican.va/content/leo-xiii/en/encyclicals/documents/hf_l-xiii_enc_18111893_providentissimus-deus.html

Pius XII (1943). *Divino Afflante Spiritu*. Encyclical of Pope Pius XII on promoting Biblical studies, commemorating the fiftieth anniversary of *Providentissimus Deus*. http://w2.vatican.va/content/pius-xii/en/encyclicals/documents/hf_p-xii_enc_30091943_divino-afflante-spiritu.html

Pollefeyt, D and Bouwens, J. (2014). *Identity in Dialogue. Assessing and Enhancing Catholic School Identity. Research Methodology and Research Results in Catholic Schools in Victoria, Australia*. Munster: LIT Verlag.

Pontifical Biblical Commission (1993). *The Interpretation of the Bible in the Church. Address of His Holiness John Paul II and Document of the Pontifical Biblical Commission*. Rome: Libreria Editrice Vaticana.

Ryan, M. and Malone, P. (Eds). (1996). *Exploring the Religion Classroom*. Wentworth Falls: Social Science press.

Sacred Congregation of the Clergy (1971). *General Catechetical Directory*. http://www.vatican.va/roman_curia/congregations/cclergy/documents/rc_con_cclergy_doc_11041971_gcat_en.html

Stead, B. (1994). *The Use of Scripture in Catholic Primary Schools in Victoria*. Unpublished thesis.

Stead, B. (1994). *A Time of Jubilee*. Thornbury: Desbooks.

Vatican II Council (1975). *Dei Verbum*. The Dogmatic Constitution on Divine Revelation. In A. Flannery, Gen ed. *Vatican Council II: The Conciliar and Post Conciliar Documents*. Collegeville: The Liturgical Press.

Vatican II Council (1975). *Gravissimum Educationis*. Declaration on Christian Education. In A. Flannery, Gen ed. *Vatican Council II: The Conciliar and Post Conciliar Documents*. Collegeville: The Liturgical Press.

Dr Margaret Carswell was born in Hamilton, New Zealand. She is currently a Senior Lecturer in Education (Religious Education) at Australian Catholic University, following a career in Primary and Secondary Catholic Education including working as an adviser and consultant in Australia and the United Kingdom. She remains a consultant to the Catholic Education Service of England and Wales. Margaret's first publication, *Teach Scripture: the Gospel of Mark,* introduced and demonstrated use of the Composite Model, a method for teaching scripture which has since been adopted for use in dioceses here and overseas.

Correspondence to:
215 Egerton-Ballark Road, Mt Egerton Victoria 3352
Email: margaret.carswell@acu.edu.au

Chapter 7

Missing in Theory and Praxis? – Teaching Spirituality in the Catholic Classroom and Beyond

Peter Mudge

Introduction

The reality of a Catholic spirituality in its broadest sense, and the need to treat it as an important pedagogical concern, is one of the most urgent yet hidden challenges within the ambit of Catholic schooling. Urgent because spirituality in its various guises (e.g. Catholic, ecumenical, interfaith, ecological) is an essential glue and *lingua franca* that holds all aspects of Catholic education together. Hidden or 'missing' because it is not openly engaged, not explicitly taught in schools, and subsists as 'the elephant in the room' – everywhere discussed and navel-gazed, or packaged as 'values' but rarely taught and applied to its full potential – as an interconnected and practical study of topics, practices and values. Consequently, few in the classroom or in executive groups choose to address the amorphous area of spirituality directly or practically, whether within the teaching of religious education, across the curriculum, within leadership teams or as part of teacher formation.

Spirituality as praxis-oriented and life-giving has largely gone missing or is reduced to theoretical musings, and the quandary is how to make it more visible and engaging in the classroom and school milieu. This chapter is written with the beginning and experienced teacher in mind, and seeks some possible solutions to this quandary through an examination of three broad areas – What is spirituality? How do we teach it? Challenges for the future. Throughout the chapter some authentic teacher reflections on spirituality are included for the benefit of the K-12 classroom practitioner. Its closing summary is presented as a revision activity for the reader.

What is spirituality? – 'the spiritual elephant in the room'

Mother Teresa, canonised on 4 September 2016, once said: 'We ourselves feel that what we are doing is just a drop in the ocean. But the ocean would be less because of that missing drop' (Chopra in Canfield, Hansen & Newmark, 2013, p. 22). The same analogy might be applied to spirituality. Spirituality is unquestionably a rather large drop in the ocean, and an indispensable one – however, it is often missing, ignored or rejected, even absorbed without trace into an ocean of other pursuits and disciplines (for example, religion, theology, ethics, values education, service learning, prayer, scripture, sacraments).

What do a range of classroom practitioners say about the nature of spirituality? In this and subsequent sections I include a range of 'teacher voices' on spirituality. Permission has been granted from all cited teachers to reproduce their views in this chapter (all from Mudge, 2016b). After considering these views, we will reflect on what is present and missing in such definitions, and then propose a number of further insights into the nature of spirituality.

A primary teacher from Newcastle, NSW defines spirituality as 'a feeling of presence, something beyond or bigger than my physical being. I believe spirituality to be your innermost feeling of a connection with more than our immediate reality. In my case, this is God'. Another primary school teacher situated in far North Queensland reflects:

> Spirituality is defined not so much in words as in actions. It is our desire and deliberate action to link all we do to our personal relationship with God. As a community, spirituality underpins celebrations, ceremonies and times of hardship ... In short our school's spirituality is each

individual's relationship with God that underlies their actions, interactions and personal growth.

For a secondary teacher in the Diocese of Broken Bay and her students, spirituality is 'that search [for] wonder and awe of, and experience of something outside of yourself that speaks to your innermost longings and deep questions of life'. Many teachers commenting on the nature of spirituality observe that their own and their students' spiritualities is characterised by the customary demarcation: 'Miss, I'm not religious, I'm spiritual.' Some commentators, however, would argue that religion and spirituality are sometimes not always mutually exclusive but often overlap and inform each other (Altmeyer et al, 2015, pp. 547-549). For example, some students and teachers meditate and use rituals and creeds from traditions in which they were brought up.

Our final reflection, from another secondary teacher, responsible for Year 8 in the Diocese of Maitland/Newcastle, relates issues arising from presentation of a unit on Prayer and Spirituality. She reflects: 'It is a difficult concept [unit] to teach with a lively bunch of students in a mixed ability class. Our program is specific but I have found the concept of "where is their soul" to have engaged the students best.' It is often the case that a topic such as prayer and spirituality cannot be engaged directly but more often 'through the back door' – meaning that other topics lead into it obliquely or by association, such as this discussion about 'soul', or perhaps other possible conversations on 'the purpose of life', 'what happens to the human spirit after death?', 'happiness' or 'flourishing'.

What is present and what is absent from the above and other typical definitions of spirituality? *Present* are aspects such as – spirituality's elusiveness and mystery, its link with values and practices (e.g. mindfulness and meditation, prayer and sacraments), its capacity to elicit awe and wonder, and the many ways in which spirituality can inform ritual, meaning, community and praxis (an ongoing cycle of action and reflection). What is typically *absent* from such definitions of Christian spirituality are what Bregman (2014) and others identify as a lack of reference within many definitions to faith, belief or practice, to the living of the spiritual life itself as 'of the Spirit', or to the persons of the Holy Trinity (Father, Son and Holy Spirit) (p. 2).

In many cases, any particular 'description' of spirituality can also be classified as 'missing'. As the aforecited teachers have found, spirituality is notoriously difficult to define, and often it is not even attempted. It resembles 'the elephant in the room' – invisible, surly, rich in memory, mysterious and yet there, ready to charge at us without warning. Lucy Bregman (2014) titles one of her chapters 'Definitions of spirituality: Ninety-two and still counting' (pp. 9-22). At the outset she reflects: 'Spirituality today has become newsworthy and glamorous, and yet it remains confusing and mysterious' (2014, p. 9). She acknowledges, in the process of critiquing a number of definitions, that spirituality commonly embraces some kind of reference to – one's basic life orientation; one's patterned ways of life; verbs like thinking, feeling, experiencing and nurturing; transcendence; the deeper meanings of human existence; and connectedness to some or all elements of the cosmos such as self, nature, and the sacred (2014, pp. 2-3). The remainder of this theoretical section will consider various descriptions of spirituality including its specifically Australian context.

Towards an understanding of Australian spiritualities?

In a general sense, Australian spirituality, and spirituality in general, can be encapsulated by Mason's (2004) description: 'spirituality is a conscious way of life based on a transcendent referent' where he understands 'way of life' as 'a worldview, an ethos and a set of practices' (p. 9; see more on worldview below). The expansiveness of such a spirituality is sketched by Groome, citing St Augustine –'All good and true Christians should understand that truth, wherever they may find it, belongs to their God' (Saint Augustine, *Teaching Christianity*, 144, cited in Groome, 1998a, fn. 31, p. 65). This expansive archetype of spirituality is echoed in Connolly's (2013) plea for a spirituality that is formed within a learning community which is at the same time a humble, respectful and sometimes silent community (pp. 11-12). These aforementioned notions of spirituality are reflected in the title of this chapter where it talks about 'the Catholic classroom and beyond' (see website for more on this topic).

Finally, in light of all the above, spirituality needs to be presented as *an interconnected study of topics, practices and values* (e.g. monastic spirituality linked to the practice of solitude and to the value of humility). In schools, parishes and elsewhere, it is often represented solely in the form of information, or as an isolated value or technique. As Nancy T. Ammerman (2014) observes, spirituality is not just a topic or discourse. It is a living, interconnected reality comprising history, topics, practices and values (pp. 56-57). Here she follows theorists such as Riesebrodt in adopting 'an "inside view" that takes the content of the action seriously in defining a practice as spiritual' (p. 57). How should this type of spirituality that intentionally morphs tradition, practices and values be taught? If I can adapt Groome's (1998b) comments on religious education, I would assert that the pedagogical purpose of spirituality is 'to engage the whole "being" of [students], their heads, hearts, and lifestyles, [and] to inform, form, and transform their identity, agency [and spirituality] in the world' (p. 2). This assumes that spirituality is linked to praxis, which is understood as action and reflection leading to transformation.

Let us now conclude this theoretical section by returning to the image of spirituality as 'the elephant in the room.' Sire (2015) argues that any worldview (of which spirituality is a part and a driver at the very least) involves an acceptance on our part of certain pre-suppositions, an interpretative framework, so that after a while we dwell in these as we do in our own body (p. 140, citing Polanyi). Spirituality is like a house we build. When our understandings, practices or values are challenged, we might be forced to leave home and search for another (cf. Fleming & Lovat, 2015; Fleming & Mudge, 2014). Spirituality is a crucial element of 'worldview' because it is essential to Christian theory and practice. As part of this worldview, as Sire (2015) avers, spirituality involves 'commitment', it assumes 'a fundamental orientation of the heart', it is expressed in stories, and it 'provides the foundation on which we live and move and have our being' (p. 141). It is imperative to embody and teach these aspects of spirituality if it is to endure within the knowledge, practices and values of both teachers and students.

Spirituality – how do you put it into practice? RE units and the teaching of spirituality

In this more practical section we explore various concrete responses to the teaching of spirituality. The section commences with a brief examination of those typical diocesan units that can promote teaching of spirituality. It concludes with a number of topics and strategies that could assist the practical teaching of spirituality. Most primary and secondary units taught throughout Australian dioceses are linked in some way to spirituality, whether

Year/Level → Prayer Types ↓	K-2	3-4	5-6	7-8	9-10	11-12
Breathing prayer	Learning to breathe; basic deep breathing	Breathing and silent prayer in presence of Holy Spirit	'Maranatha' or Come Lord Jesus prayer	Jesus prayer as breathing prayer	Combining previous with praying with icons	Former combined with 'Focusing' and other styles
Jesus as the model of Prayer	Jesus and God as Father; Moses and God as friend	Our Father as model of prayer; personal prayer	Jewish models of prayer; scripture texts; communal prayer	Parables and their teachings on prayer; penitential prayer	Prayers of the saints; Intercessions; mystical prayer	Prayer and mysticism throughout history; prayers from other traditions
Formal prayer	Sign of Cross; Grace before & after meals	Our Father and other formal prayers	Hail Mary; Glory be to the Father	Nicene Creed, Acts of contrition	Eastern orthodox prayers; Jesus Prayer; Examen of Conscience	Praying the psalms through different prayer techniques
Psalms and prayer	Rhythmic prayer; child friendly versions of Psalms	Types of psalms; e.g. Creation, Penitential	Singing Psalms; basic settings or context of psalms	Psalms and liturgical season; Australian style psalms	Psalms and social justice; interfaith uses; Psalms of Lament	Brueggemann (2007) and psalms; cycle of security, disorientation & reorientation

Year/Level → Prayer Types ↓	K-2	3-4	5-6	7-8	9-10	11-12
Liturgical and sacramental links	Structure of Liturgy;	Children's Mass responses; Advent and Christmas	Sacraments of Penance, Eucharist	Different rites of Reconciliation	Deeper study of sacraments	Marriage and other sacraments of Order; vocations
Schools or types of prayer	Prayer by key OT figures (Moses, Abraham, Hannah, Ruth)	Prayer by key NT figures (Jesus, Mary, Paul, Peter, John)	Franciscan prayer	Ignatian prayer; Prayers based on Desert fathers & mothers	Trinitarian prayer	Augustinian and Benedictine prayer
Sacred Space (SS)	Personal SS; Creation as SS	Use of colour and liturgical elements in SS	Using symbols in SS; Constructing SS in groups	Setting up SS combined with prayer ritual	Singing, art and other forms used within SS	More complex creations of SS such as interfaith setting
Links with CCC	n. 2589	2599-2606	2607-2613	2614-2616	2617-2619	2623-2625

Table 1 – Suggested Cycle for Teaching Prayer across K to 12

implicitly or explicitly, or have the potential to be so linked. Two of the dioceses that I am most familiar with (Broken Bay and Maitland/Newcastle, both in NSW) have developed standard units on Jesus, Covenant, Creation, the Church and so on. Perhaps primary units on prayer and the liturgical seasons, and secondary units titled as Youth spirituality, the Journey of Catholic faith, and Serving as a disciple, would be the most productive contexts in which to explore themes of prayer and spirituality.

One Stage 4 unit in the Maitland/Newcastle diocese is titled 'Prayer and spirituality' and, like similar units in other dioceses, explores some specific themes raised in this chapter. These include the nature of prayer and spirituality, links between them, different types of prayer in the Catholic tradition, and so on. It contains some excellent resources but has less to say on the origins of Christian and Eastern prayer which is 'breathing' (see below), although it does have a section on praying with icons. Nevertheless, many such units need to expand their topics to include, for example, the Jesus Prayer, ecological prayer (e.g. through the Lord's Prayer), walking meditation, journaling, haiku, labyrinth, types of spirituality (not just formal prayer types), kataphatic and apophatic spiritualities, and many other topics, practices and values.

However, apart from units related to spirituality and all the programming and assessment paraphernalia that accompany them, what else does a nascent, practising teacher of spirituality need to know? One suggestion that I would put forward is a more systematic treatment of spirituality across Years K-12 and followed by a similar circular treatment throughout Years 7 to 12. These suggestions are based on some earlier work I completed in Wilcannia-Forbes Diocese. I have summarised some key points and selected ideas from that document along with some insights from subsequent years in the chart below. Each stage is linked to the *Catechism of the Catholic Church (CCC)* (The Holy See, 1993) and reinforces the previous years and adds complexity to its ideas and practices for prayer (see Table 1). Tracking has been completed for other areas not mentioned in the chart, such as journalling, Jewish prayer, interfaith prayer, *lectio divina,* and many more.

We have already heard above from a range of teachers on their definitions of spirituality. Now we turn to how they teach spirituality in the classroom. Perhaps you would think that this latter topic would be more clear-cut than the former in relation to practical teaching? This is not always the case. Sometimes there are clear strategies and types of prayer. These could include the teaching of practices such as mindfulness, focusing, haiku, labyrinth, journaling, praying with icons, and many others. At other times the teaching of spirituality is part of a more general, evolving and trepidatory approach.

Plotting spirituality – four different types

In order to expand the above reflections on spiritual practice, this section explores a range of spiritual profiles that might be helpful for teachers and students in order to diagnose their own particular strengths and weaknesses? This would appear to be an essential diagnostic component of any teaching on or about spirituality. In doing so, I draw upon two spirituality taxonomies – one from Holmes that classifies spiritual types, and the other from Sheldrake that analyses the ways in which four types of spirituality that operate transformatively in the world.

Included below (Figure 1) is a chart adapted from the writings of Urban T. Holmes III (1980, pp. 3-5) which describes *four general spiritual profiles or types*. Your particular type can be located with a consideration of the chart's two axes and where they intersect to form a particular quadrant. For example, first you plot your spirituality tendency along the vertical axis between thinking and feeling. Then you do the same along the horizontal axis between k/cataphatic and apophatic. Sheldrake (1998) clarifies the relationship between these complementary forms of spirituality: 'Cataphatic theology is what we affirm about God [e.g. God is like light] and apophatic theology reflects the fact that when in the presence of God we are reduced to silence [e.g. no image can fully capture God]' (p. 200). This plotting, for example, might locate you (see cross shape) within the Type 3 'Mystic' category (circled Figure 1). Your type might tend towards the apophatic or the affective/feeling direction. You notice that the extreme for this spiritual type is possible escapism or reclusivity. Each spirituality type has its strengths and weaknesses. It also needs to engage and empathise with other spirituality types and be lived out in a concrete context. Other technical terms in the chart can be clarified through sources such as Livingstone (2000, pp. 191, 451-452).

What types of spirituality might be assumed or invisible in the above diocesan units and teacher statements? A second model based on the writings of Philip Sheldrake (2012, pp. 24-41) proposes *four types of spirituality* – ascetical, mystical, active-practical, and prophetic-critical. It provides a resource whereby the teacher can discuss different profiles of spirituality with their students. The chart provides examples of each, and addresses the where, how, and what of the transformation generated by each type. In general, the ascetical and active-practical appear to be the more visible types in society, whereas the ascetical and prophetical-critical seem to be more notable by their absence.

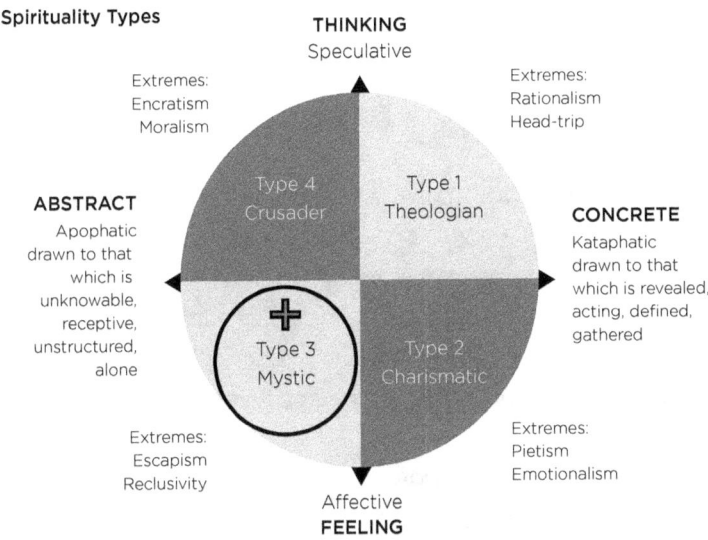

Figure 1: *Spirituality types, based on the work of Urban T. Holmes*

Spirituality – challenges for the future

Guided by a spirit of inquiry, let us consider some areas of spirituality that are typically 'missing' from normal classrooms. Reflection on *'threshold concepts' or TCs* was initially promoted by Meyer and Land (2006) who describe them as having the potential to shift any area of engagement to a new locus of reflection and praxis. TCs do this by challenging students, in this case, to cross a threshold or portal, to enter a previously inaccessible way of thinking about something. Engaging with a TC is variously described as troublesome, problematic, liminal, and hitting a brick wall (see p. 2). Whether in spirituality or other areas, TC theory is particularly interested in what TCs the student is encountering, why they choose to cross them, how they cross them, and what evidence is available to show that students have actually crossed them. Examples of spirituality TC transitions (sometimes referred to as Threshold Transitions or TTs) include – from pride to humility, from hardheartedness to mercy, and from apathy to service and praxis (refer also to Mudge).

Philip Sheldrake (2007) raises a number of *challenges for spirituality* in his *Brief History of Spirituality,* simply on account of the vast number of topics that he covers and thus deems worthy of comment and interpretation. He refers to numerous areas that are typically absent from school and in some cases tertiary consideration. These include Eastern perspectives such as the Syrian and Egyptian ascetics (pp. 43-45), the city as a sacred area (pp. 80-81), and the need to appreciate other non-Catholic Christian spiritualities – knowledge of which is essential for participating in dialogue, ecumenism and cooperation – Lutheran, Anglican, Quaker, Wesleyan and many more (pp. 106-138). Other absent spiritualities include Pietism, Orthodox (see 'breathing prayer' above), and that of John Henry Newman (pp. 143-171).

In a world where many claim to be spiritual and not religious, to find God more easily in nature rather than in a church, and to draw wisdom from multiple faiths and belief systems (confirmed by Australian ABS and CRA figures), Carl McColman (2008) has issued *a challenge about the values that we ought to teach and cultivate.* Recall that any integrated presentation of spirituality should include a fusion of topics/traditions, practices and values (see above). He calls first of all for a reinstatement of the primacy of *breathing* for prayer and spirituality. 'Breath' is at the heart of prayer and the nature of the Holy Spirit. The Greek word for 'breath' and 'spirit' is *pneuma,* while the Hebrew word is *ruach.* This same breath is linked to forgiveness in John 20:22 where 'Jesus breathed on them and said to them, "Receive the Holy

Spirit'" (p. 9). Examples of breathing prayers are the Jesus Prayer, the Rosary, and the Lord's Prayer (note the role of 'breathing' in Table 1 on p. 148).

McColman also champions other values and concepts such as wonder, change, equipoise, community, and sacrifice (pp. 37-210 passim). He asserts that the foundational challenge for Christian spirituality is that of 'cultivating practice'. Included below is a summary of the disciplines that he puts forward for nurturing the discipline of wonder.

1. Pray or meditate daily	7. Tithe or give part of your income to those in need
2. Engage in spiritual reading or study	8. Honour some form of the Sabbath
3. Find an *anamchara* or soul friend/mentor	9. Relate charitably to those who are needy
4. Join a healthy faith community	10. Actively seek political solutions to complete the ministry of charity (combine contemplation and relationships with social justice and praxis)
5. Cultivate beauty in your life	11. Seek ways to interact with persons from other traditions (ecumenical, interfaith, other)
6. Engage in some sort of personal improvement program	12. Maintain equilibrium and a sense of humour regarding your spirituality

(McColman, 2008, pp. 226-229.)

One final challenge is the urgent need for use of a *'pedagogical cycle'* in the teaching of spirituality. In my opinion, one of the most dangerous 'species of teacher' is one operating in spirituality, religious education or any other subject area, *without an explicit pedagogical framework or cycle*. Groome (1998b) understands such a cycle as a meta-approach, an overarching perspective and mode for proceeding that leads students into dialogue with Christian tradition and society in order to reflect and respond in a practical and transformative manner (praxis) (pp. 2-3).

Teachers need to base their planning, teaching, assessment, evaluation and reporting (everything) on a pedagogical cycle. Here I define 'pedagogical cycle' as a cycle of present continuous verbs that assists the teacher in planning, resourcing, and communicating spirituality to his/her students. God is a dynamic verb and not a static noun (Cooper, 1998, pp. 69-79). Examples of a series of verbs comprising a pedagogical cycle (typically four or five verbs are recommended as manageable) are: *naming* students' experience – *cultivating* the Christian tradition on the topic – *integrating* connections between the last two processes – *contemplating* wisdom insights arising from the topic – and *responding* in a practical way to the topic. Many more such verbs are possible, including analysing and working cooperatively.

Summary and conclusions

Allow me to approach this final section from a slightly different angle. Ask yourself this question – 'Based on the insights in this chapter, what would I recommend to teachers of spirituality as resources or tools within a hypothetical *Survival Kit for Teaching Spirituality*?' What is absolutely essential not only for teaching lessons or running activities on spirituality but also for having 'something up your sleeve' for those classroom emergencies when Plans B and C are required? Take time to write a list of these. Note that this kit should also include ideas for cultivating wisdom or what Groome (1998b) calls 'conation' (pp. 26-32).

Here are my suggestions. Compare them to your own. The *Survival Kit* should include at least two definitions of spirituality – but both should, as Groome and St. Augustine assert, accommodate 'truth wherever it may be found [and which] belongs to God' (compare Pope Francis' comments below). It should also contain quotes, objects and technological tools that remind the owner that their spirituality is Australian, and that they need to take account of the latest statistical insights on religion and spirituality (ABS and CRA) in the context of a highly technologised society.

In addition, the *Survival Kit* should include pictures of the Australian wilderness and ocean, a list of key values (e.g. wisdom, humility, wonder, questioning), and a reminder of Aboriginal and Torres Strait Island spiritualities that existed before the first 'boat people' arrived. Perhaps it could also boast a set of Russian or *babushka* dolls, symbolising the multivalent, Pandoran, and often surprising nature of spirituality. A Yin-yang symbol would serve to trigger memories of the complementary kataphatic and apophatic (*plerosis* and *kenosis*) dimensions of spirituality, while a model of the globe with pieces missing would remind the owner of the recurring need to 'accept exile' and to 'leave home'.

Pictures of students, staff, families and society would remind the owner of the *real* focus of spirituality, a small plant requiring constant watering would concentrate their mind on 'the spiritual life as a process of flourishing', while a list of values and practices would prompt the kit owner to review these constantly. The *Kit* would be completed by a copy of the Jesus Prayer, the charts included above by Holmes and Sheldrake, and a recording by Pope Francis entitled: 'Listen, Expand your ideas, Go to the frontiers, Dialogue, Be Transformed'. All of which leads us to the final reflection for this chapter.

In a luminous September 2013 interview, Pope Francis revealed some pathways of religion and spirituality that he believed were yet to be explored. His response below is an important contribution to the topic we raised in the title of this chapter – what does spirituality look like in the 'Catholic classroom and beyond'? He is also instructing us in a particular method, in that he employs a Socratic technique, or the answering of a question with a question, in some of his responses (similar to Jesus' Jewish parabolic teaching method). The following exchange took place as part of an interview with Eugenio Scalfari, an atheist Italian intellectual and founder of the newspaper *La Repubblica*. Are we prepared to engage in the same type of probing and courageous discourse that Pope Francis is modelling here?:

[Scalfari asks the pope a question ...]

Pope Francis: But now let me ask you a question: you, a secular non-believer in God, what do you believe in? ...

Scalfari: I am grateful for this question. The answer is this: I believe in Being, that is in the tissue from which forms, bodies arise.

Pope Francis: And I believe in God, not in a Catholic God, there is no Catholic God, there is God and I believe in Jesus Christ, his incarnation. Jesus is my teacher and my pastor, but God, the Father, Abba, is the light and the Creator. This is my Being. Do you think we are very far apart? ... [later he adds] This is important: to get to know people, listen, expand the circle of ideas (Dias, 2013, pp. 1-2).

NOTE: The above is an abridged version of a longer paper that includes additional insights, sources, teacher observations, and so on. This version also includes a list of recommended extension readings, additional charts, and a fuller list of sources for teachers of spirituality. It can be located at www.garrattpublishing.com.au

REFERENCES

Altmeyer, S., Klein, C., Keller, B., Silver, C. F., Hood, R. W. & Streib, H. (2015). Subjective definitions of spirituality and religion: An exploratory study in Germany and the US. *International Journal of Corpus Linguistics, 20*(4), 526-552.

Bregman, L. (2014). *The Ecology of Spirituality: Meanings, Virtues, and Practices in a Post-Religious Age.* Waco, TX: Baylor University Press.

Brueggemann, W. (2007). *Praying the Psalms: Engaging Scripture and the Life of the Spirit.* Eugene, OR: Cascade Books.

Chopra, D. (2013). Introduction. In J. Canfield, M. V. Hansen & A. Newmark, *Chicken Soup for the Soul, 20th Anniversary Edition.* New York: Chicken Soup for the Soul.

Connolly, N. (2013). New Evangelisation in Australia. *SEDOS Bulletin, 45*(4), 128-139.

Cooper, D. A., Rabbi. (1998). *God is a verb: Kabbalah and the practice of mystical Judaism.* New York: Riverhead Books.

Dias, E. (2013). Pope Francis Talks Spirituality in New Interview. *TIME,* 1 October 2013. Retrieved on 15/9/16 from: http://world.time.com/2013/10/01/pope-francis-talks-spirituality-in-new-interview/

Fleming, D. & Lovat, T. (2015). Learning as Leaving Home: Fear, Empathy, and Hospitality in the theology and religion classroom. *Teaching Theology & Religion, 18*(3), 207-223.

Fleming, D. & Mudge, P. (2014). 2014a. Leaving home: A pedagogy for theological education. In L. Ball & J. R. Harrison (Eds.). *Learning and teaching theology: Some ways ahead* (pp. 71-80). Northcote, Victoria: Morning Star Publishing.

Groome, T. H. (1998a). *Educating for life, a spiritual vision for every teacher and parent.* Allen, TX: Thomas More.

Groome, T. H. (1998b). *Sharing faith: A comprehensive approach to religious education and Pastoral Ministry.* Eugene, OR: Wipf and Stock Publishers.

Holmes, U. T. III. (1980). *A History of Christian Spirituality: An Analytical Introduction.* Minneapolis, MN: Seabury.

Kuchan, K. L. (2006). *Visio Divina: A New Practice of Prayer for Healing and Growth.* New York: Crossroad.

Livingstone, E. A. (2000). *The Concise Oxford Dictionary of the Christian Church (2nd Edition).* New York: Oxford.

Mason, M. (2004). *Methods for exploring primordial elements of youth spirituality.* Melbourne: ACU.

McColman, C. (2008). *Spirituality: A Post-Modern and Interfaith Approach to Cultivating a Relationship with God.* White River Junction, VT: White River Press.

Meyer, J. H. F. & Land, R. (2006). Threshold concepts and troublesome knowledge: An Introduction. In J. H. F. Meyer & R. Land (eds.), *Overcoming Barriers to Student Understanding: Threshold concepts and troublesome knowledge* (pp. 3-18). London & New York: Routledge.

Mudge, P. (2014). 'Crossing frontiers without a map' – the role of threshold concepts and problematic knowledge in religious education and spirituality. *Waikato Journal of Education, 19*(2), 51-67.

Mudge, P. (2016b). Unpublished responses from EDUC6043, RELT6016 & RELT6044 students on What is spirituality? and How do you teach spirituality? (25 pages). Used with permission. Received 10-16 May 2016 at: Pennant Hills, NSW: Broken Bay Institute.

Mudge, P. & Kupkee, C. (2010). *K-6 Framework for Prayer, Spirituality and Resources: A Proposal for the systematic K-6 teaching of Prayer based on the Catechism of the Catholic Church*. Forbes, NSW: Diocese of Wilcannia-Forbes.

Sheldrake, P. (1998). *Spirituality and History: Questions of interpretation and Method*. Maryknoll, NY: Orbis.

Sheldrake, P. (2007). *A Brief History of Spirituality*. Carlton, Vic: Blackwell.

Sheldrake, P. (2012). *Spirituality: A very short introduction*. Oxford: OUP.

Sire, J. W. (2015). *Naming the Elephant: Worldview as a Concept (2nd Edition)*. Downers Grove, IL: IVP Academic Press.

The Holy See. (1993). *Catechism of the Catholic Church*. Homebush, NSW: St Paul Publications.

Dr. Peter Mudge is Senior Lecturer in Religious Education and Spirituality at The Broken Bay Institute, Diocese of Broken Bay, and Conjoint Lecturer, School of Humanities and Social Science, The University of Newcastle, both in NSW, Australia. Peter's areas of interest and research include: religious education, spirituality, threshold concepts, connected knowing, transformative, critical and subversive pedagogies, Studies of Religion, interfaith/interbelief dialogue, philosophy in the classroom, and the role of the arts and spirituality in religious education. He has received formal training in drawing and painting which he pursues in his art studio.

Correspondence to:
Dr Peter Mudge
The Broken Bay Institute
PO Box 662, Pennant Hills NSW Australia
Email: pmudge@bbi.catholic.edu.au

Chapter 8

Teaching Ecological Themes in Religious Education

**Shane Lavery, Debra Sayce
and Sandra Peterson**

Introduction

The concept of 'Sustainability' is one of three cross-curriculum priorities mandated by the Australian Curriculum, Assessment and Reporting Authority (ACARA) (2016), the Federal organisation responsible for national curriculum from Kindergarten to Year 12. Central to this priority is that students appreciate the necessity of acting for a more sustainable future so that the Earth can maintain all life, meet the needs of the present and not compromise the needs of future generations. It is ACARA's hope that addressing this priority 'will allow all young Australians to develop skills, value and world views necessary for people to act in ways that contribute to more sustainable patterns of living'. Religious education curricula within Australian Catholic schools are well situated to support the sustainability cross-curriculum priority, especially when one considers the importance placed on stewardship and care for creation in recent papal documents. However, a Catholic school approach to sustainability is wider that the religious education program. The Sacred Congregation for Catholic Education (1988) stressed that the distinctive nature of Catholic schooling was its religious dimension. In particular the Sacred Congregation emphasised 'the illumination of all knowledge with the light of faith' (para. 1). This statement is further developed in the Bishops of Western Australia's Mandate document (2009), which requires that the 'Catholic school curriculum will be distinctive by the ways in which the Gospel values are integrated into the outcomes and content of all Learning Areas' (p. 34). This chapter initially explores the Catholic Church's teaching on stewardship of creation, both from an international perspective and within the Australian context. This discussion is followed by a review of *On Holy Ground*, an Australian Catholic educational initiative towards education for the environment. Finally, the chapter considers approaches to ecological education from Catholic Education Western Australia (CEWA) and Catholic Education South Australia (CESA), both within the religious education curriculum and through a whole school perspective.

Stewardship of Creation

The Catholic Church's teaching on responsibility towards God's creation is principally linked with the writings of Popes John Paul II (1978-2005), Benedict XVI (2005-2013) and Francis (2013-). In his very first encyclical, *Redemptor Hominis,* John Paul II (1979) raised concerns about humanity's use of the environment. He commented adversely on 'the exploitation of the earth', noting the disturbing tendency to view the environment simply for 'immediate use and consumption'. Moreover, he remarked that 'the Creator's will' was that humanity should "communicate with nature as an intelligent and noble "master" and "guardian", and not as a heedless "exploiter" and "destroyer"'. Using his 1990 New Year Message, Pope John Paul emphasised the need for a conscientious attitude towards the environment: 'Christians, in particular, realise that responsibility within creation and their duty towards nature and the Creator, are an essential part of their faith' (para. 15). The following year he raised the 'ecological question' in his encyclical, *Centesimus Annus* (1991), where he warned against the problem of consumerism, decried the 'arbitrary use of the earth' (para. 37) and warned against the subsequent 'irrational destruction of the natural environment' (para. 37). In his 1995 encyclical, *Evangelium Vitae*, John Paul II indicated that humanity 'has a specific responsibility towards the environment ... not only for the present but also for future generations' (para. 42). Perhaps John Paul II's strongest statements came in his January 2001 General Audience where he stated: 'If one looks at the regions of our planet, one realises that humanity has disappointed the divine expectation ... humiliating ... the earth, that flower-bed that is our dwelling' (para. 4). Further, he articulated the need to 'stimulate and sustain the "ecological conversion"... which has made humanity more sensitive when facing the catastrophe toward which it was moving' (para. 5).

Pope John Paul II's successor, Pope Benedict XVI, continued this pro-active stance on environmental issues. In his message to the Director General of the FAO, October 2006, the Pope stated, 'the order of creation demands that a priority be given to those human activities that do not cause irreversible damage to nature but which instead are woven into the social, cultural and religious fabric of the different communities'. In January, 2008 he highlighted the need for ecological responsibility: 'We need to care for the environment; it has been entrusted to men and women to be protected and cultivated with responsible freedom, with the good of all as a constant guiding criterion' (Caritas Internationalis, n.d., para. 1). In his 2009 encyclical *Caritas in Veritate*, Pope Benedict XVI clearly reiterated the Catholic Church's environmental commitment when he noted: 'the Church has a responsibility towards creation and she must assert this responsibility in the public sphere' (para. 51). Further, the Pope pointed out that the Church is required to 'defend not only earth, water and air as gifts of creation that belong to all', but must 'above all protect mankind from self-destruction' (para. 51). Pope Benedict XVI's most definitive statements come in his message for the celebration of the World Day of Peace, January 2010, where he focused on the theme 'If you want to cultivate peace, protect creation'. In this message he commented on the 'downright misuse of the earth' (para. 1), highlighted the need 'to exercise responsible stewardship over the environment' (para. 7), and remarked on the fact that 'the issue of environmental degradation challenges us to examine our life-style and the prevailing models of consumption and production' (para. 11). January 2010 also saw the Pope denounce the failure of world leaders to agree to a new climate change treaty in Copenhagen, criticising the economic and political resistance to addressing environmental degradation (Willey, 2010).

Pope Francis began his papacy with a strong message on the need for environmental responsibility. His apostolic exhortation *Evangelii Gaudium* (November 2013), stressed that human beings 'are not only the beneficiaries but also the stewards of other creatures' (para. 215). He urged all people, in the spirit of St Francis of Assisi, to 'watch over and protect the fragile world in which we live, and all its peoples' (para. 216). However, it was in his sweeping encyclical on the environment, *Laudato Si*, (2015) that Pope Francis clearly detailed humanity's environmental responsibilities for present and future generations. For example, he highlighted as 'urgent' the 'challenge to protect our common home' (para. 13), commenting on the need for 'a new dialogue about how we are shaping the future of our planet' (para. 14). He raised concerns regarding pollution, climate change, water, the loss of biodiversity, as well as global hunger and poverty. Moreover, he criticised a lack of any concerted world leadership 'capable of striking out on new paths and meeting the needs of the present with concern for all and without prejudice towards coming generations' (para. 53). In this respect he questioned: 'What kind of world do we want to leave those who come after us?' (para. 16), intimating that 'we may well be leaving to coming generations debris, desolation and filth' (para. 161).

Duncan (n.d.) notes that Pope Francis' message about the urgent moral dimensions of the present environmental crisis is not entirely new given previous comments by Popes John Paul II and Benedict XVI. However, what is unique is that he, as pope, would devote an entire encyclical to the issue (Duncan, n.d.). In such a way, Pope Francis (2015) clearly publicises his belief in the need for concerted world action, that is, 'a global consensus' (para. 164) for positive action through sustainable and diversified agriculture, renewable and less polluting forms of energy, the better management of marine and forest resources, and universal access to drinking water.

An Australian Catholic Perspective on Care of the Earth

The Australian Catholic Bishops have also raised concerns over the need for humanity to take a more concerted approach to the care of the earth, God's creation. Their 2002 Social Justice statement, *A New Earth,* stressed the environmental challenge facing Australians and called for an 'ecological conversion' through the exercise of good stewardship. In 2004, the Catholic Bishops of Queensland published a pastoral letter focusing on the preservation of the Great Barrier Reef, noting that 'care for the environment and a keener ecological awareness have become key moral issues for the Christian conscience' (p. 3). The Australian Catholic Bishops' 2005 Social Justice Statement raised alarms concerning 'a culture of waste' (p. 9) in Australian society, emphasised creation as a gift of God, and encouraged all to care for the earth. Rue and Brown (2006) writing on behalf of the Australian Bishops with respect to Climate Change, noted, 'the right to a safe ecological environment is a universal human right' (p. 19). Moreover, these authors stressed that 'future generations should not be robbed or left with extra burdens' (p. 18) as a consequence of the actions of current generations. Edwards (2012), an Australian theologian, highlighted that the

Incarnation concerns God embracing the entire created world (Rom 8:18-25).

He discussed the need for a 'planetary spirituality' (p. 58) where he believed that, in Australia, much could be learned from the spirituality of Indigenous people who see the land as a nurturing mother and the natural world as sacred.

A significant Australian Catholic educational initiative towards education for the environment was the 2006 publication *On Holy Ground*, co-authored by Catholic Earthcare Australia and the Catholic Education Offices in Queensland and New South Wales (Rue, 2009). Bishop Toohey established the direction of the publication in his 'Greeting' (Catholic Earthcare Australia, 2006, p. 2), when he stated, 'Catholic educators have a critical role to play in promoting the Church's call to "ecological conversion" which finds its ground in our faith.' Concerns were raised in the publication over the deteriorating environmental situation in Australia regarding 'our rivers, soil, land, air and oceans' (p. 4). Further, the publication presented a long-term vision for Catholic ecological education that involved embedding ecological values into school programs and practices. Three specific goals were detailed: (a) to foster in students an appreciation of creation as a gift, their relation with creation, and their responsibility as co-creators for its future; (b) to develop in students the knowledge, skills attitudes, values and commitment to initiate individual and collective responses that are environmentally responsible and reflective of their ecological vocation; and (c) to inspire students to decrease their ecological footprint and increase their spiritual one, as creatures made in the image and likeness of God (p. 6).

The South Australian edition of *On Holy Ground*, published in 2010, reiterated the need for Catholic schools to take seriously the protection of the environment. Archbishop Wilson of Adelaide and Bishop O'Kelly (Port Pirie Diocese) highlighted in their 'Greetings' (Catholic Earthcare Australia, 2010) that 'caring for the God's creation and respecting our fragile ecosystems are now acknowledged as core elements of Christian social teaching'. They observed that *On Holy Ground* encompassed 'all aspects of Catholic education, from the classroom curriculum to the ethical use of resources". To this effect the South Australian version introduced the concept of the ASSISI program, A Strategic Systems-based Integrated Sustainability Initiative designed as 'a strategic pathway for Catholic schools to engage with answering the call for ecological conversion and sustainability' (Catholic Earthcare Australia, 2010, p. 22). ASSISI has six components: Whole School Planning, Religious Dimension, Teaching and Learning, Ethical Resource Use, Cultivating Grounds and Buildings, and Community Relationships (Catholic Earthcare Australia, 2010, pp. 20-21). Such a broad approach to environmental education addressed concerns previously raised by commentators such as Orr (2004) that the words 'environmental education' implied 'education about the environment, just another course or two, a curricular outbuilding to the big house of formal schooling where the really important things go on' (p. 18). ASSISI suggests a deeper transformation of the substance, practice and scope of education to prepare students as ecologically aware citizens.

Catholic Education

What is clear from the *On Holy Ground* publications is that any attempt to teach ecological themes in Catholic schools must entail a whole school approach. That is, there is need to involve students in direct contact with the environment, practice in ecological decision-making, and participation in liturgy, prayer, justice initiatives, scripture as well as study. All three versions emphasised that effective ecological education involves an integration of various disciplines, with an application of the knowledge and skills 'from across key learning areas, especially the religious education curriculum of each Diocese' (Catholic Earthcare Australia, 2010, p. 6). Each publication included a detailed list of ecologically active Catholic schools in the respective states.

The fact that the religious education curriculum was specifically referred to in all three *On Holy Ground* publications is noteworthy. There has been a tendency for the ecological debate to be dominated by the language of science (Millais, 2006). Yet as Toohey (2008, p. 55) observed, issues surrounding the welfare of the natural environment 'are not simply scientific, technical, political or economic'. Rather, he postulated that at their core 'is the very nature of the person and our relationship with our Creator' (p. 55). It is critical, therefore, that Catholic schools identify and integrate areas of the religious education curriculum pertinent to ecological education. In such a way, Catholic schools can provide a religious and spiritual perspective regarding stewardship for the earth. Key focus areas might include spirituality, moral teaching, liturgy, prayer and social and ecological justice concerns (Catholic Earthcare Australia, 2010). In this regard, religious educators play a vital role in developing an informed ecological awareness and participation in young people. Through their training and expertise, religious educators are in a significant position to lead their school communities, both in the classroom setting and in the wider school environment (Lavery, 2011). What now follows is a brief outline of approaches whereby Catholic education in Western Australia and South Australia attempt to promote the Catholic Church's call to 'ecological conversion'.

Catholic Education Western Australia

Catholic education in Western Australia (CEWA) consists of 163 school and early learning sites that cater for over 73 000 students. With over 13 000 staff, schools are located across four dioceses (Broome, Geraldton, Bunbury and Perth). These schools are served by the Catholic Education Commission of Western Australia (CECWA) and one Catholic Education Office, which operate three satellite offices in the three regional dioceses and one main office in the Archdiocese of Perth (CECWA, 2015). Two examples are provided as to ways CEWA promotes ecological awareness.

First, in response to Francis' encyclical *Laudato Si*, the primary religious education program in Western Australia incorporates a strong sense of responsibility for God's creation. The primary religious education units of work consist of three key processes: A – Wondering about the Creator; B – The Promise of Christian Salvation; and C – Christian Response (Catholic Education Office of Western Australia, 2016). Within the process *Wondering about creation*, students are encouraged to marvel at the world around them; see and appreciate the many aspects of creation; celebrate God who is creator; understand how God is revealed to them through creation; and see the power of God. Back in 1972, the United Nations Declaration of the UN Conference on the Human Environment sought to improve common preservation and enhancement of the natural world. In particular, Principle 19 promoted education as an important means in which to inform future generations on ecological issues but also provide the understanding of the impact human development has on the environment (United Nations, 1972). The primary RE curriculum addresses these concerns by encouraging students to:

- Care for creation as God wants.
- Learn about and understand the importance of creation ... for example that water sustains life.
- Know God's power as revealed through the forces of creation.
- Be aware that creation is a sign of God's presence.
- Consider that the abundant resources of the earth are created by God and ways these resources may not be shared fairly as there are many on earth who lack the basic necessities of life (Catholic Education Office of Western Australia, 2016).

In order to support student learning, teachers of religious education are encouraged to use appropriate contextual examples that may include current local, national and international means to illustrate the ecological reality that humanity is facing. Such meaningful examples on the effects of climate change on the earth also highlight how the poorest communities often suffer the most. Further, students can come to appreciate very real threats to the future of our common home if humanity continues to exploit the earth and its resources.

The Promise of Christian Salvation, the second process in the teaching of primary religious education, invites students to explore how Jesus exemplified the Christian promise of salvation and how each person is empowered to live like him. The purpose of this process is to demonstrate Jesus as the model of human behaviour. That is, Jesus offered salvation by modelling how to live in a truly human way. Christians are empowered to live by the power of the Kingdom of God through participation in the life of the Church, especially through the Eucharist, the other sacraments, prayer and the ways Jesus taught and interacted with people. This process focuses upon the contemporary world of the student and how it can be experienced positively by accepting the promise of salvation. Students are introduced to examples of Jesus as the model of authentic human life. They are presented with what it looks like to draw on the power of the Kingdom fully in one's life through an understanding that: (a) Jesus wants people to experience the joy of creation as he did; (b) followers of Jesus pray like him and give thanks for creation; (c) Jesus appreciated the beauty in creation as a sign of God's presence; (d) followers of Jesus have a relationship with God and pray when they are reminded of God's presence; and (e) Jesus taught people to care for those in need and all of God's creation (Catholic Education Office of Western Australia, 2016).

The final process, *Christian Response*, considers Christ's power through His Church and how people can continue to wonder at Christian possibilities and become the person God wants us to be. In *Laudato Si*, Francis (2015) calls for every living person on the planet to engage in dialogue and action in response to the ecological and human crises of our times. This response can be personal or as a collective inquiry into the reality and implications of this encyclical for the community of life. Through the process, *Christian Response*, the Western Australian Religious Education curriculum supports, Pope Francis' call to an eco-conversion firstly, by asking students to listen to the cry of the earth and the poor, and secondly by encouraging students to look at how they continue to respond through: (a) experiencing the joy of creation; (b) expressing ideas about the world God created; (c) wondering about God who created the world; (d) showing appreciation and care for all of God's creation; (e) remembering to adore and worship God, especially through the Eucharist; (f) being empowered through prayer, to live like Jesus and respect the integrity of creation; and (g) continuing to meet the needs of all, especially the poor (Catholic Education Office of Western Australia, 2016).

It is, however, not enough to promote ecological awareness solely within the religious education curriculum. A second means by which CEWA promotes ecological awareness is through encouraging schools to adopt a whole school approach towards the New Testament imperative of stewardship of creation and Francis' call to the Church (and the world) to acknowledge the urgency of our environmental challenges (Laudato Si, 2015). As way of example, St Brigid's Primary School, Middle Swan, is presented as a case study in educating Catholic primary school students in ecological and sustainable practices.

Since 2007, St Brigid's School, has developed a holistic vision towards ecological education and sustainable practices within our school community. At the heart of this approach is developing an understanding of 'stewardship' and the clear link between our present critical environmental situation and the social justice impact on others. Staff members assisted in developing an ecological school policy during a retreat held at Rottnest Island. The school has intentionally focused on becoming more efficient with waste, water and electricity use. The Year Six Ministry Model allows students to rotate through five areas of school responsibility, including the Environmental and Christian Service Councils. The activities of these two Councils connect the practices of sustainability and social justice. Students are responsible for waste paper and cardboard recycling, mixed recycling, each class's food scraps, maintenance of the chicken coop and selling the eggs, establishing worm farms and vegetable gardens, battery and ink cartridge recycling, along with working in the St Vincent De Paul store in Midland.

St Brigid's is recognised as a Waste-Wise, Water-Wise and Energy efficient school having completed the required audits by local authorities. A Water-Wise school is required to reduce, reuse, re-cycle while developing positive environmental values within the school community. The types of activities include: incorporating rainwater tanks, waterless urinals, new technology cisterns, bore water conservation and installation of more efficient drinking taps, solar panels (60 Kw), efficient lighting, and underfloor gas heating and natural lighting via solar tubes in some buildings have also assisted with reducing energy costs. Developing a Sustainability Vision and then implementing the associated ecological practices provides a small, but observable means of bringing 'ecological conversion' to reality (Personal communication, Mike Sibbald, Assistant Principal, September, 2016).

Catholic Education South Australia

Catholic Education in South Australia (CESA) operates within the Archdiocese of Adelaide and the Diocese of Port Pirie. It employs over 6000 staff and caters for more than 48 000 students in 103 Catholic schools (Catholic Education South Australia, 2016a). Two examples are also offered as to ways CESA promotes environmental awareness. Firstly the CESA website advertises and provides a link for the document *On Holy Ground*. Viewers are told that the document 'outlines an ecological vision for Catholic schools in South Australia, which seeks to help guide them towards sustainability' (Catholic Education South Australia, 2016b). Appendix 3 of the document provides a list of 'Good News Stories' (2010, pp. 36-38) of South Australian Catholic schools working with the Religious Education Team (CESA) in an inquiry project on sustainability.

The second way that CESA promotes ecological awareness is through its religious education program. This program is based around five 'Essential Learnings for Religious Education' listed as futures, identity, interdependence, thinking and communication (Catholic Education South Australia, 2016c). The third 'Essential Learning', interdependence, considers the knowledge, skills and dispositions required for students to understand 'the interconnectedness of God, humanity and creation and to reflect, plan and take action to shape local and global communities' (Catholic Education South Australia, 2016c, p. 16). There are four learning objectives linked with the theme of interdependence. These learning objectives focus on developing (a) relationships with others and creation, (b) a sense of being connected with God, humanity and creation, (c) awareness that people are stewards of creation and co-creators with God, and (d) the ability to read the signs of the times, reflect on them in the light of the Gospel and take action to bring about justice (Catholic Education South Australia, 2016c). The other four 'Essential Learnings' also provide potential links that incorporate care for creation.

Conclusion

In 2004, the Pontifical Council for Justice and Peace presented an overview of the Catholic approach to environmental awareness in four themes: biblical awareness, humanity and creation, a crisis in the relationship between humanity and creation, and responsibility for creation. These themes have subsequently been expanded, principally through the work of Popes Benedict XVI and Francis and now provide a strong rationale for Catholic schools to address issues of creation and care for the earth. Within the Australian educational context, Catholic schools have developed curricula that promote humanity's responsibility to care for God's creation, the ethical use of resources and appropriate lifestyle choices. Moreover, this approach fits well with the ACARA (2016) cross-curriculum priority of sustainability. But of equal importance, many Australian Catholic schools are developing a more holistic attitude to 'ecological conversion' by translating the theory of the classroom into practical, real-life activities.

REFERENCES

Australian Catholic Bishops Conference (2002). *A new earth: The environmental challenge*. Retrieved from https://www.scribd.com/document/48605078/A-New-Earth-The-Environmental-Challenge

Australian Catholic Bishops Conference (2005). *Jesus, light of the world: Living the gospel today*. Retrieved from http://www.acsjc.org.au/files/SJSandresources/2005_SJSS_Statement.pdf

Australian Curriculum, Assessment and Reporting Authority (2016). *Cross-curriculum priorities*. Retrieved from http://acara.edu.au/curriculum/cross-curriculum-priorities

Benedict XVI (2006). *Message of his holiness Benedict XVI to the Director General of the Food And Agriculture Organization for the celebration of World Food Day*. Retrieved from http://w2.vatican.va/content/benedict-xvi/en/messages/food/documents/hf_ben-xvi_mes_20061016_world-food-day-2006.html

Benedict XVI (2009). *Caritas in veritate: Encyclical letter of Pope Benedict XVI*. Retrieved from http://www.vatican.va/holy_father/benedict_xvi/encyclicals/documents/hf _ben-xvi_enc_20090629_caritas-in-veritate_en.html

Benedict XVI (January 2010). *Message of his holiness Pope Benedict VXI for the celebration of world day of peace*. Retrieved from https://www.scribd.com/document/48605078/A-New-Earth-The-Environmental-Challenge

Bishops of Western Australia (2009). *Mandate 2009 – 2015*. Leederville, WA: Catholic Education Office of WA.

Caritas Internalionalis (nd.) *Climate change papal and bishops' statements*. Retrieved from http://caritas.org/activities/climate_change/its_the_climate_stupid.html?cnt =418

Catholic Bishops of Queensland (2004). *Let the many coastlands be glad! A pastoral letter on the Great Barrier Reef*. Retrieved from http://catholicearthcare.org.au/wp-content/uploads/2015/02/Let-The-Many-Coastlines-Be-Glad-A-Pastoral-Letter-on-the-Great-Barrior-Reef.pdf

Catholic Earthcare Australia (2010). *On holy ground: An ecological vision for Catholic education in South Australia.* Retrieved from http://catholicearthcare.org.au/project/on-holy-ground-south-australia/

Catholic Earthcare Australia (2006). *On holy ground: An ecological vision for Catholic education in New South Wales.* Retrieved from http://catholicearthcare.org.au/wp-content/uploads/2014/09/On-Holy-Ground-New-South-Wales.pdf

Catholic Earthcare Australia (2006). *On holy ground: An ecological vision for Catholic education in Queensland.* Retrieved from http://catholicearthcare.org.au/wp-content/uploads/2014/09/On-Holy-Ground-Queensland.pdf

Catholic Education Commission of Western Australia [CECWA] (2015). *Annual report 2015*. Retrieved from http://internet.ceo.wa.edu.au/Publications/Documents/Annual%20Report/Annual_Report_2015.pdf

Catholic Education Office of Western Australia (2016). *Primary Religious Education Curriculum.* Perth, Western Australia: CEOWA

Duncan, B. (n.d.). *Pope Francis on avoiding environmental catastrophe.* Retrieved from http://www.cssr.org.au/justice_matters/dsp-default.cfm?loadref=656

Edwards, D. (2012). *Jesus and the natural world: Exploring a Christian approach to ecology.* Mulgrave, Victoria: Garratt Publishing,

Francis (2013, November). *Evangelii Gaudium,* Retrieved from http://www.vatican.va/holy_father/francesco/apost_exhortations/documents/papa-francesco_esortazione-ap_20131124_evangelii-gaudium_en.html

Francis (2015). *Laudato Si*. Strathfield, NSW: St Paul's Publication.

John Paul II (1979) *Redemptor Hominis*. Retrieved from http://w2.vatican.va/content/john-paul-ii/en/encyclicals/documents/hf_jp-ii_enc_04031979_redemptor-hominis.html

John Paul II (1990). *Message of his holiness Pope John Paul II for the celebration of the world day of peace.* Retrieved from http://www.ewtn.com/library/PAPALDOC/JP900101.HTM

John Paul II (1991). *Centesimus Annus.* Retrieved from https://w2.vatican.va/content/john-paul-ii/en/encyclicals/documents/hf_jp-ii_enc_01051991_centesimus-annus.html

John Paul II (1995). *Evangeliium Vitae*. Retrieved from http://w2.vatican.va/content/john-paul-ii/en/encyclicals/documents/hf_jp-ii_enc_25031995_evangelium-vitae.html

John Paul II (January 2001). *General Audience*. Retrieved from http://w2.vatican.va/content/john-paul-ii/en/audiences/2001/documents/hf_jp-ii_aud_20010117.html

Lavery, S. (2011). Religious educators: Promoting an ecological balance. Religious *Education Journal of Australia, 27*(2), 16-20.

Millias C. (2006). The faith dimension. In Climate Institute (Australia). *Common belief: Australia's faith communities on Climate Change* (p. 5). Sydney: Climate Institute Australia Ltd.

Orr, D. (September/October, 2004). The learning curve. *Resurgence, 22*, 18-20.

Pontifical Council for Justice and Peace. (2004). *Compendium of the social doctrine of the church.* Strathfield, N.S.W: St Pauls Publishers

Rue, C. & Brown, C. (2006). Climate change: Future generations should not be robbed. In Climate Institute (Australia). *Common belief: Australia's faith communities on Climate Change* (pp. 18-19). Sydney: Climate Institute Australia Ltd.

Rue, C. (2009). *Let the Son shine: An Australian Catholic response to climate change.* Strathfield, NSW: St Pauls Publications.

Sacred Congregation for Catholic Education (1988). *The Religious Dimension of Education in a Catholic School.* Retrieved from http://www.vatican.va/roman_curia/congregations/ccatheduc/documents/rc_con_ccatheduc_doc_19880407_catholic-school_en.html

Toohey, C. (2006). Greetings from bishop Christopher Toohey. In Catholic Earthcare Australia. *On holy ground: An ecological vision for Catholic education in South Australia.* Retrieved from http://catholicearthcare.org.au/wp-content/uploads/2014/09/On-Holy-Ground-Queensland.pdf

Toohey, C. (2008). Stewardship and God's creation: A theological reflection. In A. Benjamin & D. Riley (Eds.). *Catholic schools: Hope in uncertain times.* Mulgrave, Victoria: John Garrett Publishing.

United Nations (1972). *Declaration of the United Nations Conference on the Human Environment (Stockholm).* Retrieved from http://www.unep.org/Documents.Multilingual/Default.asp?DocumentID=97&ArticleID=1503&l=en

Willey, D. (2010). *Pope Benedict XVI lambasts Copenhagen failure.* Retrieved from http://news.bbc.co.uk/2/hi/8452447.stm

Wilson, P. & O'Kelly, G. (2010). Greetings. In Catholic Earthcare Australia. *On holy ground: An ecological vision for Catholic education in South Australia.* Retrieved from http://catholicearthcare.org.au/project/on-holy-ground-south-australia/

Associate Professor Shane D. Lavery is Coordinator of Postgraduate Education, in the School of Education, The University of Notre Dame Australia. He teaches social justice, service-learning, and ecological studies at undergraduate level. His postgraduate teaching areas are educational leadership, religious education and ecological studies. Shane's areas of research include: educational leadership, service-learning and ecological education.

Correspondence to:
Email: shane.lavery@nd.edu.au

Dr Debra Sayce is the Director of Religious Education for Catholic Education in Western Australia. She is a member of the Catholic Education Commission of Western Australia and a member of the Faith Formation and Religious Education Committee of the National Catholic Education Commission. Debra completed her doctoral studies at The University of Notre Dame in the field of Educational Leadership.

Correspondence to:
Email: sayce.debra@ceo.wa.edu.au

Sandra Peterson is a consultant in the Religious Education and Faith Formation Team at the Catholic Education Office Western Australia. Her work is to provide leadership and support to principals and staff in Catholic schools in Western Australia. She has thirty years classroom experience and was an Assistant Principal. Sandra has completed a Masters of Educational Leadership and Management.

Correspondence to:
Email: Peterson.sandra@cathednet.wa.edu.au

Chapter 9

The Religious Education Curriculum in Australian Catholic Schools: An Overview

John McGrath

CHAPTER 9

The Catholic school participates in the evangelising mission of the Church (Congregation for Catholic Education, 1997, para. 11). The person of each individual human being is at the heart of Christ's teaching and the promotion of the human person is the goal of the Catholic school. It is committed to the integral formation of the whole person. Its task is fundamentally a synthesis of culture and faith, and a synthesis of faith and life (Sacred Congregation for Catholic Education, 1977, para. 35 - 37 and Congregation for Catholic Education, 1997, para. 9). The totality of school life gives witness to and supports students on the path towards a personal integration of faith and life. This is manifest in the various inter-related components of the Catholic school's participation in the evangelising mission of the Church. These components include its Catholic identity and culture; the religious life of the school outside the classroom; an overall curriculum imbued with a Catholic worldview; and religious education, the classroom learning and teaching of religion.

Over the last 30 years, religious education progressively has come to be seen as a learning area with educational aims, academic expectations, assessment and reporting of achievement akin to other learning areas. (Consequently, this chapter refers to students as 'learners', while acknowledging that teachers too are learners and co-inquirers in a different sense.) This evolution drew on Vatican educational documents which acknowledged that 'a scholastic discipline with the same systematic demands and the same rigour as other disciplines' (Congregation for the Clergy, 1997, para. 73). In the 1980s the term 'catechesis' still was being connected to the classroom learning and teaching of religion. The distinctions made by Vatican documents became important in light of the developing diversity that could not presume shared faith and practice among all learners. Religious education complements catechesis but is distinct from it. There 'is an absolute necessity to distinguish clearly between religious instruction and catechesis' because religious instruction focuses on 'knowledge' while catechesis 'presupposes that the hearer is receiving the Christian message as a salvific reality' (Congregation for Catholic Education, 1998, para. 68 and Congregation for the Clergy, 1997, para. 73). By 1999, Gerard (now Bishop) Holohan in his Australian commentary on the *General Directory of Catechesis* could reference the NCEC national religious education curriculum project finding (unpublished) that 'no current diocesan RE programme seeks to offer catechesis. Each seeks to meet educational aims. None reflects confusion between religious education and catechesis' (Holohan, 1999, p. 34). This does not necessarily mean that all teachers comprehended or designed religious education in that way.

The emergence of an educational focus and the distinction between and complementarity of religious education and catechesis led to clarification about the learning area's relationship to faith development and the wider religious life of the school, parish and broader Church. Their inter-relatedness is paramount if the Catholic school is to be faithful to its evangelising mission. The best articulation of this today is found in 'Brisbane Catholic Education (2008). Modelled on Moran, 1991, these guidelines present two dimensions: 'teaching people religion' (the classroom teaching and learning of religion) and 'teaching people to be religious in a particular way' (the religious life and Catholic ethos of the school). There are four components of the latter: religious identity and culture, evangelisation and faith formation, prayer and worship, social action and justice, with each one 'interrelated and mutually reinforcing' (p. 11). McGrath (2012, pp. 289-295) outlines a range of their expressions across Australian schools.

CHAPTER 9

2008 NCEC monograph

A current overview of religious education in Australian Catholic schools is best introduced through reference to the NCEC monograph *Religious Education in dialogue: curriculum across Australia* (NCEC, 2008) as many of the characteristics continue to this day, albeit with more advanced curriculum and pedagogical sophistication. It set out to examine how classroom religious education interrelated with the designated curriculum structure and framework for other learning areas in each state and territory. In its concluding chapter (pp. 85-89) it identified seven characteristics evident across Australia. They were premised on two foundational understandings:

1. *Religious Education has its purpose in the mission of the Church.* It was a vital, educational and formational activity. Depending upon its orientation at specific times, it can engage with learners as an action of the Church as a means of evangelisation, an introduction to mission, a part of broader formation and faith development, and as formative and invitational.

2. *Religious Education is a distinct area of learning.* Classroom Religious Education was identified across Australia as an area of learning on a par with the learning and teaching characteristics of other defined areas of learning.

The characteristics were:

Responsibility of the diocesan bishop. The bishop in each diocese has primacy in responsibility for religious education in a diocese and authorises the curriculum.

Religious education is informed by various sources. These sources, among others, include Scripture and Tradition, Church documents, especially the *Catechism of the Catholic Church*, national and state developments in curriculum design and pedagogy, educational and Australian sociological research.

Religious Education and State and Territory curriculum. Generally the educational approach was reflective of the state or territory curriculum frameworks for learning. Assessment and reporting practices were generally similar to other learning areas.

Diversity. In some places a common religious education curriculum was shared across a whole state. Some dioceses had collaborated with or adopted and adapted programs of other dioceses. Some dioceses (generally the larger ones) developed their own religious education curriculum and resources. A variety of resources were used across the country both as core texts and resources for teachers and learners.

Relationship between religious education and State curriculum. Some programs met state credentials and did so without compromise to Catholic beliefs, values and understanding.

Quality religious education resources. There were high quality resource modules and units equal to or superior to those in other learning areas. Some quality student texts had been developed and promulgated in some dioceses. On the whole there were not enough well-developed Australian online learning materials.

Teacher formation and learner background. Diocesan authorities had implemented religious education accreditation processes and study sponsorship programs to continue to develop the competencies of religious education teachers.

The monograph concluded by stating that the changing

background of learners and their families and their participation in the life of the Church will impact upon the religious education curriculum of the future. This raises questions about the assumptions religious educators make about the prior knowledge and experience of their students as they attempt to provide learning opportunities that are rich, relevant and real. They provide reality checks about what can be realistically expected of religious education in Catholic schools of today and tomorrow.

Contemporary contexts of religious education

As the monograph noted, religious education operates in changing contexts. As Pope Francis (2013, para. 41) has emphasised, today's 'vast and rapid cultural changes demand that we constantly seek ways of expressing unchanging truths in a language which brings out their abiding newness'. Australian society is increasingly less religious and has experienced an erosion of tradition, authority and confidence in religion and an indifference or even hostility to it. Processes of increasing pluralisation and secularisation and a focus on the pursuit of individual meaning making and autonomy effectively make being religious one choice among many. Jim and Therese D'Orsa (2013) state that the mission of Catholic schooling is now in a 'liminal period' between cultural eras; nevertheless, 'the Catholic school remains the only plausibility structure for faith that many young people and their parents encounter' (p. 249).

Australia also is a relatively affluent, consumerist society and the young in particular have a high level of digital capability and interest in immediate online communication and social media. Across Australia 69% of students in Catholic schools identify as Catholic (NCEC, 2016). Most of their families are not regular participants in the life and worship of a parish. On average three out of ten religious education learners are not Catholic.

Education in Australia is increasingly complex and there are changing societal and political expectations relating to comparative achievement internationally, preparation for employment and its contribution to the economy in terms of productivity and return on investment. At the same time, educational discourse is becoming increasingly richer, focusing increasingly on the learner and on learner agency and construction of meaning; on learning to learn, think and collaborate; on pedagogies and individualised learning; and on technologies for learning.

Learners come to learning in religious education with diverse religious, cultural, and personal profiles. They come with varying degrees of knowledge of Catholicism or religion in general, with a range of faith affiliations, with a variety of religious experiences, and in different stages in their religious journeys. Irrespective of their situations, all learners have an entitlement to learning in religious education that seeks to develop deep knowledge, understanding and skills. Its Achievement Standards describe what learners are typically able to understand and do. They are not reliant on nor are they expressions of the learners' religious dispositions or practices. At the same time, depending on learners' individual religious biographies, religious education variously is capable of being primary or first proclamation, or new evangelisation, or catechesis, or ecumenical and interfaith dialogue.

Religious education also operates in an environment of enhanced focus on mission and identity in Catholic schools. Pollefeyt and Bouwens (2014) report on the 'Enhancing Catholic School Identity Project (ECSIP)', a partnership since 2006 of the Catholic Education Commission of Victoria and Catholic University of

Leuven. It has expanded to dioceses in Queensland and South Australia. It provides a hermeneutic and an empirical methodology to assess and enhance Catholic identity in the context of pluralised, secularised contexts mentioned above. It proposes that the teacher should be a witness to the faith tradition, a specialist with a deep understanding of it, and a moderator who can engage learners with it, that is one who creates 'spaces that provide deep encounters with both the cultural and faith traditions and encourage the students to wrestle with their own issues in their search for meaning' (Sharkey, 2015, p. 26). In a different style, the Bishops of NSW/ACT in 2007 established indicators of progress (p. 18) towards schools that 'are truly Catholic in their identity and life, are centres of "the new evangelisation", enable our students to achieve high levels of 'Catholic religious literacy' [and] are led and staffed by people who will contribute to these goals' (p. 3 & p. 5).

The formation of staff is a high priority for systems and schools (NCEC, 2015). Dioceses financially support postgraduate studies in religious education and theology and provide significant professional learning and advisory support for religious education teachers. There are increased expectations for formal accreditation of teachers, especially for religious education. For example, NSW/ACT has a common framework that accredits staff to work, teach, coordinate, teach religious education and lead in Catholic schools and systems (Catholic Education Office, Sydney, 2011).

The sample of statements of purpose and aims of the most widely used religious education curricula outlined in the box below demonstrate the same systematic demands and rigour as other learning areas in ways responsive to the religious, cultural and educational contexts of the learners.

The purpose and aims of religious education

Religious education seeks to develop the religious literacy of students in light of the Catholic Christian tradition, so that they might participate critically and authentically in contemporary culture. Students become religiously literate as they develop the knowledge, skills and dispositions to interpret and use language confidently in and for faith contexts and the wider society (Brisbane Catholic Education, 2013).

The Religious Education Curriculum [K-6] through the seasons of the Liturgical Year, aims to assist the students to reflect upon, make sense of, celebrate, (and) live more deeply the mystery of Christ as revealed in each person and in relationship with others, the Church, and Creation (Catholic Education Office, Sydney, 2006, p. 12).

The purpose of religious education is to deepen students' understanding of the Tradition and to develop an appreciation of its significance in their lives, so that they may participate effectively in the life of the Church and wider society (Catholic Education South Australia, 200, p. 5).

The religious education learning area focuses on the knowledge and understanding of the Gospel as it is handed on by the Catholic Church to those who follow Christ in today's world. The outcomes and processes of the learning area are intended to ensure that students through a process of cultural, systematic and critical reflection, learn the teachings of the Gospels and understand what it means to be a Christian and how Christians live their lives (Catholic Education Office of Western Australia, 2006, p. 7).

Religious education in a Catholic School aims to ensure that students develop:

- Appreciation and deep understanding of the richness of the Catholic Tradition.
- Religious self-understanding and spiritual awareness.
- Openness to religious questions and a religious interpretation of the world.
- Awareness of the diversity of voices in society and among themselves.
- Discernment in decision-making and action informed by the Catholic Tradition.

(Catholic Education Melbourne, 2016, p. 3)

Curriculum collaboration and commonalities of content

Interdiocesan collaboration has been a feature of religious education curriculum over the last 20 years. At various times there has been partnerships, generally within the same ecclesiastical province, involving:

- Sydney (*religious education Curriculum*) and Armidale, Lismore and Wollongong, and more recently Bathurst.
- Parramatta (*Sharing Our Story*) and Wagga Wagga and Wilcannia Forbes; and originally but no longer with Canberra-Goulburn (*Treasures New and Old*).
- All NSW dioceses in the development of K-6 Foundation Statements in the format of other learning areas.
- Melbourne and Sydney in development of the student textbook series, *To Know, Worship and Love*, and then with Melbourne's adaptation of Sydney's curriculum strands for 7-10 in *Coming to Know, Worship and Love* in 2006.

- Hobart (*Good News for Living*), Ballarat (*Awakenings*), Sale (*Journeying Together in Hope*) and Sandhurst (*Source of Life*) developing individual diocesan curricula around common principles, content strands and agreed educational approaches.
- Brisbane and the four other Queensland dioceses at various times beginning with the joint project on a curriculum profile (1993-97); currently Brisbane (*Religion Curriculum P-12*) with Cairns, Townsville and Toowoomba; and Rockhampton has its own *Religion Curriculum P-10*.
- Adelaide and Port Pirie (*Crossways*), with Darwin (*Journey in Faith*).
- Catholic Education Western Australia (*Religious Education*) for Perth, Broome, Bunbury, and Geraldton.

Only two dioceses - Broken Bay *K-12 Religious Education Syllabus* and Maitland-Newcastle *K-12 Religion Syllabus* - have not had some form of partnership with another diocese or dioceses.

Careful analysis of all these curriculum documents demonstrates a remarkable degree of commonality in content. This may not be readily apparent because of the range of titles for learning strands. Analysis of their sub-sections points more clearly to a significant congruence, something that should not surprise given each document's stated base of Scripture and the *Catechism of the Catholic Church*. This commonality is not news: it was noted at NCEC level in the 1990s in the unpublished mapping of content as part of religious education's attention to the frustrated National Curriculum Statements and Profiles venture.

Some examples of content strands shared across dioceses

7-12 Sydney & Melbourne & Armidale, Bathurst, Lismore, Wollongong	Parramatta, Wagga Wagga, Wilcannia-Forbes, Hobart, Ballarat, Sale, Sandhurst	Brisbane, Cairns, Toowoomba, Townsville
Scripture and Jesus Church and Community God; Religion and Life Prayer; Liturgy and Sacraments Morality and Justice	God Jesus Church Scripture Sacraments Prayer Christian Life Religion and Society (7-12)	Sacred Texts Beliefs Church Christian Life

Western Australia	*Adelaide, Port Pirie & Darwin*
Discovering God Drawing on human experience Knowing Jesus Living like Jesus Catholic Practices	Believing Living Celebrating Praying (integrated across all)

Other features

Curriculum Structure. As NCEC (2008) noted, religious education generally adopts the structure of the local state or territory curriculum. In line with other learning areas, most curricula have tended to specify knowledge and understanding, skills and capabilities, and values, attitudes or dispositions; or 'learn about' and 'learn to'. Furthermore, they provide standards or performance descriptors or progress maps. Melbourne's religious education curriculum framework draws on the wider Victorian Essential Learning Standards and has three dimensions: religious knowledge and understandings, reasoning and responding, and personal and communal engagement. Hobart's revised curriculum has the dimensions of knowledge and understanding, inquiry and communications, and discernment and making connections.

Pedagogies and paradigms. Many jurisdictions see that a natural corollary of the educational focus of religious education is that it does need a pedagogy unique to itself but employs the best learning and teaching practices of the wider curriculum. Sydney and associated dioceses employ the Emmaus Story as an overarching paradigm rather than a learning model. It has four interconnected movements of making sense of experience, gaining access to the tradition, celebrating and responding. Melbourne uses Emmaus in three movements: to 'know', 'worship' and 'love'. Thomas Groome's Shared Christian Praxis has been a pedagogical approach in Parramatta, Wagga Wagga and Wilcannia Forbes; and in Canberra-Goulburn; and in Hobart, Ballarat, Sale and Sandhurst. In response to their ECSIP data Victorian dioceses are reflecting on the best pedagogical approaches to develop religious education. Melbourne is in the midst of a significant and innovative renewal of its framework which includes a 'pedagogy of encounter' in order to develop 'a post-critical believing, recontextualising, dialogical stance' (Catholic Education Melbourne, 2016, p. 6).

Textbooks & online resources. Modules or units of work often accompany or are part of diocesan curriculum material. These frequently have links to a range of print and online resources. Western Australia and some other jurisdictions have a cloud-based platform for digital resources. *To Know, Worship and Love* is the most well-known textbook and has been mandated for use in Melbourne and Sydney. It is now available in digital form. *Come and See* is a text for the Western Australian curriculum. *Understanding Faith*, an online multimedia resource originating in New Zealand and customised for Australia, is also widely used. Melbourne's *REsource* has many highly valued comprehensive digital resources (http://www.resourcemelb.catholic.edu.au/). *Together at One Altar*, the F-12 resource on the Eucharist developed by the NCEC in 2011, is arguably the most visited site (http://www.togetheratonealtar.catholic.edu.au). In 2014 it had 10 million hits from 278,000 users (NCEC, 2015, p. 5).

Religious Literacy Assessment. External standardised assessment is well established in three states. It provides snapshots of learner performance. Among other things, it can be utilised for evaluation and improvement of programs. Sydney introduced a religious education Test for Year 6 in 1998. Over time it has been used in several other NSW dioceses and been extended to Year 8 and now Year 10. Nine NSW dioceses have some form of religious literacy assessment. Parramatta (Years 4, 6, 8 and 10), South Australia (ReLAT, Year 4) and Western Australia Bishops' Religious Literacy Assessment (Years 3, 5 and 7) are undertaken online.

The early years. The interface of prior to school learning and Foundation to Year 2 learning varies across Australia. Some approaches to religious education, for example in Melbourne and Sydney, focus on early childhood pedagogy. Melbourne's 'The Good Shepherd Experience' drew on the research and work of Jerome Berryman in 'Godly Play' and the work of Sofia Cavalletti and Gianna Gobbi in 'The Catechesis of the Good Shepherd' (Archdiocese of Melbourne, 2000). While achievement standards or outcomes are specified for F-2 in these archdioceses, the teacher uses story, concrete materials and play. Brisbane provides significant resource support for the early years of religious education (http://extranetportal.bne.catholic.edu.au/re/REC/REEarlyYears/Pages/Pto2.aspx).

Matriculation and other credentials. Religious education has had a number of pathways in the senior years for many years. Catholic school authorities and teachers were heavily involved in advocacy for and development of ATAR-related courses. These exist in every jurisdiction and Catholic school students are the majority of candidates. In most cases these courses require study of at least two religions. A distinguishing feature of the Western Australian Certificate of Education Religion and Life ATAR course is that the examination accommodates those who have studied different individual religions, enabling Catholic school candidates to answer on Christianity. Across Australia these courses have enhanced the status of and learning expectations for religious education for students, teachers and parents, not only in the senior years but across all schooling. In addition to ATAR-related courses, the states and territories register or endorse the religious education course of learners not seeking that pathway. In Queensland and the Northern territory there is the opportunity to fulfil the requirements of Certificate III in Christian Ministry and Theology.

The interface with the religious life of the school, parish and wider Church. Diocesan curriculum materials, and religious institute, public juridic person and individual school documentation consistently point to the links between religious education and activities outside the classroom. One example is the interplay between teaching about the Eucharist and its celebration in the life of the school; another is learning about the Catholic social tradition as the motivating force behind social justice activities. One very specific and growing program is the Religious Education curriculum pathway of Catholic Schools Youth Ministry Australia. Over fifty secondary schools across many dioceses are offering a four-phase model which includes the youth ministry curriculum pathway, generally in Year 9-10 which might lead on to involvement in a senior youth ministry team post-school involvement (http://www.csyma.com). The significance lies in the curriculum differentiation, the fact that the learner chooses that pathway, one that enables religious education appropriately to be a vehicle for catechesis and mission.

Impact of the Australian curriculum

The Australian Curriculum was developed progressively from 2009. Responsive to the practice of Religious Education being aligned to state and territory curriculum frameworks, the NCEC wrote to all diocesan Catholic Education Offices in 2009 to canvass issues relating to a possible national Religious Education framework. When this was met with some openness, the NCEC issued 'A Position Paper on an Australian Framework for Religious Education' (unpublished) in 2011. It identified a continuum of possible responses ranging from doing nothing to developing a prescribed national curriculum. It sought responses to its preferred middle position, 'an approved framework'. The structure and language of the framework would broadly paralleled terms employed in the wider Australian Curriculum documents so that religious education would continue to have the same systematic demands and same rigour as other learning areas. It would include content strands and achievement standards. However, content elaborations and more detailed elements of the curriculum would be developed at diocesan level. This proposal gained very strong endorsement from state and territory commissions, dioceses and the Catholic universities. The NCEC's Religious Education Committee did some significant internal work in shaping such a framework. However, this work ceased at the end of 2012 due to the review and restructure of the NCEC. All states and territories had begun to implement the Australian Curriculum by the time the NCEC's Faith Formation and Religious Education Standing Committee first met in 2015. Its work plan (NCEC, 2015) includes a strategy for a Religious Education framework. It could become a preferred national resource for local curriculum evaluation and an enabler of prospective curriculum redesign responsive to local contexts.

In the meantime, some dioceses have worked on aligning religious education with their state or territory's manner of implementation of the Australian Curriculum. Brisbane embedded its curriculum in the online ACARA format (http://www.rec.bne.catholic.edu.au/Pages/Religious-Education.aspx). Likewise Hobart's *Good News for Living* has been refreshed to align with the language and frameworks of the Australian Curriculum and published online in the ACARA template alongside the other learning area on its curriculum portal (http://curriculum.catholic.tas.edu.au/).

These online curricula show how the learning area serves the general capabilities and cross curriculum priorities of the Australian Curriculum. They are a timely reminder of how religious education contributes to the Melbourne Declaration (MCEETYA, 2008), not just in moral and spiritual development but in the goal that all young Australians become successful learners, confident and creative individuals and active and informed citizens. The learning area contributes to the mission of the Church and the formation of the young. Irrespective of the religious commitments of the learners it can be a meaning making resource agent (Hack, 2011, pp. 61-67) that aids development of their identity and sense of purpose in life (Crawford and Rossiter, 2006, pp. 401-408). It can expand their spiritual awareness and religious identity, foster their capacities and skills of discerning, interpreting, thinking critically, seeking truth and making meaning in light of the Gospel. It should challenge and inspire their service to others and participation in the Church and society. There are many indications across Australia today that show these possibilities are in the process of being realised.

CHAPTER 9

REFERENCES

Archdiocese of Melbourne (2000), *To know, worship and love teaching companions: Levels 1-2*. Melbourne, VIC: James Goold House Publications.

Brisbane Catholic Education (2008). *Religious education: Guidelines for the religious life of the school*. Brisbane: Catholic Education Archdiocese of Brisbane.

Brisbane Catholic Education (2013). Vision for Religious Education. *The shape of religious education*. Retrieved from http://www.rec.bne.catholic.edu.au/The%20 Shape%20of%20Religious%20Education/Pages/Vision-for-Religious-Education. aspx

Bishops of NSW and the ACT (2007). *Catholic schools at a crossroads: Pastoral letter of the bishops of NSW and the ACT*. Sydney: Bishops of NSW and the ACT.

Catholic Education, Melbourne (2016). *Archdiocese of Melbourne religious education curriculum framework documentation (draft as at June 2016)*. Retrieved from http://www.resourcemelb.catholic.edu.au/ckfinder/userfiles/ files/MASTER_RECurric%20document2016(4).pdf

Catholic Education Office of Western Australia (2006). *Religious education: Learning area statement and progress maps*. Leederville: Catholic Education Office of Western Australia.

Catholic Education Office, Sydney 2006. *Religious education curriculum: Primary Year 3 to 6*. Retrieved from http://www.ceosyd.catholic.edu.au/Parents/ Religion/RE/recurr/intro-curr-03-06.pdf

Catholic Education Office, Sydney (2011). *Accreditation to work, teach and lead in systemic Catholic schools*. Sydney: Catholic Education Office.

Catholic Education South Australia (2007). *Crossways - section B: The framework for the religious education learning area*. Adelaide: Catholic Education South Australia.

Congregation for Catholic Education (1998). *The religious dimension of education in a Catholic school*. Homebush, Australia: St Paul's Publications.

Congregation for Catholic Education (1997). *Catholic schools on the threshold of the third millennium*. Homebush, Australia: St Paul's Publications.

Congregation for the Clergy (1997). *General directory for catechesis*. Homebush, Australia: St Paul's Publications.

Crawford M. & Rossiter G. (2006). *Reasons for living: Education and young people's search for meaning, identity and spirituality*. Melbourne: ACER Press.

D'Orsa, J. & D'Orsa T. (2013). *Leading for mission: Integrating life, culture and faith in Catholic Education*. Mulgrave, VIC: Vaughan Publishing.

Hack J. (2011). *Meaning-making: A key pedagogical paradigm for schooling in the third millennium.* Pennant Hills NSW: Catholic Schools Office Broken Bay.

Holohan, G.J. (1999) *Australian religious education - Facing the challenges.* Canberra: National Catholic Education Commission.

McGrath J. (2012). Befriending context and tradition: Evangelisation and Catholic schools. *The Australasian Catholic Record 89* (3) 283-298.

Ministerial Council on Education, Employment, Training and Youth Affairs (MYCEETA) (2008). *Melbourne declaration on educational goals for young Australians.* Melbourne: Curriculum Corporation.

Moran, G. (1991). Understanding Religion and Being Religious, *Professional Approaches for Religious Educators, 21,* 249-252.

National Catholic Education Commission (2008). *Religious education in dialogue: curriculum around Australia.* Braddon, ACT: National Catholic Education Commission.

National Catholic Education Commission (2015). *Faith Formation and Religious Education Work Plan 2015 - 2017.* Retrieved from http://www.ncec.catholic.edu.au/resources/faith-formation-re

National Catholic Education Commission (2016). *Annual report 2015.* Sydney: National Catholic Education Commission.

Pollefeyt, D., & Bouwens, J. (2014). *Identity in Dialogue: Assessing and enhancing Catholic school identity. Research methodology and research results in Catholic schools in Victoria,* Australia. Berlin: LIT Verlag.

Pope Francis (2013). *Evangelii gaudium.* Strathfield, NSW: St Paul's Publications.

Sacred Congregation for Catholic Education (1977). *The Catholic school.* Homebush, NSW: St Paul's Publications.

Sharkey, P. (2015). *Educator's guide to Catholic identity.* Mulgrave, VIC: Vaughan Publishing.

CHAPTER 9

John McGrath is Senior Education Officer, Faith Formation and Religious Education at the National Catholic Education Commission. He is executive officer of the NCEC Faith Formation and Religious Education Standing Committee which has a work plan that includes greater national collaboration in religious education curriculum. John has extensive teaching, leadership and governance experience at school and diocesan level. Prior to his current role, he was an assistant director of the Broken Bay Catholic Schools System with responsibility for mission, staff formation and religious education. Earlier roles include leadership of secondary religious education curriculum development for the Archdiocese of Sydney, and of the NSW HSC Studies of Religion courses.

Correspondence to:
National Catholic Education Commission
PO Box R1802, ROYAL EXCHANGE, NSW 1225
Email: john.mcgrath@ncec.catholic.edu.au

Part Two: Curriculum: Overview and Focus

Chapter 10

Curriculum Overview

The RE Curriculum in a Small Rural Diocese: Focus on Teacher Capacity and Formation

Angelo Belmonte

Introduction

As 'a pastoral instrument in proclaiming the Gospel and promoting human formation' (CCS, #31), Religious Education in Catholic schools has been traditionally viewed as critical to the mission of the Church. The changing context of contemporary Australian society, influenced in particular by the growing pluralism in the Catholic Church however, has led some writers (De Souza, 2008) to suggest there is 'little agreement concerning the nature and purpose of religious education ... the most appropriate approach for religious education school programs' (p. 29). In addition, the lack of knowledge, skills and enculturation of Catholic traditions and practices of the next generation of religious educators and faith leaders (Rymarz & Belmonte, 2014; Neidhart & Lamb, 2016; Rymarz, 2016) raises concerns that future teachers and leaders may not have the capabilities to engage from a faith perspective in religious education classes or to develop the religious literacy of students.

It is from this standpoint that this chapter describes the development and implementation of the Religious Education curriculum in the small rural Diocese of Bathurst.

The Curriculum in context of a small rural diocese

The Diocese of Bathurst was created in 1865, with the first Bishop, Dr Matthew Quinn, appointed in 1866. Even prior to the establishment of the diocese, the history of Catholic education can be traced from the mid-1850s, when Bathurst was simply a church district and its Catholic schools had a roll call of 90 boys and 130 girls. Today the Diocese of Bathurst provides a diverse range of educational options with more than 9,500 students attending 33 Catholic schools.

In an area spanning 103,600 square kilometres, the smallest school in the diocese accommodates an enrolment of 23 students with the largest secondary school with over 1100 students. Almost a third of the schools are small, catering for fewer than 100 students, and are led by a teaching Principal with the dual role of Religious Education Coordinator. The majority of these schools are located in small communities, and some are located in remote and isolated environments with more than 100 kilometres distance from a significant municipality. Gradually small communities are seeing the decline of a resident priest and as a consequence a great deal of responsibility for coordinating parish pastoral activities, as well as preparation of children for the Sacraments in State schools, has become the expectation of the Principal and the staff of the school.

Typically, like many Catholic schools in Australia, diocesan schools in Bathurst are characterised by:

- Being staffed entirely by lay teachers who generally display a commitment to the teachings of the Catholic Church but may not possess the necessary background and knowledge in the area of faith (Rymarz & Belmonte, 2014; Rymarz, 2016).
- Extensively being administered by a lay Principal. One small school in the diocese is administered by a Sister of St Joseph.
- High levels of parent support and participation, but for many, have chosen a Catholic school for reasons other than religious reasons.
- Having an increasing percentage of non-Catholic, or non-practising Catholic, teachers and pupils. The attendance of a significant number of non-Catholic students may have little to do with a belief in the teachings of the

Catholic Church or, in some cases, a desire to embrace the Catholic way of life. Although academically able in terms of the formal teaching curriculum, the same students generally have little religious literacy and so bring little experience of Catholic traditions and its teaching (Engebretson, 2014).

- Becoming the major experience of Church for many students and their families; a result of the decline of participation in worshipping communities of parishes and the secularisation of Australian society (Engebretson, 2014; Rymarz, 2016).
- Increasingly seeing the evaporation of an Irish-Catholic, socio-political identity with recent large numbers of migrant families moving into rural areas.
- Being dependent on government funding to the extent that it could not exist without it (Canavan, 1999; McLaughlin, 2000), and so are required to satisfy the requirements of the Church and at the same time, conform to government accountability.

Historical development of the Religious Education curriculum

The release of the *Bathurst Diocese Religious Education Guidelines* in 1985 was significant for teachers of religious education, for not since the 'Green Catechism' and the 'Australian Catechism' of the 1960's, has material been provided centrally that set out concisely for teachers what to teach (Content) and when (Year Level). Prior to the guidelines, schools were caught up in the Kerygamatic and then the life-centred approach that seemed to have infiltrated Catholic schools in Australia during this time (Buchanan, 2006). Though both approaches were open to a variety of teaching methods and techniques, teachers become reliant on external resources and publications that were not necessarily approved by local authorities. Textbook series such as *My Way to God* and *Come to the Father*, for primary classes, and booklets like *Come Alive*, have become common place in secondary schools.

The introduction of the guidelines was provided on the presumption that teachers would develop their own school based Religious Education Curriculum; where a framework like this could be used to develop a curriculum that catered for the needs of students at their particular school (Catholic Education Office, 1985). Unlike guidelines developed by other dioceses such as Melbourne, the Bathurst guidelines provided only doctrinal statements for particular grade levels based of the hierarchy of truths developed from magisterial texts such as the catechism and other church documents. The guidelines did not employ educational language consistent with other learning areas such as objectives, learning goals, assessment or evaluation, and nor did it suggest any teaching approach or strategies that could be used in religious education teaching programs. In short, the expectations of each teacher was to cultivate a content focussed program for their class to compensate for the largely doctrinal shortcomings of the texts that were being used.

It was not until the early 1990's that it was becoming apparent to the local Bishop and among other diocesan authorities that the Bathurst Guidelines of 1985 did not provide the necessary support for teachers, who for the most part, were not trained in Catholic colleges or universities, but locally in secular institutions where specialisations in theology or religious education were not available. There was a need for supporting teachers, particularly young teachers. Rymarz (2016) even now notes, that increasingly many teachers in Catholic schools are well motivated to teach in our schools, but lack a strong sense of religious connection and less confident to the witnessing aspect of being a religious education teacher.

The Christ We Proclaim – Kindergarten to Year 12

In 1992, a working party consisting of teachers from secondary schools, and a small team from the Catholic Education Office, was established and set about to develop a scope and sequence of topics and units of work that was to be presented as a scholastic study with the same academic rigour as other key learning areas. The new curriculum was to be developed to cater more appropriately for the liturgical year, and a number of recurring themes such Lent, Easter, Advent and Mary. Most importantly and innovative at the time, *The Christ We Proclaim*, as the curriculum was to be known, was to include suggested teaching and learning strategies, as well as a bibliography of useful texts and other resources developed as background reading for teachers, and sample resource sheets for students for classroom use.

Launched in 1994, *The Christ We Proclaim* emphasised a pedagogical methodology that was influenced and adapted from Groome's Shared Christian Praxis (1991). The schema consisted of a four-step program that was identified as:

1. **Life Experience:** The teacher and students identify and examine their own life experience and related life experience of their culture. *What is my life experience?*
2. **Content (Our Faith Story):** The teacher and students recall and develop their understanding of Scripture and Tradition. *What is the Christian Story?*

3. **Internalisation:** The teacher invites students, as individuals and in a manner appropriate to their development and their stage of faith, to dwell upon their own experiences in the light of Our Faith Story. *What does Our Faith Story mean in my life?*
4. **Response:** The teachers and students respond in ways appropriate to their understanding and decisions. *What am I going to do about it?*

The Christ we Proclaim became a welcomed resource for teachers of religion in secondary schools. Teachers were introduced into an environment where the religious education curriculum was centralised and approved by the local Bishop that also reflected the standards of learning and opportunities for more creative classroom pedagogy. Teaching units were developed for each topic areas and were constructed as a ready-made teachers' register where teachers could adapt to suit their classroom needs. The syllabuses for Year 9 to 12 was also approved by the New South Wales Board of Studies as Board Endorsed courses.

In 1998, *The Christ We Proclaim* was developed for primary classes, and in similar vein to the secondary component was to be written with the least experienced teacher in mind. With a small team of religious education coordinators and one Catholic Education Office consultant, the primary program was to make improvements from lessons learnt from the secondary component. With an extensive list of teaching and learning activities that considered different teaching and learning styles; links to Scripture and Catechism of the Catholic Church; an increased emphasis on the use of music and the creative arts; a bibliography of relevant literature and the inclusion of sites on the emerging world wide web, teachers' confidence levels in teaching religious education grew exponentially. As such, a new and improved secondary program was rewritten and launched in 2000, but most importantly a basic design and philosophy for future Religious Education curricula in the diocese emerged.

Appropriating and contextualising: The Religious Education curriculum

In recent years, there has been an increasing collaboration in religious education among New South Wales dioceses. In particular, the willingness of larger metropolitan dioceses such as the Archdiocese of Sydney to make curriculum resources available, provided incentive for smaller dioceses with limited resources and personnel, to work in partnership with larger dioceses. The diocese of Armidale, Wollongong, Lismore and Sydney adopted *Religious Education K-12*, and while not associated with its original development, the syllabus and curriculum formed the basis for the current developmental framework in religious education for the Diocese of Bathurst.

The decision not to adopt the *Religious Education K-12* at that time was in essence that Bathurst had already commenced its work to respond to religious education teachers who were seeking a program that was comprehensive, well resourced, teacher friendly and so provided explicit guidance to the teaching of religious education. By 2007 however, as the Archdiocese of Sydney's curriculum was being released, it was becoming apparent, particularly through a review of the Catholic Education Office in that year, that *The Christ We Proclaim* curriculum was in need of renewal.

With the arrival of Bishop Michael McKenna in 2009 and a number of recommendations considered through various consultations and alternatives, Bishop McKenna supported and approved the recommendation that the Diocese of Bathurst would adopt *Religious Education K-12* as other rural dioceses had a few years prior, but the diocese would remain committed to contextualising the curriculum to the specific needs of Bathurst and the curriculum documentation desired by teachers. In a sense, the diocese could now avoid much of the syllabus duplication that was occurring among dioceses in New South Wales and have access to much more professional development for RE teachers, and yet maintain its own distinct way of presenting and delivering the curriculum.

The Bathurst approach to Sydney's Religious Education K-12

Sydney's *Religious Education K-12* is well known and is established in many dioceses. The curriculum documentation consists of two major components. The syllabus for each year level describes the aims, objectives and the expected outcomes. It mandates the content strands and its approach to assessment as well as key principles of teaching and learning. It provides a scope and sequence of topics and offers explanation of how teaching units should be used. As with *The Christ We Proclaim*, Sydney's curriculum employs four movements based on The Emmaus Story (Luke 24:13-35), which is the source for the experience of religious education in which students are engaged. These are:

- **Reflecting** *(making sense)* of everyday life experiences in the broader contexts of mystery, complexity, confusion and awe.
- **Catholic Story** *(gaining access)*. Understanding the Scriptures, the traditions of the Catholic community, its stories, its experiences and its teachings.

- **Responding** to the activity of God in their lives and in the whole of creation.
- **Celebrating** with others the mystery and life of the risen Christ.

The second component of the curriculum is the teaching units from which resource packages are developed from the syllabus. They contain the expected outcomes and provide scriptural and catechism references to support the teaching of the content. In addition, the units provide theological and scriptural background to support teachers' understanding of the topic. The units suggest ways pedagogy can be incorporated into the teaching of religious education in the classroom. Central to the units are clear links to the *To Know, Worship and Love* textbook. In the context of Bathurst, as in the case of Sydney, the Religious Education K-12 syllabus is core to the curriculum framework, but it is the development of the curriculum units where enhancements have taken place to better meet the needs of the teachers of Bathurst.

The Curriculum units: Building teacher capacity

The experience and learnings gained from the development of *The Christ We Proclaim* suggested that the place and respect for the work and expertise of teachers is paramount. Any curriculum change should be gauged on its potential for building teachers' knowledge and skills, as well as the sense of professionalism it could promote. The move toward a new curriculum could not only provide an opportunity for a more contemporary approach to learning, it may also cultivate an avenue of teacher formation as well as developing their own religious literacy. More so for teachers, the ready-made teacher units and program registers developed in *The Christ We Proclaim* had also created an expectation by religious education teachers that had become the benchmark of requirements for any future changes to the religious education curriculum, to point where many teachers may not cope in the religious education classroom without them.

Following a similar process to *The Christ We Proclaim,* but this time without the effort of developing a syllabus, the process of crafting detailed units commenced. Key to discussions and planning at that time was to explore ways where teachers could spend more effort on preparing and teaching effective lessons, and spend less time searching for key resources or creating documentation for supervision purposes. A vision was required as to how this opportunity to reconstruct the RE Curriculum could be best utilised to best meet not only the needs of students, but the needs of teachers as well. A focus on preparing units of work with the least confident RE teacher in mind was again at the centre of any work to be undertaken.

Preliminary work by the Catholic Education Office had to be undertaken. With fidelity to the archdiocese's syllabus paramount, and with the aim of contextualising the program to meet the needs of the Bathurst diocese, a new framework for the presentation of curriculum documents had to be established. New unit templates were personalised, not only to reflect the diocese's expectations but also reflect the curriculum designs of other key learning areas. With contextualising Sydney's curriculum at the forefront, small clusters of writing teams were established. Consisting in the main of religious co-ordinators from diocesan schools, writing teams focused on particular year levels and prepared drafts of units following templates that had been developed. Class sets of *To Know Worship* text were purchased by the diocese.

The decision to included RECs was initially made given the small number of personnel in the Catholic Education Office, but the decision was to prove invaluable with the planning and implementation process. At the planning phase, RECs were able to influence the broad direction of framing and structuring of the writing, and so foster further the needs of teachers. As integral members of writing teams, RECs were able to demonstrate greater leadership to support and guide on how to implement and use the new curriculum.

With the initial work of writing teams complete, the 88 draft units were typed and published, including the associated teacher and student resources. A small team of two from the Catholic Education Office reviewed, and in many cases, rewrote draft units. The focus for reviewers was very much on pedagogy and suggested strategies meet the needs of students, in particular in relation to the various learning styles of students. The task of reviewers was also to review and develop a large number of resources. Some of these would assist teachers with the necessary background knowledge of the topic or area being studied, while others included resources for students. A wide range of electronic and virtual resources were also included. Electronic and so editable teachers' program registers were also developed to minimise administration and supervision requirements. In all, extensive content, teaching strategies and resources were presented to allow teachers this discretion.

With the completion of the units, a local member of the clergy with doctoral qualifications in theology performed the role as imprimatur to ensure orthodoxy, where the religious education curriculum was free of doctrinal or moral error.

Godly play for young students

Based on the *Catechesis of the Good Shepherd* developed by Sofia Cavaletti (Cavaletti, Coulter, Gobbi & Montanaro, 1996), and *Godly Play* that was further refined by Berryman (2009, 2013), a key feature of the new curriculum is the introduction of this particular approach to immersing young students into biblical stories. By attempting to engage students' imaginations, its intention is to allow participants to experience faith-building stories through intentional storytelling and imaginative wondering.

Godly Play therefore is more about understanding how each story connects with the student's own experience and relationship with God than actually instructing students on what they should know. The use of visual and concrete materials, such as simple puppets, aims to assist students to depict the story as the story unfolds. For each unit in primary classes, a script is provided for the teacher to read while moving materials which take the form of the characters in the story. The teacher becomes the storyteller as the students listen to the story and watch the materials. With such a different approach to opening up the scriptures the focus for professional development of teachers and classroom support became paramount.

With the assistance from Catholic Education Sydney and members of the RE team, a number of days were organised in various regions of the diocese to introduce the Godly Play approach. With some 200 teachers attending these days, appropriate Godly Play material linked to scripts provided were modelled and the skills used were outlined and practiced. Organisation of space, suggestions for the making of concrete materials, as well as tips for storytelling became the emphasis of the professional development. Follow-up days for teachers were organised following a period of time where new learnings were shared and affirmed.

As would be expected, the introduction of Godly Play was well received by teachers and students alike. Concrete and visual materials were developed by teachers and a sense of commitment to the process was quickly established, particularly by those who had attended training days. Part of thinking strategically however, was the sustainability of inducting new teachers to the diocese who may not be familiar with the process of Godly Play. A reliance on Sydney to provide professional development on a yearly basis did not seem practical nor feasible, as was depending on existing primary teachers developing the necessary skills to new teachers. The solution was found to use cheap and easy technology that was available so that teachers could easily discover the process. The result was that 10 lessons from teachers and students were filmed specific for each grade level and followed the scripts that were provide in each unit. Once recorded, each video was edited with commentary and then placed on DVDs to be distributed to schools.

Additional support and resourcing

With the formal RE curriculum designed to provide classroom teachers with the support they need to be effective educators, additional resourcing is provided to every teacher to further enhance the teaching of religious education. One such resource is *Understanding Faith*, developed by the Catholic parish of Port Macquarie. As a comprehensive online multimedia resource, over 100 units covering themes for both primary and secondary Schools have been developed. The resource incorporates interactive activities, video extracts, radio broadcasts, music, newspaper articles, slideshows, and contemporary teaching and learning tasks for scripture study. Each unit has been meticulously linked to the Bathurst curriculum teaching program.

Two other diocesan-wide online subscriptions are also offered to all teachers; *Liturgyhelp* and *Liturgy, Ritual and Prayer*. Both resources assist teachers to prepare liturgies and prayers as well as school Masses. *Liturgy, Ritual and Prayer* in particular offers practical help in the preparation and celebration of liturgy for the whole school and for individual classrooms as well. In response to the needs of teachers, *Liturgy, Ritual and Prayer* offers a vast collection of resources for the liturgical year as well as major feasts and communal events. Teachers are able to download customable liturgies, prayer rituals and audiovisuals that not only offer practical support to teachers, but also informs and educates to promote ongoing liturgical formation.

One particular resource consistently referred to and in support of curriculum units and teacher's program registers is *Breathing Life into the RE Classroom: Creative Teaching Strategies for Religious Educators*. The text prepared in 1997 by the Bathurst Catholic Education Office, and subsequently reprinted multiple times until 2002, offers a plethora of drama, visual and discussion strategies that enhances creative and critical teaching and learning skills in an attempt to invigorate the teaching of RE, particularly in presenting and exploring the Scriptures. The text highlights the importance of the teacher's own creative engagement and shares a wealth of innovative ideas to enrich pedagogy and practice.

Challenges and the future: Religious literacy, expression of faith and engagement of youth

The challenge to the present has been to develop a curriculum that is planned, taught, assessed with the same meticulousness as other key learning areas in the school. With this in mind, with the release of *The Christ We Proclaim* the focus has also been for the religious education curriculum in the diocese to develop the capacity of RE teachers. In developing a curriculum that is well resourced, teacher friendly and provides explicit guidance to the teaching of religious education, its aim has also been to deliver the confidence for teachers to grow in their knowledge and skills to be effective teachers of religion in the classroom. In a real sense the design and implementation of the curriculum has provided a formative experience for teachers, especially for graduate teachers or other teachers who lack the background knowledge of the Catholic worldview and its teachings.

While the curriculum in recent years has developed teacher capacity in the classroom, teachers must also seek to develop their own religious literacy. It is clear that religion teachers need to understand the content in any unit of work they are developing with and for their students if they seek to increase students' religious understanding of the content, in particular with some key issues. In developing the capacity of its religious education teachers too, the diocese has invested significantly in supporting teachers obtaining formal qualifications from Catholic universities and other providers. Since 1997, the diocese has sponsored financially a large number of teachers to obtain graduate certificates and master degrees in theology and religious education, as well as degrees in Catholic school leadership. The continuance to the development of the competencies of Religious Education teachers through formal study will continue to be a high priority.

As noted earlier in this chapter, the changing background of students and their families and their participation in the life of the Church increasingly provides a challenge to parishes and school communities, and these realities appear to be escalating. Such realities will undoubtedly impact upon the religious education curriculum of the future. Questions will arise about the assumptions religious educators make about the prior knowledge and experience of their students as they attempt to provide learning opportunities that are rich and relevant. More and more they will seek benchmarks as to what can be realistically expected of religious education in Catholic schools in the future. The great challenge then will be how to engage students in making sense and meaning of this everyday life in light of the teaching of the Catholic church and the traditions of the Catholic community.

One recent development in the diocese has been the introduction of the Catholic Schools Youth Ministry Australia (CSYMA) program into secondary schools. Offered as an 'opt in', through its four-phase model, students have been introduced to teaching programs in Year 9 and Year 10 that have been merged with existing programs. The emphasis on this teaching component has been youth ministry and leadership, with its aim of finding new and creative ways to express the Catholic faith. Though in the infancy of its implementation, there have been signs of encouragement for more personal and affective responses from students, as well as providing more opportunities for students to express their faith and provide personal witness and service. There is already some evidence to suggest that CSYMA students are taking key roles in the planning of major school liturgies, taking greater involvement in social justice and service groups, as well as involvement in peer ministry such as facilitating retreats for primary and junior secondary students.

Conclusion

Catholic Schools are in privileged places where students can engage in a dialogue between faith and culture; not only through the religious education curriculum, but in all curricula and events of the day. Through the RE curriculum, however, is where students will deepen their understanding of Catholic traditions and practices, of Christian service, and of their place in a faith community of the school, parish and universal Church. More importantly, it is through their religion teachers especially that students may come to discover the signs and sacred mystery of God's presence through Word, Sacrament and Prayer and respond critically in the light of gospel values. A religion teacher well formed in the Catholic faith is best positioned for this to occur, and so it has been the motivation of this diocese in recent years, and will continue to so in the future, to build and sustain the Catholic capacity of its teachers through the development and provision of a high-quality curriculum with the added support of valuable resources and ongoing formation.

REFERENCES

Belmonte, A. & Rymarz, R. (2014). And Now I Find Myself Here: Some Life History Narratives of Religious Education Coordinators in Catholic Schools, *International Studies in Catholic Education*, 6 (2): 191-201.

Berryman, J. (2009). *Teaching Godly Play: How to Mentor the Spiritual Development of Children.* Denver: Morehouse Education Resources.

Berryman, J. (2013). *The Complete Guide to Godly Play, Volume 8.* Atlanta: Church Publishing Incorporated.

Buchanan, M. (2006). A Brief History of Approaches to Religious Education in Catholic Schools, in *Leadership in Religious Education*, Rymarz, R (Ed), St Paul Publications, Strathfield.

Canavan, K. 1999. The transformation of Catholic schools in Australia, *Journal of Religious Education*, 47 (1): 19-24.

Catholic Education Office Bathurst (1985). *Bathurst Diocese Religious Education Guidelines.* Bathurst: Catholic Education Office.

Catholic Education Office Bathurst (2002). *Breathing Life into the RE Classroom: Creative Teaching Strategies for Religious Educators.* Bathurst: Catholic Education Office.

Cavalletti, S. Coulter, P. Gobbi, G. & Montanaro, S. (1996). *The Good Shepherd and the Child: A Joyful Journey*. Chicago: Catechesis of the Good Shepherd Publications.

Congregation for Catholic Education (1988). *The Religious Dimension of Education in a Catholic School.* Homebush: St Paul Publications.

de Souza, M. (2008). Some Perspectives on the Nature and Purpose of Religious Education in Catholic Secondary Schools, in *Cornerstones of Catholic Secondary Religious Education: Principles and Practice of the New Evangelization*, Engebreston, K; de Souza M; Rymarz, R & Buchanan, M (Eds). Terrigal: David Barlow Publishing.

Engebretson, K. (2014). *Catholic Schools and the Future of the Church.* Sydney: Bloomsbury Publishing.

Groome, T. (1991). *Sharing faith. A comprehensive approach to religious education and pastoral ministry.* San Francisco: Harper.

McLaughlin, D. 2000. Quo Vadis the Catholic education? A post conciliar perspective, in *The Catholic School: Paradoxes and Challenges.* McLaughlin, D. (ed) Strathfield: St Pauls Publications, pp. 24-41.

Neidhart, H. & Lamb, J. (2016). Australian Catholic Schools Today: School Identity and Leadership Formation. *Journal of Catholic Education*, 19 (3) 49-65.

Rymarz, R. (2016). *Creating and Authentic Catholic School.* Canada: Novalis Publishing.

Dr Angelo Belmonte has been involved in Catholic education for over 30 years, during this time he has held a number of teaching and executive positions in Catholic education. During this time, amongst other roles, he las led a number of curriculum projects in religious education. At present he is Leader: Faith, Learning and Teaching for Catholic Education in the Diocese of Bathurst.

Following his initial teaching qualification, Angelo completed master degrees in Religious Education/Theology and Educational Leadership. In 2006 he completed the Doctor of Philosophy at the University of Queensland and his thesis was awarded the Bassett and Grassier Award for Academic Excellence by the University of Queensland and the Australian Council for Educational Leadership.

Correspondence to:
Catholic Education Leader: Faith Learning and Teaching
PO Box 308, Bathurst NSW 2795
Email: a.belmonte@bth.catholic.edu.au

Chapter 11

Curriculum Overview

Religious Education Curriculum in Melbourne

Rina Madden

Introduction

Religious education curriculum in the Archdiocese of Melbourne has been shaped around the mandated student texts *To Know Worship and Love*, since their publication in 2000. The secondary and primary curriculum frameworks *Coming to Know Worship and Love* were developed some time later to support teachers to implement quality religious education based on the texts. It is this framework which is currently undergoing renewal in Melbourne. This chapter describes the renewal process as a change endeavour in partnership with schools. A key learning from the process is an understanding of dialogue that characterises both the pedagogy of the renewed curriculum framework and relationships between all members of the learning community. Another key learning is the pivotal role of the leader as learner to enable the conditions for dialogue to flourish.

Enhancing Catholic identity and Religious Education

The decision to renew the RE curriculum framework offered CEM an opportunity to address key findings from the Enhancing Catholic Identity Project (ECSIP) identified in the chapter of this book written by Paul Sharkey. A draft RE curriculum framework was constructed in 2015 in consultation with 14 schools, with the intention of articulating in practical language an approach to religious education (RE) that would operationalise some of the ECSIP recommendations as identified in Pollefeyt and Bouwens (2014). In 2016 the RE team set in motion a system inquiry to identify how schools interpreted the draft curriculum and whether it was being successful in its goal of supporting schools' Catholic identity and the vision for students as articulated in the Education Framework for the Archdiocese of Melbourne, Horizons of Hope.

Specifically, this inquiry was interested to learn how best to apply the theological normative identified in the three scales of the ECSIP in our ways of working with the renewed RE curriculum framework in schools. The theological normative identifies an option which applies the insights and directions provided by the Second Vatican Council (1962-1965). It is described in the ECSI project as: "A *Dialogue School* model which *Recontextualises* the Catholic faith in a pluralising culture based on a strong *Post Critical Belief*" (Pollefeyt & Bouwens, 2014).

The first area of interest concerned a *Dialogue School* option as articulated in the Victoria Scale. As system leaders, we were interested to identify how teachers and leaders engaged students in a religious education that embraces diversity and the issues of the day in robust dialogue with Catholic faith. The second area of interest addressed *Recontextualisation* as a response to our pluralising and individualising context. We wanted to explore how best to engage teachers, leaders and students in Catholic faith in rich and personally meaningful ways. The third area concerned the *Post Critical Belief* scale. We were interested in finding what supported teachers and leaders to find a balance between confident communication of Catholic faith and humbly inviting students into a faith possibility that is open, dialogic, critical and creative. The system inquiry attended to these areas of interest in a yearlong Focus Schools Project, working in parallel to schools' own inquiries, honouring their questions and concerns about teaching and learning in RE. Dialogue emerged as a theme across the three areas and was the key driver of the process of the inquiry and a valued outcome in itself.

Empowering schools: focus schools project, 2016

The renewal process offered an opportunity to engage and empower schools in a creative process to renew their practice in RE. At the start of 2016, 10 secondary and 20 primary schools expressed interest in participating in a Focus school project. Each of these schools identified a question to inquire into their teaching practice and student learning in RE, working with the draft RE documentation to support them in renewing their practice. Focus schools were asking such questions as: 'What does inquiry learning look like in RE?' 'How can we invite student voice into the planning, learning and teaching of RE?' 'How can leadership enhance teacher confidence to open rich and challenging dialogue with students in RE?' 'What does assessment look like in RE?' 'How do we work differently to challenge values education?' 'How can we deepen effective reflective practice for all learners?' Schools' investigations were supported by the RE team through regular guided conversations with teachers and leaders which helped to move them through a cycle of self-reflection and action around their questions. In the project, schools were able to share their learning with other schools from which we gathered evidence around our areas of interest. This evidence informed the processes and content of professional learning in religious education pedagogy and faith formation offered by CEM in 2017. It also helped identify successes and challenges in ways of working with schools in religious education as we seek to bring on board more schools in an engagement model for the future.

Curriculum

Dialogue as both process and product in RE

Dialogue is the defining feature of both the way of working in the renewal process with schools and a teaching and learning approach in religious education in the renewed RE curriculum framework. Dialogue as understood here is more than conversation between teachers, leaders and students. It holds a theological dimension as expressed by Benedict XVI in Verbum Domini (2010), which uses a dialogue model of God's self-communication with humanity through the Word made flesh. Theologian Lieven Boeve (2016) encapsulates it thus: '... God is dialogue. Dialogue belongs to the essence of God.' Profound engagement in dialogue is itself a valued outcome of religious education that opens up possibilities of encounter with God and the other. To be in dialogue is to be open to the other in such a way that leads to placing oneself at the service of the other. However, the nature of dialogue is not always immediately obvious and it was important in the renewal process to create conditions and opportunities for rich experiences of dialogue with teachers and leaders. From a system perspective, the RE team was challenged to re-think leadership approaches in light of a theological understanding of dialogue. We positioned ourselves as participants in shared dialogue, modelling dispositions such as: being comfortable with sitting with silence and ambiguity; listening with respect; embracing difference and challenge; making space for all contributions and balancing divergent thinking with staying on track. Transformational learning occurred in these opportunities for dialogue.

Teachers in dialogue with their professional identity

It is well known that the quality professional skills and insights teachers use in engaging students in other learning domains are not always transferred to teaching and learning in RE, resulting in lower student engagement. Many of the Focus schools therefore had questions around ways to engage student voice in the learning about and from religion. They were asking questions around ways to use issues and big questions to invite connections between religion and student's lives. Teachers found they needed to rethink their role in the classroom and how they planned student learning experiences. They had to consider more than the religious education content areas, taking into account the school and cultural settings, the students' diverse experiences, faith traditions and current issues. Due to the multi-faith, multi-cultural context of Catholic schools in Melbourne, RE teachers needed to anticipate different outcomes for learners who are at different stages of faith, are of different faiths, or who have no religious affiliation. The General Directory for Catechesis (1998) identifies some of the outcomes possible within one group of students:

- Students become more deeply rooted in their own tradition (catechesis).
- Students discover the Christian tradition (evangelisation) or rediscover the Christian tradition (re-evangelisation).
- Students of other religions learn to become more authentically rooted in their own religion and partners in dialogue (interreligious learning).
- Students learn the Christian tradition as an important cultural and moral value in Western society (pre-evangelisation).

Teachers in the focus schools had to be aware of offering multiple entry points into conversations about God and culture in RE and to be attuned to the diverse outcomes these conversations may generate. While the curriculum content of the draft RE documentation, with its origins in the *To Know Worship and Love* student texts is consistent with the previous curriculum framework so that teachers were familiar with this content, they needed to identify the issues that mattered to students and listen to the questions students raised. They had to engage in the complex task of finding meaningful connections between the curriculum content, the theology that underpinned the content, and students' questions. For teachers it was vital to have time to develop their professional and theological content knowledge and make these connections through guided dialogue. School leaders needed to consider ways to create or enhance school structures that enabled regular collegial dialogue prior to planning. This was a challenge particularly for secondary schools needing to juggle complex timetables and accommodate teachers with responsibilities across multiple domains. However it was through their own immersion in dialogue that teachers were able to develop the skills and understanding to engage students in dialogue.

Prompted by the need to scaffold teacher dialogue, a tool was developed by the CEM team which used a range of questions to stimulate thinking and prompt ideas around the many aspects that a teacher needs to consider when they seek to engage students in RE. It finds its origins in an understanding of hermeneutics (Ricouer, 1992) and its application to teaching and learning (Pollefeyt, 2008). The tool guides teachers in opening up big questions of life, God and culture with their colleagues. It prompts teachers to identify and engage the diversity and interests of students as well as attending to the demands of the RE curriculum content. In one example of a collegial planning approach using some of the questions in the guide, year 8 teachers opened up their familiar unit on 'Martyrs' which began with the story of St. Stephen. They asked themselves: 'What's important about this? How is it relevant in our world and to our students?' Considering the current context, the teachers developed a provocation in the form of the question: 'Are all terrorists martyrs?' In this way they stimulated student interest to begin to unpack the big question: 'What do I stand for, what would I die for?' The role of the question has long been recognised as an essential element of sound pedagogy (Vygotsky, 1978; McTighe & Wiggins, 2013). Essential questions in RE have been embraced by teachers in many of the focus schools as drivers for engaging diverse perspectives and inviting student voice. In the above school example, the year 8 boys hotly debated the provocation from their various perspectives and over several weeks of learning and exploration were challenged to discern a well-articulated personal faith stance in the context of issues of the day, in dialogue with the stories of the tradition and particularly, the story of Jesus. By regularly reflecting on these classroom experiences in dialogue, teachers were able to gradually work towards building up their skills, knowledge, vocabulary and self-awareness, shifting their understanding of their role in the classroom.

The role of the teacher and leader is addressed in the RE curriculum to reflect the complex nature of being an educator in a Catholic school, identifying five key attributes. These attributes work together in all phases of the teaching and learning cycle, from planning through to assessment. Three of the attributes are drawn from a framework used in Belgium which describes the teacher as Witness, Specialist and Moderator (Pollefeyt, 2008). The final two attributes: the teacher and leader as Designer and

Co-Inquirer were developed in consultation with the CEM Learning and Teaching team. As witnesses, teachers and leaders are able to articulate their own personal faith stance in relation to the Catholic faith. As specialists, teachers and leaders are able to draw on the Catholic tradition and other sources to support learners in their ongoing exploration of their religious identity. As moderators, teachers and leaders invite all learners into dialogue, making room to consider multiple perspectives and to seek new possibilities and new understanding. As designers of student learning, teachers and leaders draw on their knowledge of learners; their interpretation of the RE curriculum and the standards; and the important issues and questions arising from students and current events to shape engaging learning. As co-inquirers, teachers and leaders model truth - seeking and lifelong learning, using powerful questions to probe meaning and deepen understanding to reach into the heart of the matter. These roles position teachers and leaders as part of a learning community responsible for providing students with opportunities to experience meaningful learning in religious education. Teachers draw on each of these roles when they plan collegially for student learning and when teachers seek to create conditions for dialogue in the classroom. They support each other to refine and extend their expertise, creating a shared understanding of what is valued learning for students in RE. One secondary school, whose focus was on planning ways to engage student voice, became critically aware of their responsibility as teachers and a new appreciation of their students' abilities. Their comments reveal insights about their role:

'Our teaching style has changed - there has been a "letting go" to move from teacher to facilitator' (co-inquirer).
'To know when is the appropriate time to explicitly teach - to be the "expert"' (specialist).

> 'We are more aware and able to honour other traditions in the classes and give these students a stronger place in the learning' (moderator).

A primary school reflected in their notes that through dialogue teachers became more confident to engage students in questions and issues that mattered to them.

> 'We feel free to respond to needs of students and their questions, really feel like we are recontextualising!'
> 'More organic approach to planning - not completing the planner prior to the term, having team dialogue around where we are headed next - what are the students asking? What are they curious about? How can we support them in this?'

Teachers in dialogue with faith

'Witnesses are open to sharing their faith position in a way that offers something of themselves to those who are encountered' (Congregation for Catholic Education, 2013). The role of witness is a critical one which addresses the central context for learning in a school - the teacher and student relationship. A pedagogy which embraces dialogue must also embrace the relationship between teacher and student as vital to the process of learning. It asks the teacher to share of themselves, even as an unfinished identity 'under construction' (Pollefeyt, 2008). Through the renewal process schools appreciated the importance of engaging teachers and leaders in dialogue with faith to come to a deeper understanding of themselves as professional educators in a Catholic school and as people of faith who are present to and care about their students' spiritual lives. The RE curriculum framework includes discussion questions throughout the text which invite professional dialogue and ongoing faith formation closely related to praxis. The content of the draft curriculum documentation is organised around five areas, consistent with the former To Know Worship and Love framework: Scripture and Jesus; Church and Community; God, Religion and Life; Prayer, Sacrament and Liturgy; Morality and Justice. Each area has a statement summarizing the theology underpinning the content with questions that act as a springboard to personal and communal faith exploration. Focus schools' stories of practice illustrate how, animated by a faith community and supported by a collegial learning environment, teachers were enabled to build their knowledge of the Catholic tradition through engagement with these questions and were encouraged by the experience to go further. Comments from one school reveal insights prompted from engagement with the Scripture and Jesus content area, facilitated by the RE Leader. They reflect learning and questions around ways their faith and engagement with scripture influences their role:

> 'Our roles as teachers are to facilitate experiences and dialogue which aid students to develop a relationship with God.'
>
> 'Will connection with other Sacred texts further enrich my understanding of my faith/spirituality?'
>
> 'Art appreciation ... a challenging/interesting way to reflect ... learn ... respond to scripture.'
>
> 'When looking at the context of the scripture, we found it gave us new understanding of how it was written and what it meant to the audience of the day.'
>
> 'This was the first time we gave ourselves permission to have a theological discussion ... to really talk about the big questions of life and God and what the Word means.'

Students in dialogue

As teachers come to a deeper understanding of dialogue a new pedagogy emerges ... pedagogy of encounter. Pedagogy of encounter stands in the Vatican II dialogical understanding of revelation articulated in Dei Verbum (1965) where God speaks to us as friends, living among us so that we might come to know and love Him. This pedagogy asks teachers to open up spaces of meaning that engage the Catholic tradition as a point of concrete reference with what matters most in the minds and hearts of the students and the big questions of life and culture (Congregation for the Clergy, 1998). It invites a humble, listening attitude that engages students' stories to allow the Catholic tradition itself to be enriched. Pedagogy of encounter is an optimistic pedagogy, one that opens up horizons of hope for the future for the individual learner, the school community and the Church. For all learners a disposition of openness to encounter is vital to engagement in religious education:

- Encounter with diverse views and cultures that shake and shift perspective.
- Encounter with creation that inspires awe and wonder,
- Encounter with the Word of God whose Spirit moves and transforms.
- Encounter with a faith community which celebrates and lives out the ongoing presence of Christ in the world.
- Encounter with the other who calls for a response of love and compassion.

To identify in practical terms what such an approach could look like in the classroom, the RE team developed over time and in consultation with schools, a learning cycle featured as a resource for teachers in the RE curriculum framework, which uses five groups of questions to invite deep encounter. The questions challenge students to be actively involved in practical theology which seeks to bring understandings of God to human experience and create new meaning as part of the ongoing dynamic of God's revelation. The learning cycle is just one way schools might approach learning in RE. Focus schools who grappled with what pedagogy of encounter might mean for their context indicated:

> 'The pedagogy of encounter has helped to make more sense of the work.'
> 'There was a merging of ideas and all questions have been addressed, and most have been answered.'
> 'Now we have clarity of vision ... we know what we want to achieve and how to go about it.'
> 'We feel like we have taken a step forward ... now ready to go from theory into practice.'

Through the learning cycle, teachers are encouraged to be questioners rather than giving answers, to be provocative rather than predictable and to practice in the classroom what they encountered in their professional dialogue - to open up talk about God with their students as discovered in the experiences of the group. In using this approach, students were able to find a voice and were listened to. Teachers began to expect students to articulate their thinking, to interpret their life through the eyes of new learning from the Tradition and to be reflective in discerning action for good. The approach demanded high order thinking and deep learning enabled by genuine encounter in the dialogue facilitated in small groups and with the teacher. Students revealed curiosity and wonder as they were positioned as active and responsible learners. One school leader noted on visiting classrooms: 'Learning is more visible in RE in classrooms - questions are visible and students are able to talk to them.'

Pedagogy of encounter has implications for how teachers assess RE. Nurturing relationship with God and noticing, naming and giving assent to encounter with Christ through relationship with others, the Word and the world are the primary concerns of religious education. However there is no form of evaluating a child's growth in faith, for this requires judgments about a person's relationship with God. In the RE curriculum, the Achievement Standards assist teachers to identify valued student learning in religious education which is observable. The Achievement Standards attend to valued student learning in RE, describing the *quality* of student demonstrations of understanding: the level of sophistication in explanation, the degree of insight and empathy in interpretation, the depth of self-knowledge in reflection and the breadth of application of new learning. The Standards describe student progress on a learning continuum from Entry Level prior to Foundation through to Post Year 12, allowing for differentiation. The Standards, like the learning content are written in terms of the three dimensions of learning in RE, reflecting a holistic approach to developing all aspects of the learner's faith identity. These three dimensions of learning in religious education find their origins in a Christian anthropology (International Theological Commission, 2004): an understanding of the human person as a seeker of truth leading to God in Knowledge and Understanding; as a maker of meaning for life in Reasoning and Responding; and as an active participant in their spiritual growth and that of the faith community in Personal and Communal Engagement. By inviting teachers to integrate all three dimensions in the learning and teaching process, both learning and assessment attends to the full flourishing of the learner.

The RE curriculum promotes formative assessment practices grounded in respectful teacher student relationships and supported by teacher strategies including conferencing, prompting self-assessment and reflection, and providing specific feedback in the context of learning. Through observation, dialogue and questioning with students, teachers gather information that reflects students' learning progress as described in the Achievement Standards. This information helps teachers make decisions that will benefit students' learning progress, providing students with descriptive feedback that guides their efforts towards improvement and advancing student learning in religious education through the continuum. One primary school illustrates how using the Achievement Standards has prompted deeper thinking around what opportunities they need to offer students to demonstrate their understanding in line with the Achievement Standards:

> 'Keeping RE explicit is really important - students need to know what they are doing'.
> 'Learning intentions and success criteria for RE can come from the content descriptors and Achievement Standards'.
> 'Assessment tasks in RE: How do they enable me to see exactly where that student is? What kind of tasks might be helpful?'.
> 'Learning and assessment are seamless'.

The Achievement Standards have required a critical shift in thinking from schools. Because the standards explicitly look at the actions of dialogue: explanation, interpretation and self-reflection, they encourage teachers to engage students in dialogue and to maintain this engagement even as they assess. One school, after doing a unit of work around liturgy, involved their year 7 students in designing their own assessment rubrics using the Achievement Standards. The teachers commented on the impact using the

Achievement Standards had on their practice:

> 'Formal assessment has changed - we are thinking about learning and understanding rather than only content'.
> 'Students are involved in designing the Rubrics.'
> 'We establish prior knowledge, check in with what they know and what they are asking.'
> 'Students now have clarity about expected standards within the learning.'
> 'Priority on checking for consistency of learning across classes.'
> 'Student feedback to date: strong indications of a change in the level of student engagement.'

Highlights

Leaders as learners: Creating conditions for dialogue

The Focus school project gave schools the opportunity to make learning through dialogue a priority. Leaders of these focus schools made time and funds available to enable dialogue to happen. Without the structures of meeting times that honoured teacher dialogue with adequate and regular time, the opportunities for change would have been limited. While not finding it easy, the schools who made the commitment found it was a worthwhile investment in terms of both teacher and student learning. The RE curriculum framework acknowledges the powerful role leaders have in creating the conditions for dialogic learning for staff as well as students. These conditions are most effective when the principal takes part in the learning with teachers, as revealed in one primary school's comments: 'Having G ... (Principal) at meetings to share understanding, has deepened his understanding of RE in learning and teaching. This process (the RE focus school inquiry) has given the principal licence to inquire with the RE Leaders. It has opened discussion with the whole school community.' Another school noted that now, 'Leaders are working with teachers in planning but also in classrooms, coaching, mentoring.' The leader as an integral part of the professional dialogue sends a clear message that learning in RE extends to the whole of the school community and that religious education is a valued learning domain. The leader as learner builds relationships through dialogue and in so doing promotes relational and dialogical learning that is at the heart of a robust Catholic identity.

Future directions

The 2016 focus school project has provided the RE team with evidence and insights to inform processes and content of professional learning in religious education pedagogy and faith formation in 2017, resulting in a suite of professional learning shaped by these findings. The project has also helped identify engagement models as we invite more schools to enter the space of renewal in 2017 and ongoing. Schools have been able to develop stories of practice which help illuminate some of their findings using the renewed RE curriculum documentation and these will find a place online to share their learning. True to the nature of a creative change process, the renewal has raised further questions for us which will form future system inquiries and forge new partnerships with schools. We have questions around the quality and kinds of resources for teachers of religious education which could be accessed. There is still much work to be done to flesh out the RE curriculum framework offerings in response to ongoing feedback.

As we prepare the renewed RE curriculum framework for an online presence, we are asking how best to partner with To Know Worship and Love student online resources being produced by James Gould House Publishing. Further questions are raised about effective ways to support school leaders in regards to ongoing capacity building in RE; employment and induction processes; and profiling of religious education in the school context. Forging deeper connections with both postgraduate and pre-service teacher education providers in the Melbourne context is also an important next phase. We look forward to schools accepting the invitation to explore the renewed RE curriculum framework and particularly pedagogy of encounter in 2017 as core to enhancing their school's Catholic identity.

Conclusion

The process of renewal has been a creative response to the needs and questions identified by CEM and schools around the goal of supporting the full flourishing of students through religious education. It was an exercise in exploration and shared learning between schools and from schools that led to building leadership capacity in leading learning in RE across the sector. Most importantly it offered an opportunity for encounter through dialogue, leading to deeper self-understanding of teachers and leaders in the mission of Catholic education.

The renewed RE curriculum framework seeks to describe learning in religious education as encounter characterised by dialogue. But the curriculum framework can only be brought to life in the work of schools who courageously undertake to engage their community in a dialogue that is the essence of God. They are the ones who can invite students into a religious education that is spiritually rewarding, challenging, rich and relevant. The process of renewal remains ongoing - cumulatively gathering insights along the way that contribute to an overall strategic approach. At CEM, we have identified the need to be vigilant in allowing insights to challenge and correct each other and to ensure that we continue to ask system questions that will push further exploration leading to deeper insights. The process of renewing religious education in the Archdiocese of Melbourne will therefore be an ongoing work; one that will continue to engage schools in sharing their learning and expertise and one that remains focused on empowering teachers and leaders to interpret the renewed RE curriculum framework for their context and students.

REFERENCES

Boeve, L. (2016). *Theology at the crossroads of university, Church and society: dialogue, difference and Catholic identity.* London: Bloomsbury.

McTighe, J. & Wiggins, G. (2013). *Essential Questions: opening doors to student understanding.* Virginia: ASCD.

Pollefeyt, D. (2008). The difference of alterity: A religious pedagogy for an interreligious and interideological world. In L. De Tavernier, et al. (Eds.), *Responsibility, God and society: festschrift Roger Burggraeve* (pp. 305-330). Leuven: Peeters.

Pollefeyt, D. & Bouwens, J. (2014). *Identity in dialogue: assessing and enhancing Catholic school identity.* Berlin: Lit Verlag.

Ricouer, P. (1992). *Oneself as another.* Chicago: University of Chicago Press.

Vygotsky, L.S. (1978). *Mind in society.* Cambridge: Harvard University Press.

Benedict XVI. (2010). Post synodal apostolic exhortation: Verbum Domini. Vatican website, accessed November 4, 2016. http://w2.vatican.va/content/benedict-xvi/en/apost_exhortations/documents/hf_ben-xvi_exh_20100930_verbum-domini.html

Congregation for the Clergy (1998) *General directory for catechesis. retrived from: http://www.vatican.va/roman_curia/congregations/cclergy/documents/rc_con_ccatheduc_doc_17041998_directory-for-catechesis_en.html*

Congregation for Catholic Education (2013). *Educating to intercultural dialogue in Catholic schools.* Retrieved from http://www.vatican.va/roman_curia/congregations/ccatheduc/documents/rc_con_ccatheduc_doc_20131028_dialogo-interculturale_en.html

Paul VI. (1965). *dogmatic constitution on divine revelation: dei verbum.* Vatican Website, accessed retrived from http://www.vatican.va/archive/hist_councils/ii_vatican_council/documents/vat-ii_const_19651118_dei-verbum_en.html

International Theological Commission (2004). *communion and stewardship: human persons created in the image of God.* Retrieved from http://www.vatican.va/roman_curia/congregations/cfaith/cti_documents/rc_con_cfaith_doc_20040723_communion-stewardship_en.html

Rina Madden works as an education officer in religious education with Catholic Education Melbourne. Her role includes: project work renewing the Religious Education Curriculum Framework for primary and secondary schools in the Archdiocese of Melbourne; contributing to key strategic documentation for CEM; and school based consultancy with a focus on professional dialogue around religious education. Rina is currently undertaking a PhD in theology at Catholic Theological College (University of Divinity, Melbourne) exploring teacher beliefs about student spirituality and its impact on teacher pedagogy. She is an experienced primary teacher and adult educator with research interests in children's spirituality, Catholic identity and pedagogy.

Correspondence to:
Email: rmadden@cem.edu.au

Chapter 12

Curriculum Overview

Religious Education in the Diocese of Rockhampton

Di-Anne Rowan and Gail Davis

CHAPTER 12

Our local context

In 1881 the Diocese of Brisbane was divided into two and the new Diocese of Rockhampton came into being. There are now five Catholic dioceses in Queensland: Brisbane, Toowoomba, Rockhampton, Townsville and Cairns. The Diocese of Rockhampton extends from Mackay in the north to Bundaberg in the south and west to the Northern Territory border. It covers some 414,385 square kilometres and has a total population of nearly 400,000 people with about a quarter of the population Catholic. This vast and beautiful area includes outback regions that can suffer from isolation, long-term drought and flash flooding; central highland regions where their prosperity is at the mercy of the weather and the fluctuating fortunes of the mining industry; and coastal regions where the population is at its most dense.

It was the vision of pioneering priests such as Father Charles Murlay and Father Pierre Marie Bucas, as well as the generosity and hard work of lay men and women and of members of religious orders such as the Sisters of St Joseph, the Sisters of Mercy and the Presentation Sisters, that the foundations of Catholic Education were laid in the Diocese. The stories of how they battled sectarianism and poverty, as well as the challenges of a hot and humid climate to provide education for children are remembered and retold in the forty-one schools and colleges in the diocese today.

The diocese has been a pioneer in many developments – the first Catholic Education Office in Queensland was opened in Rockhampton in 1966. A much more thorough history of Catholic education and its development in Central Queensland from 1863-1990 can be found in the book, *Always Mindful* by John Browning (2005). In a fitting tribute he wrote:

Throughout the process of change, Catholic schools have continued to strive to interpret and live out the Gospel values in the context of the present age. Looking back, we can see many ways in which they have been true to this call and have brought about great good to individuals, families, the Church and society at large (2005, p. 187).

Overview of the religion curriculum

By 1976, most schools and colleges in the diocese were using *Religious Education Guidelines* from the Archdiocese of Brisbane. The diocese later developed and wrote *Religious Education Guidelines* and then *Religious Education Syllabus*. When a decision was made to replace outcomes-based education with an Australian Curriculum that had a new vision and format, this posed a challenge for the format and content of the religion curriculum. In response, the Diocese of Rockhampton could have adopted the religion curriculum from another diocese.

After considerable research and thorough consultation, it was decided to write a religion curriculum that reflected the vision and format of the Australian Curriculum but more importantly one that would reflect the unique nature of the Rockhampton Diocese and its vision for teaching and learning in Catholic schools. This vision is enunciated in various diocesan documents and policies such as its *Learning Framework* and policy on *Teaching and Learning Religion in Schools and Colleges* which states that 'Religion is a specific Learning Area' and then continues:

> In the Religion curriculum, the emphasis is on knowledge of Jesus Christ and understanding his message as expressed in the Bible and through the beliefs, teachings, values and practices of the Catholic Church (2015).

This emphasis on Jesus Christ is based on many Church documents such as *Educating Today and Tomorrow: A Renewing Passion* (2014) which highlighted in Section III: Current and future educational challenges:

> At the heart of Catholic education there is always Jesus Christ: everything that happens in Catholic schools and universities should lead to an encounter with the living Christ.

It is a fact that many of the families who have enrolled their children in Catholic Schools describe themselves as Christian even though they do not participate in a parish or other faith community. This is also true of staff members. In writing a religion curriculum it was hoped that students, by the time they left our schools, would have encountered the living Christ – the mystery of the Divine in the midst of their daily life experiences.

The Rationale of the religion curriculum articulates its purpose:

> Religions attempt to answer questions about life – its meaning and purpose. Christianity claims that the answers are to be found in the person and teachings of Jesus Christ.

The Rationale then highlights the specifically Catholic expression of Christianity: 'Catholicism offers a unique approach to the development of a relationship with Jesus Christ through its rich heritage of theology, sacramentality, spirituality and morality.'

The Rationale also emphasises the benefits of teaching religion:

> Learning about religion promotes the holistic development of the students with an emphasis on the spiritual, moral, intellectual, social, emotional and aesthetic dimensions of life. It can help students, whatever their individual religious beliefs and backgrounds, to develop their knowledge,

understanding, values and skills thereby assisting them to participate effectively in Australian society.

As well as the Rationale, the Aims of the Religion Curriculum highlight that a relationship with Jesus Christ was central in this curriculum:

This curriculum is designed so that students have opportunities to develop:

- A personal relationship with Jesus Christ.
- Understanding and appreciation of the religious beliefs, values.
- Practices of Christianity and the ways that Catholics live these out.
- Respect and appreciation for the religious beliefs, attitudes and values of others.
- Age-appropriate skills to research, discuss, reflect on and critique.
- Religion in an informed, intelligent and sensitive manner.

The use of the title *Religion Curriculum* was deliberate as it was intended to complement the format of the Australian Curriculum and its learning areas. The curriculum was to be treated with the academic respect it deserved as an important and mandatory aspect of the teaching and learning that occurs in Catholic schools. Therefore, the classroom learning and teaching of religion reflects the philosophy, content, structure, academic rigour and assessment and reporting modes used in other learning areas.

Like most dioceses in Australia, the Diocese of Rockhampton identified *The Catechism of the Catholic Church* (1994) as the authoritative resource and supportive framework on which to build the Religion Curriculum. It is based on the four dimensions of Christian life as outlined in the *Catechism:*

Part one: The profession of faith
Part two: The celebration of the Christian mystery
Part three: Life in Christ
Part four: Christian prayer

The organising strands for the content of the religion curriculum were named:

Beliefs   - **Faith Professed**
Sacraments - **Faith Celebrated**
Morality   - **Faith Lived**
Prayer   - **Faith Prayed**

One of the early decisions made in writing the religion curriculum was that there would not be a separate strand devoted to Scripture. Instead, Scripture was to be incorporated into the content of all four strands. Effective teaching of religion in the classroom connects sacred texts to all aspects of the religion curriculum: beliefs about God, Jesus and the Holy Spirit; understanding sacramentality and sacraments; ethical choices and prayer. The teaching of Scripture in isolation does little to encourage a love of the Gospels and an experience of a living God if it does not connect to learners in a real-world context. Encouraging students to reflect upon and wonder about the life and times of Jesus, the mystery of the Incarnation, and the revelation of God across the centuries requires a range of learning experiences across all four content organisers of the religion curriculum. It is enriched through a variety of experiences in a Catholic school such as prayer and liturgical celebrations, pastoral care, outreach to others and care for creation. The study of Scripture is something that needs ongoing dialogue with and openness to the Spirit of God. It is a very important focus for teacher formation. The consultative process with teachers of all year levels and from all schools in the diocese was invaluable as teachers' input enabled the writers to ascertain the strengths and the concerns of teachers. As well, teachers were able to share their knowledge of how children learn. The wisdom of the teachers was distilled and added to the religion curriculum allowing them to take ownership of the document and also giving the Catholic Education Office guidance as to the professional development that teachers needed to develop their skills as religious educators in diocesan Catholic schools. The use of teleconferences, school visits and an open-door philosophy for any questions and comments highlighted their need for a religion curriculum that was able to be accessed electronically via computer, tablet and smartphone and able to be navigated easily. It needed to have everything a religious educator wanted in one place and be aesthetically pleasing. As an online document, it was easier to edit the content and add new resources. Religion curriculum is the main component of the religious education website (http://rokreligiouseducation.com) developed by the Melbourne Company *Fraynework Multimedia*. The diocese is very grateful to Rev Fr David Pascoe who reviewed the content of the curriculum to ensure it was theologically correct.

Key features

In writing this religion curriculum, it was important to mirror the organisational aspects of the Australian Curriculum to allow ease of transition from the other learning areas to the learning area of religion. For ease of use, the religion curriculum is organised in year levels from kindergarten to Year 10. This enables a teacher to locate the achievement standards, knowledge, understandings and skills which will inform their teaching and planning for students at any year level. Guided by the religion curriculum, teachers are aware of what students are to accomplish. They use the curriculum to inform their instructional decision making and plan from the curriculum by building on students' prior learning, providing opportunities for students to develop age-appropriate skills to research, discuss, reflect on and critique religion in an informed, intelligent and sensitive manner as stated previously in its aims.

In the context of learning and learners today, it was important to consider how to develop the skills and knowledge for students to successfully contribute to and participate in the global domain of their world today and in the future. Pondering on how to be able to offer experiences of success and opportunities for students to become confident, respectful, innovative, motivated, collaborative, optimistic, empathetic and enterprising was a challenge. These are the important qualifiers identified in the Diocesan Learning Framework to reflect the capabilities to develop in all learners. By looking at the variety of pedagogical practices that are transformational, it was decided that the inquiry based approach provided a scaffold that supported and engaged learners in their own enquiries and to thrive in their ever - changing world. Use of an inquiry approach aligns with the overall hopes for students when they complete their years of schooling and continue their life education.

So, an inquiry approach to teaching has been the principal pedagogy that informs the planning, teaching, assessing and evaluating of the religion curriculum.

There is a great deal of information written and published about Inquiry Learning. Kath Murdoch is one teacher who has been a significant influence in the diocese because of her writings and seminars. On her website http://www.kathmurdoch.com.au/ she has identified several phases in student learning but it must be noted they do not necessarily occur in the following sequence:

- **Tuning in to students' thinking**
  Establishing the 'known', connecting to students' lives, sense of purpose for inquiry, first thinking, first invitation for questions.
- **Finding out**
  Gathering information from a range of sources - working as researchers - continuing to raise questions, learning skills of investigation.
- **Sorting out**
  Analysing information, looking for patterns, reviewing thinking, making meaning, expressing new understandings.
- **Going further**
  Personal and small group pathways of investigation, taking learning further, personalising.
- **Synthesising and reflecting**
  Reviewing earlier thinking, identifying changes in understanding, making connections between ideas, identifying what has been learned.
- **Acting and applying**
  Sharing new learning with others, making a difference with my learning applying to new contexts, creating/constructing/doing.

Teachers guide inquiry learning to various degrees and set parameters for a classroom inquiry. However, it must be acknowledged that true inquiry is internally motivated. To implement the *Diocesan Learning Framework*, teachers are encouraged to incorporate many learning strategies in an inquiry approach that invites and challenges learners of all ages *to be and become reflective and self-directed as we journey together with Christ in our ever-changing world.*

Suggested inquiry questions and wondering questions were added to each year level of the religion curriculum to prompt teachers in the way of an inquiry learning approach to teaching and learning. Sample units, written using this approach, were also included on the religious education website as a resource for teachers to access. However, it is also worth noting here that teaching and learning are not only about the content to be taught and efficiency of the teacher's methods. Teachers' personal ideas about teaching and learning affect how they teach and with the diverse ranges in age, gender, culture, faith formation and skills of the teachers in diocesan schools, the religion curriculum has a responsibility to assist teachers using the best possible strategies that do more than transmit knowledge but also give students the opportunity to reflect upon and experience learning in the context of a Catholic school.

As well as offering a pedagogy that encourages students to become enquiring and successful learners, it is also important to remember that the role of the Catholic school is also to offer a holistic formation that opens students' hearts and minds to the mystery and wonder of the world and all of creation. Offering a holistic education, as articulated in the *Rationale* for the religion curriculum, constantly invites teachers to reflect on how to promote more than the academic achievements of students. Catholic education embraces the challenges posed by a post-modern, pluralistic society where teachers, students and their families are recognised as being part of a community of learners. Priority is given to a creative, stimulating and age-appropriate curriculum that teachers can use to guide their instructional choices.

Scripture

As mentioned earlier, the religion curriculum in the diocese emphasises that Scripture should not be studied in isolation. It is an integral part of all the strands and is also recognised and experienced in the wider context of the school community. When developing the religion curriculum, there was an opportunity to reflect on the various passages from Scripture that had been previously taught in particular year levels. In student survey responses, it seemed that by the time students had completed their years in a Catholic school, their interest in Scripture had waned considerably or, in some instances, disappeared altogether. In many cases, their knowledge was scanty. There are many possible reasons for this: perhaps their teachers lacked confidence and expertise in the teaching of Scripture. Many teachers simply did not know how to teach about Scripture. They rarely engaged with Scripture and lacked a credible pedagogy to assist them in sharing authentic interpretations and gaining some meaning from the texts.

A new approach was required. It seemed important to identify Scripture passages that were appropriate for the different ages of the children. Learners in the early years of schooling are literal believers and as Robert Keeley (2010) wrote: 'Children of this age are generally not able to think abstractly, to take someone else's perspective on things or to think through complex ideas.' (p. 22). The story of creation in the first chapter of the book of Genesis is very beautiful and poetic but young children tend to interpret it very literally and ask: How did God create the world in six days?

CHAPTER 12

The story of Noah's ark might seem a charming tale about a floating zoo to use with young children but that was not the original intention of the writers. It raises many questions: Why share religious myths with young children who tend to understand them literally and may be given an impression of God that is contrary to what the Church teaches? God is not a vengeful person who sends floods to destroy all the bad people in the world.

When sharing biblical stories, it is vital that teachers employ a pedagogy that does not focus only on the literal meaning but also allowed learners to appreciate the theology that underpins such a story.

Importantly, when teachers are introducing a passage of Scripture it is crucial that the students are not taught something that has to be untaught later. It is imperative that the teachers do not foster interpretations that make it difficult for the children to move towards a more challenging interpretation later. Marcus Borg (2002, p. 51) maintained that:

> Contemporary readers of the Bible have a serious need to move from precritical naiveté (we simply hear the Bible's stories as true stories) through critical thinking (concerned with factuality) to postcritical naiveté (the ability to once again hear the biblical stories as true stories, even knowing that they may not be factually true and that their truth does not depend on their factuality).

Postcritical naiveté is not a return to precritical naiveté. It includes critical thinking with it. It does not reject the insights of historical criticism but integrates them into a larger whole. One realises that the truth of the story lies in its metaphorical meaning. Many of the Biblical genres traditionally taught in the early years of school and the relevance for these children was questioned, including:

- When introducing the miracles of Jesus to young children is there a risk of them believing Jesus was a magician or some sort of supernatural being as depicted in the many superhero movies of which they are familiar?
- Is it possible for students in the early years to understand the genre of parables and appreciate how these stories challenged the listeners in the first century?
- How are these parables relevant to the children and their lives today?

The historical reality of God's revelation also imposes many challenges for young students and their teachers, such as:

- How do we introduce young children to the world of the Old Testament with murder, adultery, slavery, idols, sacrifices, genocide, kings, prophets and exile?
- What is gained (or lost) by introducing students in the early and middle primary school years to the idea of 'covenant' theology?

In addition, it was vital that a variety of Scripture passages were included so that students were not revisiting the same Scriptures throughout their schooling years, e.g. the story of the Prodigal Son and the Parable of the Good Samaritan. So it was decided to select Scripture for each year level that is age-appropriate and within the realms of their understanding especially in regards to the variety of literary genres found in the Bible. In the early years, the focus is on having learners meet and experience Jesus the person and listen to the narratives told about him that are found in the Gospels. They also experience God, the

Creator, through the wonder and awe of life experiences and relationships.

In the middle years of primary school, the students learn more about Jesus and the cultural, social and historical aspects of his life as a Jewish person and discern how his words and actions show us the love of God. They investigate the parables and miracles of the Gospels to ascertain the metaphorical and symbolic meaning within the texts to develop an understanding of the theological aspects of Scripture and the different images of Jesus as delivered by the Gospel authors to their communities.

In lower secondary the students learn more of the divinity of Jesus and the implications of God's story on the development of the Church today and on members of the Church. They investigate images of a Trinitarian God in the many genres of the Bible. They identify the presence of the Holy Spirit in all of creation and the people who continue to keep the story alive in the world today.

To assist teachers in the interpretation of the various relevant Scriptural texts with their students, the religious education website has utilised 'The Three Worlds of the Text' first proposed by Sr Sandra Schneiders IHM in her book *The Revelatory Text: Interpreting the New Testament as Sacred Scripture*. This framework is an invaluable tool that teachers are encouraged to use to understand the context of a text, the actual words of the text and its impact on various audiences who read or hear the text.

Godly play

Another valuable pedagogy that is included and encouraged in the religion curriculum is the use of Godly Play as a way of opening Scripture for all to interpret in their own context and to identify their experience of God. Godly Play has been received by most primary school teachers in the diocese as a surprisingly refreshing and easy way to have the students and themselves experience the mystery of God and to release them from the mistaken idea that they need to know the one true message of the Scripture to teach to students. Godly play nurtures the natural capacity that learners have to wonder, to imagine, to become curious, to investigate, to apply to their life experiences and to reflect.

Godly Play is a tool that opens the door for the students to wonder about: the story, who is in the story, when did it occur, where did it occur, and what does this mean for me? Following these wondering questions, teachers are encouraged to work with the story by reading the text in an actual children's Bible, investigating aspects of wonder that were identified, using ICTs to respond to the text and to discern the theological message of the story for them and for the community. The suggested Scripture scope and sequence that has been added to the elaborations of the curriculum includes links to Godly Play scripts for the corresponding passages and to useful background knowledge for teachers.

Sacraments

Another key feature of the religion curriculum is a stand-alone strand of sacraments. From past observations of the teaching of Sacraments the writers reflected on how well this important aspect of the Catholic faith was taught and experienced by the learners. Once again, which aspects of sacramental theology were to be taught in each year and how these aspects were to be taught needed to be considered. As Grajczonek (2007) points out:

> As student populations in Catholic schools continue to become more diverse and pluralistic, and the numbers of

Catholic children belonging to faith communities decrease, the need to find real and relevant opportunities to teach religion becomes more urgent and necessary (p. 126).

The aspects of sacramental theology that were deemed important such as sacramentality, ritual, symbols, prayer and liturgy were enhanced by the decision to allow more time on each of the sacraments over the eleven years of schooling. The notion of sacrament is central to any understanding of the Christian faith. Teachers have the opportunity to discover a wider sacramental vision that gives the seven sacraments their true meaning by teaching more than just the ritual and symbols. The sacraments of Initiation and Reconciliation are introduced in the primary years and again at the beginning of the secondary religion curriculum. The other sacraments, Marriage, Holy Orders and Anointing of the Sick, are investigated by the older students where a more relevant understanding of their lived experience can be identified and where, through this awareness of life and its complexities, they can find the grace of God.

Future directions

All the systemic schools and colleges in the Rockhampton Diocese are participating in a project known as *Enhancing Catholic Schools Identity* (http://www.schoolidentity.net/introduction/). This project began in Victoria with the Catholic Schools Commission contracting the Catholic University of Leuven to undertake research. The project has provided key insights into the faith development of students, staff and parents. It has challenged schools to consider what type of Catholic schools is most appropriate today in a secularised environment. It has highlighted the importance of understanding hermeneutics and the perils of emphasising just Christian values.

There is much to learn about the theology and the pedagogy that underpins this project. For nearly twenty years, an educational approach to teaching religion has been promoted as it allowed everyone to learn about the Christian religion. It was hoped this method would include all learners no matter their faith experience, culture, prior life experiences, and knowledge of the beliefs and traditions of the Church or lack of knowledge.

Without doubt religion needed to be planned, taught, assessed and evaluated with the same depth and rigour as other learning areas in the school's curriculum. This is evident in the description of what is taught and how it should be taught and assessed in the subject area of religion. Teachers have come to appreciate the need to have a clear and current understanding of the content contained within the religion curriculum. A solid understanding of background knowledge for teachers is not just important, it is essential for effective student learning in religion. The development of the diocese's religious education website allowed for teacher background knowledge to be available to all. This also assisted graduate teachers and teachers who do not have a great deal of practical knowledge about the Catholic Church. Formal courses of study have been an essential part in assisting teachers who did not have any formal religious education training or qualifications. This will continue to be a high priority into the future.

In seeking to increase students' religious understanding of the content, teachers must also seek to develop their own religious literacy. Whilst the contemporary, changing religious landscape makes it increasingly difficult to presume any degree of knowledge, experience and participation in the Catholic faith of those who facilitate the teaching of Religion, it is clear that religion teachers need to understand the content in any unit of work they are developing with and for their students.

This educational approach has assisted students and teachers to learn a great deal about religion. Thomas Groome (2011) in his book, *Will there be Faith? A new Vision for educating and growing disciples,* challenges teachers to consider how they and their students can learn from religion too. He maintains that such an approach highlights the contribution that religion can make to their lives.

The emphasis on religious knowledge can at times exclude any sense or experience of God. Catechesis is considered suspect in many Catholic schools. It is a concern that focussing solely on the doctrinally explicit creed of beliefs misses the reality of the Incarnation and its implications for humanity. Daniel O'Leary (2008) challenges a limited vision of religious knowledge:

'Surely [religious knowledge] can be no other than living and believing the sacramental vision of our transformed humanity in Christ, and consequently, our new empowerment to change the world so beloved of [God]' (p. 160).

So, in the future, there needs to be more conversations to evaluate the way that religion is taught in our Catholic schools. There is no doubt that the knowledge component of the religion curriculum is essential. However, there is also a challenge to move one step further 'to connect life to faith' and 'faith to life' as Groome (2011) wrote. Can we re-connect our knowledge about Christianity to a religion curriculum that poses big questions and encourages change to occur from what has been learned? Another direction for future development involves going beyond the religion curriculum and considering a Catholic perspective in other areas of the curriculum in a Catholic school. This truly takes faith beyond the religion classroom to the real world and everyday issues and would seem to be very worthwhile.

The document *Educating Today and Tomorrow: A Renewing Passion* (2014) expresses this in the following words:

> In particular, schools would not be a complete learning environment if ... what pupils learnt ... did not also become an occasion to serve the local community. Today, many students still consider learning as an obligation or an imposition: probably this depends upon schools' inability to pass on to students the passion that is absolutely required for research, in addition to knowledge. Instead, when students have the opportunity to experience how important what they learn is for their lives and their communities, their motivation does change. It would be advisable for teachers to provide their students with opportunities to realise the social impact of what they are studying, thus favouring the discovery of the link between school and life, as well as the development of a sense of responsibility and active citizenship (Congregation for Catholic Education, 2014, II: What Kind of Catholic Schools and Universities, 4, par 2).

The biggest challenge for our schools in the future was documented in the aims of the religion curriculum in our diocese - that students leave our schools with a personal relationship with Jesus. We need to look again not just at *what* we are teaching in religion and *how* we are teaching but more importantly at *who* we are teaching: building a dialogue of faith between learners.

CHAPTER 12

REFERENCES

Borg, M. J. (2002). *Reading the Bible Again For the First Time: Taking the Bible Seriously But Not Literally.* San Francisco, CA: HarperSan Francisco.

Browning, J. (2005). *Always mindful: a history of Catholic education in Central Queensland 1863-1900.* Rockhampton: Diocesan Catholic Education Office.

Catholic Education Diocese of Rockhampton. *Learning Framework.* Retrieved from http://www.rok.catholic.edu.au/wp-content/uploads/Learning-Framework.pdf

Catholic Education Diocese of Rockhampton. *Rationale.* Retrieved from http://rokreligiouseducation.com/about/rationale/

Congregation for Catholic Education. (2014). *Educating Today and Tomorrow: a Renewing Passion.* Retrieved from http://www.vatican.va/roman_curia/congregations/ccatheduc/documents/rc_con_ccatheduc_doc_20140407_educare-oggi-e-domani_en.html

Grajczonek, J. (2007). Developing Sacramental Education Using Children's Literature. In J. Grajczonek & M. Ryan (Eds.), *Religious education in early childhood* (pp. 126-135). Hamilton, QLD: Lumino Press.

Keely, R. (2010). Faith Development and Faith Formation: More Than Just Ages and Stages. *Lifelong Faith, fall 2010,* 20-27.

O'Leary, D. (2008). *Begin with the Heart: Recovering a Sacramental Vision.* Blackrock, Dublin: The Columba Press.

Schneiders, S. (1999). *The Revelatory Text: Interpreting the New Testament as Sacred Scripture.* A Michael Glazier Book: Liturgical Press.

Di-Anne Rowan has been a member of the Catholic Education Leadership Team in the Diocese of Rockhampton since 2002. Her role is described as Assistant Director: Mission. She holds a Master's degree in Religious Education from ACU as well as a BA and Dip Teaching (Primary) from CQU. She has really enjoyed working with teachers and the Faith Education Team to develop a religion curriculum that is relevant and engaging. Many valuable insights and challenges have been identified through participation in the 'Enhancing Catholic School Identity Project' with the Catholic University in Leuven.

Gail Davis is Teaching and Learning Religion Consultant for Catholic Education in the Diocese of Rockhampton, where her role includes supporting teachers in the delivery of the Diocesan Religion Curriculum P-10, as well as working with CQ University in the provision of undergraduate and postgraduate courses in religious education. Previously, Gail worked as teacher and APRE in Catholic schools in the Rockhampton Diocese. Gail finds working with the early years' teachers and students a delightful challenge.

Chapter: 13

Curriculum Overview

'The Truth will set you free': Religious Education in Western Australia

Chris Hackett, Debra Sayce and Diana Alteri

Introduction

The delivery of religious education in Western Australia is unique. There is one common curriculum that is taught throughout Catholic schools in Western Australia. The development of the curriculum has been in response to many challenges because of the state's size and the needs of students and teachers. The curriculum has a priority of place in the Catholic school curriculum and plays an integral role the evangelisation plans of schools. The formal aspects of the RE curriculum are well-resourced, the evaluation of the curriculum's literacy effectiveness is promoted and the training of qualified teachers is well supported. Into the future, the RE curriculum will incorporate the use of digital technologies and teachers will require sustained faith formation to be able to witness to the curriculum appropriately.

This chapter sets out the structural features of the religious education (RE) curriculum in Western Australia and responses to challenges confronted by the curriculum today. Firstly, the chapter outlines the local context of the teaching of RE in Western Australia. Unlike other jurisdictions, there is one common RE curriculum for all Catholic schools in WA. Secondly, the nature and philosophy of RE is described within the context of the school's Evangelisation Plan and, specifically the educational approach incorporating New Evangelisation. Thirdly, the approach to teaching and assessment in RE is described for the key years of schooling taking the starting point from the students and their needs and human heart questions. Lastly, the chapter outlines the future directions of the RE curriculum in adopting digital technologies and enhancing the professional quality and faith formation of teachers and future leaders.

Local context

For Catholic schools in Western Australia, the term 'RE' is reserved for the time set aside in the classroom for instruction. Like other learning areas in the Catholic school curriculum, RE has the 'same systematic demands and rigour' (Congregation for the Clergy, 1997, n. 73), and is promoted as the 'first learning area' within the Catholic School (Catholic Education Commission of Western Australia, 2009, n. 61). The RE Program, based on the Archdiocese of Perth's *The Truth Will Set You Free Religious Education Guidelines*, is compulsory for all years of schooling. Both the process and content of what is to be taught in RE is mandated by the Conference of Catholic Bishops of Western Australia as well as the scheduled time for teaching RE in the classroom. Complementary to this teaching are the 'activities of catechesis' (Catholic Education Commission of Western Australia, 2008, p. 2) within the religious life and non-academic curriculum aspects of the school. The activities include school and class liturgies and prayers, celebrations of liturgical feasts through the year, retreats and spirituality days, Christian service learning and student leadership and ministry. These activities are experiential and formative, that is, an 'apprenticeship' in Christian living (Second Vatican Council, 1965, para. 14).

There are four Catholic dioceses in Western Australia (WA): the Archdiocese of Perth and the dioceses of Broome, Bunbury, and Geraldton. Collectively, the Bishops form the Conference of Catholic Bishops of Western Australia and while they are responsible for the teaching of the Catholic faith in their individual dioceses (Editrice Libreria Vaticana, Canon 804, para. 4), they have agreed on mandating the same RE curriculum for their respective jurisdictions. In 1987, the Archdiocese of Perth published 'The

Truth Will Set You Free' Religious Education Guidelines, drawing upon the inspiration of John 8:32, which became the basis for the RE Learning Area today taught in Catholic schools throughout Western Australia. This decision by the Bishops makes Western Australia the only mainland State with one RE program.

The development of the Perth Archdiocesan RE Guidelines (PAREG) began in 1981 when the Archbishop of Perth, Lancelot John Goody, appointed a Director of Religious Education and established the Perth Archdiocesan Department of Religious Education (PADRE) service. The purpose of the service was to develop RE programs and support teachers in the teaching of RE. The first priority for the service was to identify the needs and challenges that schools faced in teaching RE in Western Australia. During 1981 and 1982 a number of meetings and conferences were held with bishops, school leaders and priests to identify the challenges and possible solutions for the teaching of RE in Western Australia. The main challenges identified at the time were:

- a lack of knowledge and understanding of the content and processes for RE in schools;
- the need for appropriate content outlined for the different year levels of schooling;
- catering for the range of teacher faith levels within Catholic schools, especially with the decline of numbers in teaching priests and consecrated religious;
- the problem that some teachers felt uncomfortable teaching certain areas of Church teaching;
- the distances between schools across the State and Catholic Education Offices and the support of school leaders and teachers within a growing Catholic school system; and,

- catering for the differing spiritual and faith needs of students across Western Australia.

The delegated responsibility from the bishops for the development of the curriculum and professional learning within the RE learning area lies with the Director of RE. As an appointment of the bishops, the Director is a member of the Catholic Education Commission of Western Australia (CECWA) and has been part of the executive management team within the Office of Catholic Education Western Australia (CEWA) since 1986. The responsibility of the Director of RE is a broad and complex one that includes managing accreditation of staff, evangelisation planning, faith formation of leaders and staff, campus ministry and service learning. These responsibilities emerge from how RE is understood in the WA context.

At a school level, the principal is responsible for RE within the broader context of the School's Evangelisation Planning. The aim of Evangelisation Plans in WA Catholic schools is to articulate the Catholic identity and mission of the school and ensure that the religious dimension of the curriculum and the essential faith formation of students is systematically planned and implemented by school leaders and their staff. These plans demonstrate the school's contribution to the lifelong formation experiences and living of faith bringing not only the students but also the whole school community to 'communion and intimacy with Jesus Christ' (Congregation for the Clergy, 1997, n. 80).

RE, as part of the school's Evangelisation Plan, aims to contribute to students' choices about their personal commitment to Christ (Congregation for Catholic Education, 1977, n. 40). The learning area focuses on developing students' religious knowledge and understandings which are important for developing faith. The beliefs and values studied in RE inspire and draw together every aspect of the life of a Catholic school. The content of RE draws together the content of the rest of the curriculum and every life of a Catholic school. RE, then, is considered to be the first curriculum priority in a Catholic school (CECWA, 2009, n. 62).

While the challenges presented in the last century continue to be addressed, there exists today a number of positive strategies that maintain and enhance the teaching of RE in WA Catholic schools today. Some of these strategies include:

- the development of a state-wide RE Policy by the Catholic Education Commission of Western Australia;
- the development of systematic RE Guidelines and, more recently, generic year-based units of work and student resource materials which are reviewed and updated;
- the development of senior secondary RE materials in line with the School Curriculum and Standards Authority's university-entrance and general course called Religion and Life;
- development of an understanding of the need to assess and report on RE within the classroom and through a system-wide standardised assessment called the Bishops Religious Literacy Test;
- the development of an Accreditation Framework, including the professional requirement that RE teachers have tertiary theological background and training in RE pedagogy;
- the appointment of principals and leaders of RE in each school with postgraduate studies in theology or RE as part of Accreditation for Leadership;
- ongoing professional learning courses through CEWA in RE; and,

- the provision of initial teacher education units and post-graduate units and courses in theology and RE through the Catholic Institute of Western Australia within public universities and at The University of Notre Dame Australia, Fremantle.

Overview of the curriculum

The goal of RE in Western Australia is for students to know and understand 'the Gospel as it is handed on by the Catholic Church, and of how those who follow Christ are called to live this Gospel in today's world' (Congregation for Catholic Education, 1988, paras 69, 73). As a learning area, the focus is on the acquisition of knowledge (Congregation for Catholic Education, 1988, para. 69); that is, an educational approach that is as demanding and rigorous as other subjects, presenting Catholic Church teachings with the same seriousness and depth as other disciplines. The presentation of this Catholic 'content' works in an integrative way such as dealing with significant life experiences from the purpose and meaning of human bodies and emotions to the meaning of work and vocation with the Christian vision of the whole person and Christian moral principles and decision making.

The intent is that young people will be enabled to study, research and learn what the Catholic Church teaches about the distinctive vision of living the Gospel. Such an intent is coupled with an invitation to students to reflect and discern a response to this vision that they may want to enact in their lives whether they be an active Church believer, searcher or doubter or non-believer (Congregation for the Clergy, 1998, para. 75). In particular, the teaching of RE is mindful of the predominant numbers of students in the latter categories mentioned. Consequently, the RE approach in

Western Australia is one of New Evangelisation (Congregation for the Clergy, 1998, para. 58c). This approach acknowledges that Catholic schools today are increasingly dealing with students who come from families for whom religion is irrelevant and from families who are not Catholic. Within the context of New Evangelisation, the RE curriculum in WA seeks to cater for all students. It does not assume students are adherents to an active involvement in the Catholic faith. Furthermore, the content of RE in WA Catholic schools is based on the following contexts:

- All people have the basic need of Salvation.
- In Jesus Christ, Salvation is offered to everyone as a gift.
- The Catholic school presents a Gospel teaching as 'transmitted through the Catholic Church' (Congregation for Catholic Education, 1977, para. 49).
- There must be an 'unceasing interplay' of the Gospel and the hearer's 'concrete life, both personal and social' (Paul VI, 1975, para. 29).
- A Gospel vision of the total human person (Paul VI, 1975, paras 35-36).
- Human freedom, which includes spiritual, economic, political, social and cultural freedom (Paul VI, 1975, paras 35-36).
- There is a Hierarchy of Christian Truths, whereby some Truths are more fundamental than others (Vatican Council II, 1964, para. 11).

The underlying teaching process for RE in Western Australia provides opportunities for students to develop an understanding of the Christian Promise of Salvation and the implications of this Promise for the lives of people, both personal and social. Learning and teaching is directed towards enabling students to progress in developing a sophisticated understanding of how Jesus' Gospel can satisfy the deep questionings and yearnings of people and provide a sense of purpose and meaning to life. As St Augustine of Hippo proclaimed, '... our hearts are restless till they find rest in You.' (Knight, 2009, Chapter 1, para. 1). Therefore, students explore how the Jesus' message and his Church supports human development and the universal human search for meaning.

In WA Catholic schools, classroom time is set aside each day in the primary years or over a week for the secondary years for RE as shown in Table 1. In addition to this scheduled time, 'at least 60 minutes per week of [activities of catechesis] averaged over the particular year level's academic year' (Catholic Education Commission of Western Australia, 2008, p. 2) is provided. For three and four-year-old children, the focus of the early childhood years RE program is on raising their religious awareness by 'providing an atmosphere where "God-talk" permeates all leaning experiences as a natural part of the day' (Catholic Education Commission of Western Australia, 2008, p. 2).

Primary schools (Minimum Time)		Secondary schools (Minimum Time)	
Years Pre-Primary – 1	15 minutes per day	Years 7 - 10	160 minutes per week
Years 2 – 6	30 Minutes per day	Years 11 - 12	220 minutes per week

(Catholic Education Commission of Western Australia, 2008, p. 2)

Table 1: Religious Education instruction in Catholic Schools in Western Australia

Key features

The starting point for RE in WA Catholic schools is always the students and their needs, their human heart questions and yearnings (Congregation for the Clergy, 1998, para. 152a). RE is developmental and addresses the various needs of students at different phases of schooling, that is, the early childhood years contribute to the primary school experience which, in turn, is foundational to secondary learning. In Western Australia, there are resources for the different phases of learning with these being developed into more digital on-line materials. Over the years the focus of programs has always been educational engagement between the students, the teacher and the authentic subject material. Students are drawn into a systematic study of the teaching of the Church and the saving mystery of Christ which the Church proclaims.

The Early Childhood Years of Schooling and Religious Education

The early years learning environment plays an essential role in laying the foundations for later learning and for life-long engagement with the mystery of God. The Western Australian resource for the early years in Catholic schools is 'Let the Little Children Come to Me'. This resource is available to teachers both as a hard copy and online with added videos and songs. Early years teachers provide children with a range of experiences to nurture and develop each child's sense of wonder in God's presence and creation. Spiritual, social and emotional growth are fostered as children learn about God's great love and presence and integrates closely with the domains of the Early Years Learning Framework (Australian Government Department of Education, Employment and Workplace Relations for the Council of Australian Governments, 2009).

Teachers in Western Australia develop the spiritual and religious awareness of children in the early years by providing learning environments that create opportunities for children to:

- wonder within God's presence and creation;
- explore God's creation;

- engage in human experiences that relate to spiritual and religious concepts;
- engage in role-play that helps develops spiritual and religious awareness;
- see and emulate how to relate with others in the way Jesus taught and modelled by the teacher;
- recall and retell scripture stories; and,
- be introduced to simple rituals and symbols.

With careful planning in the early years, teachers assist children to learn about God and how to live as God wants through all aspects of their environment. Through play-based learning, children are encouraged to understand and apply Catholic beliefs and values in meaningful ways. For example, children learn about Jesus teaching to love and care for others through engaging in Gospel stories. Children then apply their learning through activities, they are guided to take turns, share and listen to others, and they are given the opportunity to practise the teachings of Jesus. One of the ways teachers engage children in the stories from the Bible is by using 'Godly-play' activities (Hyde, 2011).

Primary and Middle Years of Schooling and Religious Education

The key content for RE in the primary and middle years of Catholic schooling is presented in a systematic way. Sequenced along year levels, students explore how the Gospel vision of relating with God and communion with others expresses itself in Catholic Church teachings and practices. Students are provided with activities that stimulate thought and inquiry and develop their understanding of how those who follow Jesus are called to live the Gospel in today's world. Students develop these understandings through the study of Scripture and a systematic study of the teachings of the Church. The RE program enables students to progressively develop and extend their knowledge, understanding and skills.

Through their study, students develop a sense of God's vision in creating and sustaining the universe and the human person. They explore how human experiences, and today's societal and secular values, pose challenges to those who seek to live the Gospel vision. In particular, as children mature in the later primary years and into middle years of schooling, they are able to develop the critical skills to challenge what is contrary to the teachings of Jesus. Teachers use the CEWA's generic year level units of work that follow a process of integrating life, faith and culture (Congregation for Catholic Education, 1997, para. 11); there are three key 'steps' to this process.

1. The first step is to assist students to wonder about God the Creator who loves people so much that they are surrounded by the experiences of creation in people and the environment. Students are taught about wondering about the God who created them, others and the world around them, and importantly, to wonder at the different attributes of God.

2. In the second step, Jesus is offered as the truly human way to live the Gospel and the Promise of Christian Salvation. This step usually includes Gospel stories of Jesus and focuses on practical applications of the different gifts God offers as people discover and experience God. These gifts are shown through Jesus, the Church, the Scriptures, the Sacraments and Christian prayer.

3. The third step teaches about elements of Catholic belief, the Creed, Sacraments, the Moral Life and Prayer which relate to parts of the Catechism of the Catholic Church. This step explains how Catholics respond to the Christian

message and how this message can relate to the real life situations of people.

In the secondary school, the units of work are supplemented by the student resource book, 'Come follow me'. The resource books provide the key content, class activities and other stimulus materials to support the teaching of the RE teacher.

Senior secondary years of schooling and Religious Education

Following a review of senior secondary courses eight years ago, the Curriculum Council of Western Australia (now called the School Curriculum and Standards Authority), introduced a number of new courses. At the time, the Catholic Education Office of Western Australia (now referred to as Catholic Education Western Australia) proposed during the review to introduce a course that would enable students who attend religious and state schools to use the study of religion as a way of gaining secondary graduation for the Western Australian Certificate of Education (WACE) and the option of using the course towards university or technical education entrance. After consultation with representatives of these schools, a course called 'Religion and Life' was introduced (School Curriculum and Standards Authority, 2014). The course was designed to provide students with opportunities to gain an understanding of religion and of how religion can give people meaning and purpose in their lives. The Religion and Life course was examined externally by the Curriculum Council for the first time in November 2010.

For Catholic schools in Western Australian, Religion and Life has become a compulsory subject for senior secondary students. The subject fulfils the CECWA's RE policy requirements and allows students, aspiring for university entrance, to have their Tertiary Entrance Exam (TEE) and school results contribute towards an Australian Tertiary Admission Rank (ATAR). Initially, there were some misgivings about the compulsory introduction of the course (Perth Now, 2010); however, the course quickly gained appeal with RE teachers and students (Berlach & Hackett, 2012). Today, 82.49% of year 12 students in WA Catholic schools who studied the subject found their results were used towards their ATAR score for university entrance (McDonald, 2016).

Students of the course are able to develop knowledge, skills and values in order to understand the different visions of life found in the culture in which they live. Their learning enables them to develop an understanding of how religion influences the major moral questions confronting humanity today giving them the tools necessary to understand and value different cultural views and perspectives at the local, national and international level. Students also gain an understanding of the ways religious knowledge, skills and values contribute to an understanding of the origins of the world, history, ethical values, the function of religion in culture, human relationships and the destiny of people, and humanity's relationship with nature.

Senior secondary students in Catholic schools who study this course are directed to a systematic and critical reflection of what it means to be a Catholic in Australia and the rest of the world today. Students are guided through study and research to learn what the Catholic Church teaches about the distinctive vision of how Christian people live. Students use a range of inquiry skills to explore the Catholic religious worldview and to investigate characteristics of Catholicism, its origins, foundations, cultural influences and development over time. They also use these skills to critically analyse the role religion in general plays in society and to consider the challenges and opportunities religions face in the future.

Ensuring rigour in Religious Education through assessment

A key feature of RE curriculum in WA is to evaluate the effectiveness of the school's RE program and to ensure that RE is taught with the same depth and rigour as other subjects (Congregation for the Clergy, 1997, para. 73). At the request of the Catholic Bishops of Western Australian, a formal large-scale standardised assessment in RE was introduced in 2006. The assessment is known as the Bishops' Religious Literacy Assessment (BRLA) and is complementary to the national testing of literacy and numeracy in Australian schools (NAPLAN). The BRLA provides a 'point in time' snapshot of student performance. Student knowledge and understanding of the content of the RE curriculum is assessed using a combination of multiple choice questions, as well as short and extended response items. The role of this formal external assessment is to complement the school based assessment programs. In 2016, the BRLA was completed online for the first time.

Before its introduction, there was extensive professional learning for teachers and leaders to develop their understanding of RE and what should be assessed and methods of assessment. A key focus was the importance of making clear to the Catholic school community that only student knowledge, and understandings and skills of Catholic beliefs and practices is assessed. Staff, parents and students also needed to understand that the student's own faith tradition or practice cannot be formally assessed or reported upon. The BRLA developed by the Office of Catholic Education Western Australia is diagnostic in nature and is not designed to display benchmark standards in RE.

Students in Catholic schools in years 3, 5 and 9 across the state take part in the BRLA each year in term 3. Only students who are following a regular classroom program are expected to participate. The purpose of testing is to measure student learning of the content of the RE Curriculum. The test items are developed and marked under the supervision of staff at the Office of Catholic Education Western Australia. Following testing, formal school and student reports similar to those for NAPLAN are produced for students in Years 5 and 9. Year 3 tests are marked by the classroom teacher within the school for their own analysis. The student performance data from these tests are provided to schools in the form of individual school and student reports. These reports provide schools with an opportunity to help teachers diagnose student learning in RE. Schools conduct in-depth test item analysis in conjunction with an analysis of classroom assessment data in RE to understand and improve the quality of student learning in RE.

Year 11 students in WA Catholic schools are also required to complete common assessments developed under the supervision of staff at the Office of Catholic Education Western Australia. All Year 11 students completing a pair of Religion and Life units are required to complete a Common Assessment Task for each unit. These tasks are similar in style to those set by the School Curriculum and Standards Authority. Tasks are administered by school staff under invigilated conditions following set protocols and then marked by school staff using marking keys that are provided by the Office of CEWA.

Future directions

Digital transformation of teaching and learning

The challenge into the future is to continue to contextualise programs for Western Australian schools across a large state with differing needs. The aspiration of Catholic Education in Western Australia is to provide for the contemporary needs of students in rapidly changing times. At present, the focus is on digital transformation to reimagine teaching and learning. RE needs to reflect the same teaching and learning situations as other subjects so that students and the community appreciate its value. While the content of RE is ageless, it will always need to be addressed to the real life of students and their situations and to reflect evidence based best-practice in methodologies, technologies, resources and professional learning.

RE programs in Western Australia are currently being reviewed to ensure that the content is at the appropriate year level for today's students and conditions. Online resources are being developed with clearly outlined content at each year level along the lines of the rest of the Western Australian Curriculum. Grade descriptors are being developed as well as access to digital resources and tools to progressively develop and extend student knowledge, understanding and skills.

The Christian witness of leaders and teachers

The success of classroom RE in WA Catholic schools depends on the professional quality and faith formation of teachers. It is important for evangelisation and the teaching of RE to have mature adults who have a good understanding of their own faith. The RE Policy stipulates that teachers of RE in Western Australia need to be 'committed Catholics and ... give active Christian witness to Catholic beliefs' (Catholic Education Commission of Western Australia, 2008, p. 2). The need to recruit, educate and support such teachers is critical to the teaching of RE. There needs to be clarity of expectations for teachers of RE and opportunities for them to continue their own life-long formation in faith as well as for their professional development.

Staff in Catholic schools were surveyed to understand how they regard faith formation and the different formation needs of staff depending on their roles and circumstances. Key factors that enhance and challenge faith were identified and work has begun to develop clear strategies for formation based on different needs. The '... divine power of the Message ...' (Paul VI, 1975, para. 18) seems to pervade such formation as evidenced by the depth of individual staff formation and length of service in a Catholic school. A significant finding was the contribution of postgraduate units in RE and theology, as offered by The University of Notre Dame Australia, the Catholic Institute of Western Australia and other tertiary providers, to the critical reflection of teachers and leaders for their own faith formation. More recently, a spiritual and faith formation program called *'Galilee'* is being trialled by the Catholic Institute of Western Australia to support and enhance the spiritual and faith formation of school staff.

Conclusion

The RE curriculum in Western Australia is characterised by high levels of collaboration between the Conference of Catholic Bishops, Catholic Education Western Australia, and Catholic school communities. There is one common RE program taught throughout WA which is well resourced and supported by suitably qualified staff. The RE program is adapted to the needs of students, and especially focuses on New Evangelisation. The learning area is the priority in WA Catholic schools and integral to the implementation of schools' Evangelisation Plans. Furthermore, like any other learning area, RE is scheduled on the classroom timetable, complemented by catechetical activities and assessed formally. At the senior school level, students can use RE in the guise of the WACE Religion and Life as part of the ATAR score. In the future, digital technologies will increasingly serve the teaching and learning needs of teachers and students alike.

The importance of RE in WA Catholic schools needs to continue to be a priority into the future. Parents, school leaders, staff and students need to appreciate its value and role and not succumb to the pressure of being private schools rather than Catholic schools. Church documents as reflected in the RE Policy state that RE is to be taught, developed and resourced with the same commitment as any other subject. RE sometimes suffers from a lack of expectation and challenge. It requires the support of leaders and the community of every Catholic school in Western Australia.

REFERENCES

Australian Government Department of Education, Employment and Workplace Relations for the Council of Australian Governments (2009). *Belonging, being, becoming: The early years learning framework for Australia*. Retrieved from https://www.coag.gov.au/sites/default/files/early_years_learning_framework.pdf

Berlach, R. G. & Hackett, C. (2012). Upper secondary school religion and life course: Perceptions of the inaugural cohort. *Religious Education Journal of Australia, 28*(1), 9-15.

Catholic Education Commission of Western Australia (2008). *Education: 2B5 – Religious Education policy*. Retrieved from http://internet.ceo.wa.edu.au/AboutUs/Governance/Policies/Documents/Education/Policy%202B5%20Religious%20Education.pdf

Catholic Education Commission of Western Australia (2009). *Mandate of the Catholic Education Commission of Western Australia 2009-2015*. Retrieved from http://internet.ceo.wa.edu.au/AboutUs/Documents/Bishops%20Mandate%202009-2015.pdf

Congregation for Catholic Education (1977). *The Catholic school*. Retrieved from http://www.vatican.va/roman_curia/congregations/ccatheduc/documents/rc_con_ccatheduc_doc_19770319_catholic-school_en.html

Congregation for Catholic Education (1988). *The religious dimension of education in a Catholic school*. Retrieved from http://www.vatican.va/roman_curia/congregations/ccatheduc/documents/rc_con_ccatheduc_doc_19880407_catholic-school_en.html

Congregation for Catholic Education (1997). *The Catholic school on the threshold of the third millennium*. Retrieved from http://www.vatican.va/roman_curia/congregations/ccatheduc/documents/rc_con_ccathed uc_doc_27041998_school2000_en.html

Congregation for the Clergy (1998). *General directory for catechesis*. Retrieved from http://www.vatican.va/roman_curia/congregations/cclergy/documents/rc_con_ccatheduc_doc_17041998_directory-for-catechesis_en.html

Editrice Libreria Vaticana. (1983). *Code of canon law*. Retrieved from http://www.vatican.va/archive/ENG1104/_INDEX.HTM#fonte

Hyde, B. (2011). Berryman and the purpose of religious education: The significance of Berryman's approach to religious education for Catholic schools. *Journal of Catholic School Studies, 83*(1), 20-28. Retrieved from http://www.ceoballarat.catholic.edu.au/media/uploads/rec_godly_play/JournalofCatholicSchoolStudiesarticle2011withpermission.pdf

Knight, K. (2009). *Nicene and Post-Nicene Fathers, First Series*, Vol. 1. Edited by Philip Schaff. (Buffalo, NY: Christian Literature Publishing Co., 1887.) Translated by J.G. Pilkington. Revised and edited for New Advent by Kevin Knight. Retrieved from http://www.newadvent.org/fathers/110101.htm

McDonald, T. (2016). *Media release: Catholic Education sustains improved WACE performance*. Retrieved from http://internet.ceo.wa.edu.au/Publications/Documents/MediaStatements/MediaRelease_WACE%20results%202015.pdf

Paul VI (1975). *Evangelii Nuntiandi (On evangelization in the modern world). Apostolic exhortation of his Holiness Pope Paul VI to the episcopate, to the clergy and to all the faithful of the entire world*. Retrieved from http://w2.vatican.va/content/paul-vi/en/apost_exhortations/documents/hf_p-vi_exh_19751208_evangelii-nuntiandi.html

Perth Now (2010). *Catholic schools force religion as TEE subject*. Retrieved from http://www.perthnow.com.au/news/catholic-schools-force-religion-as-tee-subject/story-e6frg12c-1225825009570

School Curriculum and Standards Authority (2014). *Religion and Life*. Retrieved from http://senior-secondary.scsa.wa.edu.au/syllabus-and-support-materials/humanities-and-social-sciences/religion-and-life

Vatican Council II (1964). *Unitatis Redintegratio (Decree on ecumenism)*. Retrieved from http://www.vatican.va/archive/hist_councils/ii_vatican_council/documents/vat-ii_decree_19641121_unitatis-redintegratio_en.html

Professor Chris Hackett is the Director of the Catholic Institute of Western Australia and the Associate Dean (Religious Education) in the School of Education at The University of Notre Dame Australia, Fremantle Campus. He is responsible for undergraduate and postgraduate teacher education programs in religious education, pastoral care, spirituality education and values education. He also supervises research students in these areas. Chris has published academic articles and book chapters on religious education, teacher formation and student ministry and presented at conferences on the formation of RE teachers, student ministry and the spirituality of young people.

Dr Debra Sayce is the Director of Religious Education for Catholic Education in Western Australia. She is a member of the Catholic Education Commission of Western Australia and a member of the Faith Formation and Religious Education Committee of the National Catholic Education Commission. Debra completed her doctoral studies at The University of Notre Dame in the field of Educational Leadership.

Email: sayce.debra@ceo.wa.edu.au

Diana Alteri is the Team Leader for Religious Education and Faith Formation for Catholic Education in Western Australia. She has worked in the area of religious education for over 40 years. For the past 26 years she has been responsible for leading a team that develops Religious Education materials for Catholic schools in Western Australia and works in the area of formation for teachers.

Chapter 14

Curriculum Focus

Old Wine in New Wineskins? A Comparison of Approaches to Religious Education in Catholic schools in Four Australian Dioceses

Brendan Hyde

Although it was published in 1997, *The General Directory for Catechesis* reminds us that the Church does not utilise any one single method for transmitting the faith, but rather that it 'discerns contemporary methods in the light of the pedagogy of God … It avails of the pedagogical sciences and of communication, as applied to catechesis, while also taking account of the numerous and notable acquisitions of contemporary catechesis' (GDC, 1997, para. 148). The many and various dioceses in Australia have certainly taken heed of this statement, with each developing its own philosophical stance and pedagogical practices to meet the needs of the diocese in the religious education of its students in Catholic schools. The purpose of this chapter is to briefly compare the approaches to religious education in Catholic schools in four Australian dioceses to illustrate the variety of philosophies and pedagogical practices that have been employed to meet the needs, both educational and pastoral, of those dioceses. The approaches compared are those from the Archdiocese of Brisbane, the Archdiocese of Sydney, and the Dioceses of Broken Bay and Lismore.

Since 2008, the classroom learning and teaching of religion in the Archdiocese of Brisbane has been characterised by a reconceptualist approach. In short, it operates from an educational framework rather than from a catechetical framework. The most prominent proponent of the reconceptualist approach has been Gabriel Moran upon whose work the Brisbane Catholic Education *Model for Religious Education* is based. Moran (1991) distinguished clearly between two contrasting processes within the meaning of the term 'religious education' – teaching people religion, and teaching people to be religious in a particular way.

In this reconceptualist approach, the classroom religion program becomes a primary arena for teaching students about the Catholic tradition in a systematic and rigorous manner – that is, teaching students religion. The Catholic ethos of the school as a whole becomes the arena in which opportunities are provided for teaching people to be religious in a particular way. This is represented visually in Figure 1 below.

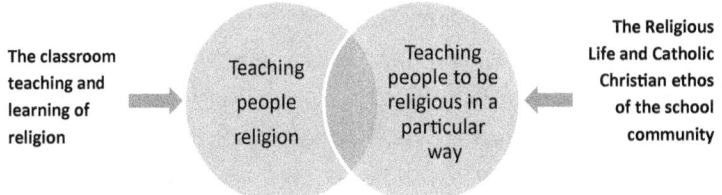

Brisbane Catholic Education (2008)

Figure 1. Relationship between the classroom religion program and the religious life of the school

In effect, this means that the learning and teaching that takes place in the classroom has an educational focus rather than a catechetical one. It is not assumed that students are faithful Christians, or that they have any affiliation with faith communities. Material in the religion classroom is presented and explored in the same way that other subject areas of the curriculum present and explore the content in their disciplines, drawing on contemporary pedagogy that informs learning and teaching (cf GDC, 1997, para. 73). This has significant ramification for the classroom program. For instance, teachers need to be cognizant of the language they use to ensure that it does not assume belief on the part of the students (for instance, 'Catholics believe ...' rather than 'we believe ...'). As well, opportunities for prayer and liturgy are not part of the classroom program in the reconceptualist approach. Rather, opportunities for faith formation are provided by the religious life of the school, which aims to promote the Catholic ethos of the school as a whole.

A reconceptualist approach requires powerful pedagogies that engage students with the richest resources of the tradition. The pedagogical practices embedded in the Brisbane Catholic Education's classroom religion program are consistent with a reconceptualist approach to the teaching of religion. Five practices provide a common language for planning and reflecting on learning and teaching in the religion classroom: focusing on learners and their learning; establishing clear learning intentions and success criteria; activating multiple ways of knowing, interacting and opportunities to construct knowledge; responding with feedback to move learning forward; and evaluating learning with students as activators of their own learning and as resources for others.

The organization of the religion curriculum itself includes a number of features that can be found in other subject areas, and are reflective of the Australian Curriculum. These include Year Level Descriptions, Content Descriptions, Achievement Standards, Content Elaborations, General Capabilities and Cross Curriculum Priorities. General capabilities comprise an integrated and interconnected set of knowledge, skills, behaviours as well as dispositions that students develop and use in their learning across the curriculum, in co-curricular programs and in their lives outside of school. There are seven general capabilities: literacy, numeracy, information and communication technology (ICT) capability, critical and creative thinking, personal and social capability, ethical understanding, and intercultural understanding. The general capabilities are further outlined within other learning and teaching documents provided to schools by Brisbane Catholic Education.

In short, religious education that occurs in the classroom is understood by the Archdiocese of Brisbane to be an educational activity. At the classroom level contemporary learning and teaching pedagogies are utilised in the same way as other disciplines to present and explore the content of the unit of work. Opportunities for faith formation are taken up by the religious life and ethos of the Catholic school, rather than as a part of the classroom religion program.

Religious education in the Diocese of Broken Bay

The centrepiece of Catholic life and mission in the Diocese of Broken Bay is the call to Catholic discipleship. It calls for an individual commitment realised in active membership of the Catholic Church, demonstrated by love, compassion, hope, reconciliation, transformation, prayer, respect for life and a desire to bring about justice for all (Diocese of Broken Bay, 2004).

Understanding the study of religious education to be at the heart of the Catholic curriculum, the approach to religious education in the Diocese of Broken Day, under the guidance and influence of Bishop David Walker, is, then, to educate and form young people in Catholic discipleship, offering them experiences of following Jesus as members of the Catholic community. This educational activity is not simply a human activity, but is understood as a genuine Christian journey of faith (Diocese of Broken Bay, 2004).

The curriculum documentation itself consists of three major parts. The Foundations introduce the context of the curriculum and place religious education firmly, but not exclusively in the Catholic School. It identifies the Catholic school as a place where students are offered experiences of Catholic discipleship, and suggests ways that schools can promote those experiences in everyday school life. An appreciation of the relationship between school and home, school and parish, and school and the wider community is essential for a clear understanding of religious education in general and classroom religious education in particular.

The Syllabus describes aims, the objectives and the expected outcomes of classroom religious education in the diocese of Broken Bay. It mandates the content and the progressive teaching and learning that takes place in classroom religious education from kindergarten to the completion of school education. Consistent with contemporary education, it is an outcomes-based syllabus and seeks to ensure a breadth and depth of coverage of content over the thirteen years of schooling.

The modules are resource packages developed from the syllabus. They contain the expected outcomes, and provide Biblical and references to the Catechism to support the teaching of various topics. As well, they provide theological and education background material to support the teachers' understanding of the topic and suggest ways contemporary pedagogy can be incorporated into the teaching of religious education in the classroom.

While the syllabus maintains a well-defined focus on an outcomes-based approach to religious education, the intent of the curriculum as a whole is clearly catechetical, aimed at the faith formation of students. Such an approach reflects the importance of the Catholic school to participate in the evangelising mission of the Church (cf Congregation for Catholic Education, 1997, para. 11) which fulfils in the tasks of catechesis and religious education undertaken by both volunteers and trained professionals, such as teachers. Indeed, the document reiterates that within the Catholic school teachers have a vital role in the mission of evangelisation:

> Teachers must remember that it depends chiefly on them whether the Catholic school achieves its purpose. They should therefore be prepared for their work with special

care, having the appropriate qualifications and adequate learning both religious and secular. They should also be skilled in the art of education in accordance with the discoveries of modern times. Possessed by charity both towards each other and towards their pupils, and inspired by an apostolic spirit, they should bear testimony by their lives and their teaching to the one Teacher, who is Christ.

(Pope Paul VI (1965), para. 8)

In short, religious education in the Diocese of Broken Bay is understood to be an activity that educates and forms young people in Catholic discipleship, offering them experiences of following Jesus as members of the Catholic community. This is achieved through an outcomes-based approach, although the curriculum itself is clearly catechetical in intent.

Religious education in the Archdiocese of Sydney

One of the first attempts at instigating an outcomes-based approach to religious education occurred in the Archdiocese of Sydney in 1996 (Ryan, 2007) with its revised curriculum guidelines for Catholic secondary schools, titled *Faithful to God, Faithful to People*. The outcomes-based approach was modelled on the one of the proposed NSW Board of Studies curriculum guideline documents, and contained statements relating to outcomes at the level of bands (strands) and classroom.

This curriculum was revised and republished in 2006, incorporating a New South Wales edition of the texts, *To Know, Worship and Love* (2000, 2001), that were collaboratively developed with the Archdiocese of Melbourne as the major resource for each year level from K-12. While maintaining its outcomes-based approach to ensure that religious education reflects 'the same systematic demands and the same rigour as other disciplines' (GDC, 1997, para. 73), this revised document places an emphasis on the religious formation of students. Although the sections that form the basis of teaching and learning in religious education include aims, objectives, outcomes and unit content (including identified scripture and doctrine), the inspiration for religious education continues to take its impetus from the Emmaus Story (Luke 24:13-35), emphasising students finding meaning in the light of God's Revelation. For instance, the K-2 Primary Levels of religious education aim to 'lay foundations for learning about and engaging with the mystery of God and the faith of the Church.' (CEO, 2006, p. 10). Through the seasons of the Liturgical Year, religious education aims to assist the students to reflect upon, make sense of, celebrate and live more deeply the mystery of Christ as revealed in each person and in relationship with others, the Church, and Creation. The religious education Curriculum K-2 in the Archdiocese of Sydney has been developed with a particular focus on the particular ways young children learn. Research on the spirituality and faith development of young children has also informed its development.

As such, the curriculum draws on the research and work of Jerome Berryman's (2003) *Godly Play* approach to religious education, and the work of Sofia Cavalletti and Gianna Gobbi in their approach to religious education, titled 'The Catechesis of the Good Shepherd' (1996), both of which were influenced by the work of Maria Montessori in the early 20th century. As well, the curriculum draws on the Archdiocese of Melbourne's adaptation of these works in 'The Good Shepherd Experience' *To Know, Worship and Love* student textbooks and teaching companions (2000). These resources are used to support the curriculum.

In this way, the religious education curriculum K-2 lays the foundations for later learning and for life-long engagement with the mystery of God. A key part of laying the foundations is telling the stories of the Catholic community – stories from sacred Scripture and stories about how the Catholic community celebrates, prays and lives the Christian life. These are termed as (1) Narrative Stories – people's experience of Gods' activity in their lives from the Old and New Testaments; (2) Parables – the stories of Jesus that challenge listeners to understand situations in a new way; and (3) Liturgical Signs, Symbols and Actions – stories and activities through which children learn the language of liturgy and have an appropriate place to experience it, so they can enter more fully into the liturgical experience of the Church.

In short, religious education in the Archdiocese of Sydney emanates from an outcomes-based approach, reflecting the intent of previous curriculum documentation, namely *Faithful to God, Faithful to People*. However, it too has a clear catechetical intent, with the impetus of the curriculum coming from the Emmaus story in Luke's Gospel. At the K-2 levels, the curriculum is influenced by Berryman's *Godly Play* and Cavalletti's *Catechesis of the Good Shepherd*, both of which, while being significantly researched and highly worthwhile approaches, are aimed at faith formation.

Religious education in the Diocese of Lismore

In taking its impetus from the The Bishops of New South Wales Pastoral Statement, *Catholic Schools at a Crossroads* (2007), the Diocese of Lismore understands religious education and catechesis to be activities of evangelization, aimed at building a stronger Catholic community founded on deeper commitment to the mission entrusted by Jesus Christ to the Church. At the heart of this statement, then, is a faith view of the world, which animates and sustains the community – a Catholic worldview, focussed on the six Christocentric foundational values of tradition, evangelisation, worship, witness, community and service, expressed in Figure 2 below.

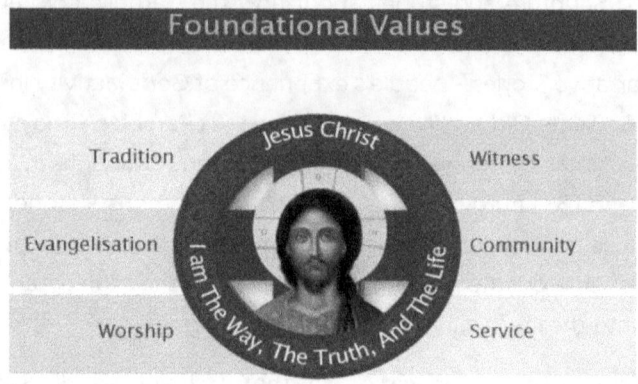

Figure 2: Foundation values underpinning a Catholic worldview

In terms of Catholic education, a Catholic worldview means that those who develop, design and implement curriculum in Catholic schools must 'do so in a manner that draws explicitly on Catholic beliefs, values and worldview' (Catholic School's Office, Diocese of Lismore, 2013, p. 3), since religion cannot be separated or divorced from the rest of the curriculum. In the Diocese of Lismore, this is addressed through the notion of *Catholic permeation* of the curriculum, a process which understands the curriculum as 'the school's planned educational experiences and connection between faith and life, church and school, learning and Catholic teaching both moral and social' (Catholic School's Office, Diocese of Lismore, 2015, p. 10).

In practice, this means that units of work that are developed by teachers in both religious education *and* the broader curriculum will include opportunities for the Catholic worldview to explicitly permeate those units of work. A number of auditing and planning tools have been developed by the Diocese of Lismore to enable classroom practitioners to work towards this aim (Catholic Schools Office, Diocese of Lismore, 2013). Curriculum design templates have been designed for units of work in the general curriculum where permeation is being undertaken, and include opportunities for naming and recording the Foundational Values applicable to that unit, as well as direct scripture quotation and clear statements on Church teaching that might influence or be taken into account in the development of particular units of work. For catechesis in schools such design templates include the opportunities for naming the Foundation Values and Mission, and, at the secondary level of schooling, the opportunities to name particular religious education priorities that might influence the development of particular units of work.

It is important to note that, in keeping with the heart of the bishops' pastoral statement, the term 'catechesis' is often used rather than the term 'religious education'. Indeed, personnel in Catholic primary schools who hold responsibility for curriculum development in this area are referred to as Leaders of Catechesis, charged with the responsibility of integrating Catholic beliefs and practices into all aspects of catechesis by, for example, assisting in the integration and permeation of the Catholic worldview across the various Key Learning Areas. Such an understanding reinforces the notion of religious education as an activity of evangelization and as a means of handing on the Christian faith. Within the content and environment of the Catholic school, it makes the Gospel present in a personal process of cultural, systematic and critical assimilation. It helps students to learn the teachings of the Gospel and to develop a sense of the nature of Christianity and of how Christians are trying to live their lives (cf. Religious Dimension of Education in a Catholic School, 1998).

Old wine in new wineskins – comparisons and issues

By way of summary and comparison, Table 1 below presents the approach to and intent of (that is, the purpose of) religious education in each of the four dioceses that have been explored in this chapter.

Diocese/Archdiocese	Approach	Intent (Purpose)
Brisbane	Reconceptualist	Teach students *about* the Catholic tradition
Broken Bay	Outcomes-based/faith forming	Educate and form young people in Catholic discipleship
Sydney	Outcomes-based/faith forming	Lay foundations for learning about and engaging with the mystery of God and the faith of the Church
Lismore	Catholic Christian (worldview) permeation of the curriculum	Build a stronger Catholic community founded on deeper commitment to the mission entrusted by Jesus Christ to his Church

Table 1: A comparison of the approaches to classroom religious education

While three of the dioceses have similar (although not identical) approaches, the intention or purpose of religious education in the classroom context in each diocese is quite different. The question arises as to whether this represents a case of old wine (the content of religious education) being re-cased, or re-packaged, in new wineskins (approaches and purposes). In other words, does the difference simply represent an attempt by each diocese to assert its political influence over how the content of this subject area is delivered? The answer to this question is far more complex, and lies in the understanding that each of these dioceses has in relation to the nature and purpose of religious education, based on various examinations of the relevant Church documents that inform this understanding.

Of the four, the Archdiocese of Brisbane is the only one to clearly separate the study of religion at the classroom level from the opportunities for faith formation that it understands to be located in the broader spheres of the Catholic school and its relationship to the parish community that calls the school into being. Influenced by the Religious Dimension of Education in a Catholic School (1988) which makes a clear distinction between religious instruction and catechesis, and Moran's (1991) understanding of teaching people religion and teaching people to be religious in a particular way, the Archdiocese of Brisbane understands the purpose of religious education at the classroom level to be concerned with an academic study of religion, in which the Catholic tradition is given a privileged position. Opportunities for faith formation occur in coordinated efforts the broader spheres of the Catholic school and in parish communities.

The Dioceses of Broken Bay and Lismore, as well as the Archdiocese of Sydney, have different understandings of the purpose of religious education, largely influenced by the General Directory for Catechesis (1997). While this particular Church document acknowledges the distinction between religious instruction and catechesis, its focus is largely upon the complementarity of these two activities. Both are moments of evangelization, both contribute to the development of Christian faith, and the handing on of Christian faith. Therefore, at the classroom level, these three dioceses emphasise the complementarity between religious instruction and catechesis. The curriculum design in these dioceses then provides a systematic approach to the study of the Catholic tradition as well as opportunities for sharing faith. Such an understanding echo's Groome's (2003) notion of total catechesis in which both religious education and catechesis are posed together as two symbiotic and necessary emphases within education in faith:

> Catholics tend to use the term *catechesis* to describe the *formative* process of nurturing Christian identity, and *religious education* as *informative* pedagogy in a faith tradition ... Both religious education and catechesis are necessary for educating the Christian person and community. With an appropriate pedagogy ... both can be done as dual emphases within the same enterprise (p. 1).

While these three dioceses share a common catechetical approach to religious education, the intent of the approach in each diocese is quite different. In the Diocese of Broken Bay the intent is to educate and form young people in Catholic discipleship. Within the Catholic school, religious education then aims to provide students with 'a total learning environment in which they experience what discipleship of Jesus means to those who are committed to the Catholic faith' (Catholic Schools Office, 2004, p. 17).

In the Archdiocese of Sydney, the intent of religious education is to lay the foundations for students to learn about and engage with the mystery of God and the faith of the Church. Each of the Content Strands – Church and Liturgical Year, Creation, Self and Others – around which the content for classroom religious education is arranged is designed to provide such a foundation. Further, the learning and teaching activities that are planned within each of these Content Stands will comprise both education and catechetical pursuits that will enable students to learn about as well as to engage in the faith of the Catholic church.

In the Diocese of Lismore, the intent of religious education is explicitly catechetical. Its intent is to build a stronger Catholic community founded on deeper commitment to the mission entrusted by Jesus Christ to his Church, achieved through a process in which the Catholic Christian (worldview) permeates the whole of the curriculum. Therefore, at the classroom level, the curriculum will be organised to as to provide students with both education and catechetical pursuits to facilitate the personal process of cultural, systematic and critical assimilation.

For some, however, the approaches and intents that are expressed by the Dioceses of Broken and Bay and Lismore, along with the Archdiocese of Sydney, can be problematic. For instance, Ryan (2007) and Rossiter (1985, 2002) question the extent to which it might be reasonable to assume that students who compulsorily attend religious education classes in a Catholic school are ready, willing or able to share their religious faith during the class. Students who attend Catholic schools in Australia today come from a range of multi-faith and secular backgrounds. Even among those who come from Catholic families, many, for a range of reasons, have little or no connection with their local parish communities. It is unreasonable, Ryan and Rossiter would therefore argue, to expect that such students are in a position to be able to share faith in the religious education classroom.

There is also a feature of all four diocesan sets of religious education syllabi that may prove to be problematic. In their attempts to ensure that religious education is systematic, coherent and coordinated, each syllabus has been broadly developed within parameters similar to those set by the Board of Studies in both New South Wales and Queensland. This may appear to be educationally sound since it ensures that religious education is viewed as being a subject with the same academic demands and expectations as other subjects in the curriculum – criteria which are expressed in The Religious Dimension of Education in a Catholic School (1988). However, assuming religious education to be the same as other subject areas, by, for instance, applying the outcomes-based philosophy and the language of other subject areas to religious education, may render a category mistake (Hyde, 2013) in which facts of one kind are presented as if they belong to another type or grouping. Church documents, while they may differ in their emphases, view religious education as a means to faith formation. This is true even of the The Religious Dimension of Education in a Catholic school (1988), which states that religious instruction 'assists in and promotes faith education' (para. 69). The emphasis on religious education as a vehicle for faith formation renders this activity significantly different from other subjects which comprise the curriculum, since other subjects do not share this same aim. The aim of mathematics, geography and English are not to increase students' faith. They do not share the aim of religious education. Therefore, to equate religious education with other subjects comprising the curriculum could be to make a category mistake.

A close examination of the curriculum documentation of The Archdiocese of Sydney, along with the Dioceses of Broken Bay and Lismore, suggests, on the one hand, that there is a clear recognition that religious education is quite distinct from other subjects that comprise the curriculum. Yet developing the syllabus within the parameters of the New South Wales Board of Studies – applying the outcomes-based philosophy and the language of other subject areas to religious education – may render a category mistake.

Similarly, a close examination of the curriculum documentation from the Archdiocese of Brisbane also suggests a recognition that religious education is distinct from other subjects that comprise the curriculum. In envisioning religious education as an 'umbrella' term, the Archdiocese is able to include both the systematic study of the Catholic faith tradition at the classroom level, and opportunities for faith formation at the broader level of the Catholic school. A separate document, titled *Religious Education: Guidelines for the Religious Life of the School* (2008) has been developed for this purpose, and addresses the ways in which elements such as prayer, liturgy and worship might be addressed s part of the religious life of the school. This would seem to be an effective means by which to address the aims and purposes of religious education.

Conclusion

The religious education syllabus documents in the Archdioceses of Brisbane and Sydney, along with those in the Dioceses of Broken Bay and Lismore, represent genuine attempts to 'discern contemporary methods in the light of the pedagogy of God' (GDC, 1997, par 148). In designing their curriculum, each diocese has drawn on the pedagogical sciences, as well as communication, as applied to catechesis, and has taken into account the many advances of contemporary catechesis to meet the education and pastoral needs of students. While the approaches and understood purposes differ, the religious education syllabus and accompanying documentation in each of the four diocese explored in this chapter have resulted in successful attempts to ensure the prominence and centrality of religious education within diocesan schools at both the curriculum and whole school levels to support students in developing a Christian interpretation of life.

CHAPTER 14

REFERENCES

Archdiocese of Melbourne (2000). *To know worship and love teaching companions Levels 1-2*. Melbourne, VIC: James Goold House Publications.

Archdiocese of Melbourne (2000/2001). *To know worship and love textbook series*. Melbourne, VIC: James Goold House Publications.

Barry, G. & Brennan, D. (2008). *Religious education: Guidelines for the religious life of the school*. Brisbane, Qld: Archdiocese of Brisbane.

Berryman, J. (2003). *The Complete Guide to Godly Play Vol 1-5*. Denver, Colorado: Living the Good News.

Bishops of NSW and the ACT (2007). *Catholic Schools at a Crossroads: Pastoral letter of the Bishops of NSW and the ACT*.

Brisbane Catholic Education (2005). *Model for religious education*. Retrieved from http://www.rec.bne.catholic.edu.au/The%20Shape%20of%20Religious%20 Education/Pages/Model-for-Religious-Education.aspx

Catholic Education Office, Sydney (2006). *Religious education curriculum, Primary K-2*. Leichhardt, NSW: Catholic Education Office, Sydney.

Catholic School's Office, Diocese of Broken Bay (2004). *K-12 religious education curriculum: Foundations and syllabus*. Waitara, NSW: Catholic School's Office, Diocese of Broken Bay.

Catholic School's Office, Diocese of Lismore (2013). *Catholic education in the Diocese of Lismore: Catholic worldview permeation statement*. Catholic School's Office, Diocese of Lismore.

Catholic School's Office, Diocese of Lismore (2015). *Catholic education in the Diocese of Lismore: Foundational values for Catholic identity and mission*. Catholic School's Office, Diocese of Lismore.

Cavalletti, S, Coulter P, Gobbi G, and Montanaro S. Q. (1996). *The Good Shepherd and the Child: A Joyful Journey*. Chicago: Liturgy Training Publications.

Congregation for Catholic Education (1997). *The Catholic school on the Threshold of the Third Millennium*. Homebush, NSW: St. Paul's Publications.

Congregation for Catholic Education (1988). *The religious dimension of education in a Catholic school*. Homebush, NSW: St. Paul's Publications.

Congregation for the Clergy (1997). *General Directory for Catechesis*. Homebush, NSW: St. Paul's Publications.

Groome, T. (2003). Total catechesis/religious education: A vision for now and always. In T. Groome & H. Horell (Eds.), *Horizons & Hopes: The Future of Religious Education* (pp. 1-29). New York/Mahwah, NJ: Paulist Press.

Hyde, B. (2013). A category mistake: Why contemporary Australian religious education in Catholic schools may be doomed to failure. *Journal of Beliefs and Values, 34* (1), 36-45.

Moran, G. (1991). Understanding religion and being religious. *Professional Approaches for Christian Educators, 21*, 249-252.

Pope Paul VI (1965). *Gravissimum Educationis (Declaration on Christian education)*. Homebush, NSW: St. Paul's Publications.

Rossiter, G. (1985). The place of faith in classroom religious education. *Catholic School Studies, 59* (2), 49-55.

Rossiter, G. (2002). Addressing an apparent crisis for Catholic school religious education: The importance of "relevance" and the theme of "searching for meaning". *Journal of Religious Education, 50* (2), 53-70.

Ryan, M. (2007). *A common search: The history of and forms of religious education in Catholic schools*. Brisbane, QLD: Lumino Press.

Brendan Hyde is an Honorary Fellow of Australian Catholic University, and an Honorary Senior Research Fellow of Federation University Australia. He is also a Fellow of the Centre for the Theology of Childhood (Denver, Colorado, USA).

Dr Hyde is the co-editor of *International Journal of Children's Spirituality*, and has research interests in hermeneutic phenomenology, children's spirituality, and in how Godly Play (an approach to religious education in early childhood) nurtures the spirituality of children in both parish and school contexts.

Chapter 15

Curriculum Focus

K-2 Religious Education in the Archdiocese of Sydney

Anthony Cleary and Sue Moffat

On becoming Archbishop of Sydney in 2001, Archbishop George Pell commissioned a review of the Religious Education (RE) curricula, *Celebrating Our Journey* (K-6) and *Faithful to God: Faithful to People* (7-12), which had been developed in the 1990s by the Catholic Education Office, Sydney.

The revised K-12 curriculum is closely aligned to the *To Know, Worship and Love* textbooks, which were adopted as the principal resource. It also incorporates key elements of the Melbourne Archdiocese RE curriculum.

The RE curriculum brings together the essential components of knowledge, understanding, appreciation and celebration of the Catholic Tradition. Its principal objectives are that students will be provided with opportunities to develop:

- An openness to the presence and activity of God.
- A sense of wonder, joy and delight in responding to the mystery of God.
- Knowledge and understanding of the traditions, beliefs, Scripture and stories of the Church.
- An appreciation of the richness of Scripture and Tradition.
- Active participation in the celebrations, prayer and liturgical life of the Church and communities.
- Knowledge and understanding of the Church's activity in continuing the mission of Jesus to build the reign of God.
- An awareness of, and commitment to their role in the life of the Church community.
- The capacity to engage with, explore, and find meaning in the traditions, stories and beliefs of the Catholic Church.
- Confidence in communicating and expressing the traditions, stories and beliefs of the Catholic Church.
- Critical thinking and reflection on life experience and faith.

The Emmaus story

As with *Celebrating Our Journey* and *Faithful to God: Faithful to People*, the revised RE curriculum draws inspiration from the structure and activity of the *Emmaus Story* (Luke 24:13-35), which has four distinct movements or stages.

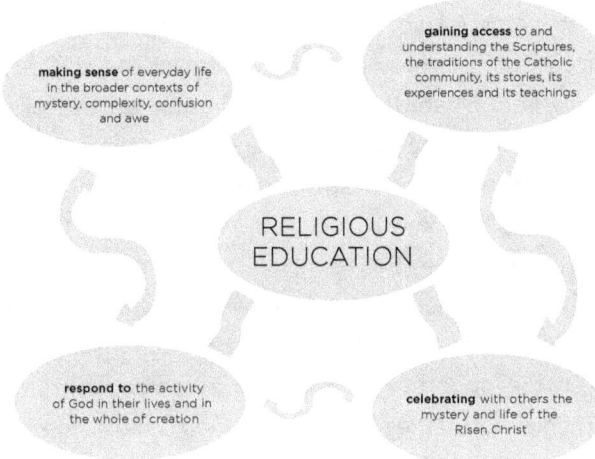

making sense of everyday life in the broader contexts of mystery, complexity, confusion and awe

gaining access to and understanding the Scriptures, the traditions of the Catholic community, its stories, its experiences and its teachings

RELIGIOUS EDUCATION

respond to the activity of God in their lives and in the whole of creation

celebrating with others the mystery and life of the Risen Christ

These movements are not a sequential lock-step process. Rather, they are part of a fluid and dynamic process in which each of the four movements are interconnected, each enriching the other movements. The movements of the *Emmaus Story* highlight that 'the communication of faith in catechesis is an event of grace, realised in the encounter of the Word of God with the experience of the person' (Congregation for the Clergy, 1971, no. 150), and so, by its very nature, effective RE enables young people to integrate faith and life. A dichotomy doesn't exist between faith and life. Rather, the meeting and integration of the two is essential to catechesis. The revised RE curriculum features both deductive and inductive catechetical methodologies.

The spirituality of young children

The Archbishop's request to review the RE curricula provided an opportunity for system personnel and teachers to evaluate the nature and scope of the existing content, the quality and suitability of pedagogical practices, and the overall engagement of students in RE. Central to the review, was the recognition of the changing nature of students' religious contexts. While the revised curricula sought to respond to these changes, and meet the religious and spiritual needs of all students, particular attention was given to the spiritual nature of the young child and the particular ways that young children learn. At that point in time the spirituality of children had increasingly become a focus of research and theoretical inquiry, particularly in relation to moral and faith development and approaches to RE. Emerging from the research was the view that children have an innate awareness of the spiritual realm, and will, when given the opportunity, 'explain their perception of God's self-communication in their lives' (Westerhoff, 1985, p. xxxiii).

The spirituality of children does not seem to be directly dependent upon their cognitive and verbal development but rather, 'religious awareness, the religious imagination, and the experience of the holy or sacred is natural to childhood.' (Westerhoff, 1985, p. 145). This is made ostensible in the research of Bradford (1995) who explored spirituality amongst those with an intellectual disability. Bradford noted the innate curiosity of young children with a disability, who like those of the mainstream, were 'spiritual seekers', except for possessing a language by which to express it.

In listening to the stories of young children, Harvard psychiatrist Robert Coles (1989) noted that they 'try to understand, not only what is happening to them, but why, and in doing so they call upon the religious life they have experienced and the spiritual life they have received' (Coles, 1989, p. 100). Coles' research was undertaken with individuals and small groups, capturing the immediacy of the spiritual experience through personal story, as the young children engaged in a process of meaning-making in which they 'struggled to figure out the world ... human nature ... and faith' (Coles, 1989, p. 39) Significantly, Coles (1989, pp. 10-21) came to the realization that it was through their spiritual experience and development that many children found psychological stability and personal fulfilment and meaning.

In contrast with Coles (1989), Robinson (1977, 1983) and Farmer (1992) explored the complexity of childhood spirituality from an alternative perspective, surveying and interviewing adults for their recollection of spiritual experiences. Both researchers found that the original vision of childhood had never wholly faded. The respondents clearly articulated a connection between imagination and spontaneous moments of wonder, with spiritual awareness (Hyde, 1990).

For many respondents, early spiritual awareness was the beginning of a healthy lifelong development, whereas others complained bitterly that the validity of their spiritual experiences was questioned, and on occasions denied, by an education that stifled rather than stimulated their imagination and creative spirit.

The researchers, Hay and Nye (1998), espouse the view that 'for many children in primary school, their natural spiritual awareness undergoes a process of becoming orphaned and steadily isolated' (p. 6) This process stems from the fact that many adults merely impose the language and norms of the culture and religion a child has been born into, rather than drawing forth and engaging the child's inherent spirituality. This is not a relatively recent concern but was foreshadowed by the ancient Roman philosopher, Plutarch (cited in Erricker & Erricker, 1997), who warned that 'a child's mind is not a vessel to be filled, but a fire to be kindled' (p. 43).

In their research on the spirituality of children, Hay and Nye (1998) identified what they called *relational consciousness* as the most fundamental feature of children's spirituality. This was observed in children's conversations, as an unusual level of consciousness or perceptiveness in certain instances and in all these cases was qualified by reference to a specific relationship with either self, others, God or the world (Hay & Nye, 1998, p. 109).

The data gathered and discussed in Hay and Nye's (1998) research supports the view that 'spirituality in its full range, including religious awareness, is entirely natural' (p. 141). However, it was also noted that most children by the age of ten were shy and embarrassed about their spiritual lives as are many adults in contemporary society.

These researchers suggested that the spirituality of children could be nourished by:

> '... directing formal attention daily (sometimes several times a day) to those aspects of human experience through which spiritual awareness most easily comes to light (e.g. worship, prayer, silence, contemplation, meditation etc.)'; and,

> the provision of a context of ritual, communal narrative, doctrine and social teaching which both focuses attention on and gives concrete expression to spiritual insight. In this way spirituality diffuses through and influences the whole of life in a coherent manner' (p. 141).

Madeleine Simon (1993) argues that 'there is a certain capacity for learning which is unique to childhood and these experiences sink deeply into the very core of a child's being in a way that is not possible in later life' (p. 46). Perhaps the most notable capacity of young children is their ability to be drawn into the present moment, whereas adults tend to become preoccupied with either the past or the future, which 'inhibits them from enjoying the vividness of the here and now' (Hay & Nye, 1998, p. 74).

As people age they are often drawn less into the *mystery* of God and instead become pre-occupied with having the answers and being in control. By contrast 'children are not afraid of questions without answers', and instead are fascinated by a world filled with mystery (Sasso, 2007). According to Kerrie Hide (1991), 'young children are natural contemplatives with great capacity for wonder and awe. They are naturally aware of the small moments in life and see the connectedness with creation' (p. 20). Such a view is strongly supported by Sofia Cavalletti (1996) and Jerome Berryman (2009) and underpins their respective approaches to the religious and spiritual development of young children.

It was these two approaches that influenced the Archdiocese' of Melbourne's approach to the development of their *To Know Worship and Love* resource books and accompanying *Teaching Companions.*

Cavalletti (1996) suggests that, 'when we are proclaiming the Christian message it is helpful to give children the opportunity to reflect and meditate on it' (p. 39). She also believes that children have a capacity for stillness and silence. Hence her approach, *The Catechesis of The Good Shepherd,* has specific times and ways of engaging children in stillness and reflection.

In the last few years in Australia, teachers and catechists have looked at approaches to RE and catechesis that recognise and nurture children's innate spirituality. Cavalletti (1996) stresses the importance of ensuring that the *method* of speaking about God with children is compatible with the *religious message*, 'one that conveys rather than limits the content, especially as the content we are referring to is the mystery of the infinite God, revealed as an inexhaustible richness' (p. 38).

The Catechesis of the Good Shepherd was developed by Sofia Cavalletti with Gianna Gobbi (1996) over the last fifty years in collaboration with catechists and children all over the world. Its basis is in the work of Maria Montessori. Sofia Cavalletti was a biblical scholar in Rome who first discovered the natural religious nature of the child when she agreed to teach a friend's nephew about the Bible. She noticed that her young student displayed great interest and joy as they together pondered God's word. She then sought the help of Gianna Gobbi, an experienced Montessori educator, to work out what particular aspects of God and the Christian Tradition met the child's needs at particular stages of their development.

The result, developed over many years, was a body of presentations from Scripture and liturgy that seemed to satisfy the deep spiritual needs of children at three different stages of development (aged 3-6, 6-9, 9-12). The key elements of this approach include 'telling the story', 'listening and reflecting together', 'presenting materials that accompany the story', 'praying together' and a 'response time' for children to explore and internalise the story. The teacher's role is that of guide or facilitator, preparing the materials and presenting the stories to 'call forth' the child's response rather than 'pouring in' information. The adult is a co-wonderer with the child.

A similar approach known as 'Godly Play' was developed in the United States by Dr Jerome Berryman who studied under Cavalletti in Bergamo, Italy and was a Montessori teacher and headmaster. One of his departures from Cavalletti's approach is his use of a carefully chosen sequence of Old Testament stories, as well as ones from the New Testament. Godly Play includes the same essential elements as the Catechesis of the Good Shepherd; telling the story, wondering and responding.

Both these approaches were originally developed for religious education/catechesis in the church environment but have been used and adapted to other environments including the school. A number of dioceses in Australia have adopted their principles and pedagogy and have incorporated key aspects in their RE curricula for young children.

What do these approaches offer to the teaching of RE and why are they so suited to it?

Religious Education and young children

Telling the story

Story is a key part of our faith tradition. In every age people have sought to relate their own story to the larger story of faith.

Young children, with their capacity for intuitive learning, are particularly able to find meaning through story and symbol. Stories carry deep insights, which young children are often unable to verbalise. However, the stories help them to make sense of their experience and relate to the mystery of God.

In telling the stories of faith, adults pass on to children the sacred story of salvation. Catechists and teachers often exhort children to love God and Jesus. But do they firstly help children to *know* God and Jesus? If catechesis is to put people 'not only in touch but in communion, in intimacy, with Jesus Christ' as John Paul II (1979, no. 5) explained, then telling the story offers a method for doing this 'that avoids putting ourselves and our experience between God and the child' (Cavalletti, Coulter, Gobbi & Montanaro, 1996, p. 38).

The style of biblical stories is particularly suited to young children because it uses only actions and descriptions essential to the story. This engages the imagination and invites the young listeners to relate the stories to their own lives and experience. In the Catechesis of the Good Shepherd/Godly Play approach the story is told, not necessarily 'by heart' but 'from the heart'. Well tested scripts are provided that stay close to the biblical texts and include gestures and silence with which children quickly engage.

The stories are accompanied by the use of simple but substantial concrete or visual materials. We know that young children learn through the senses. Concrete materials such as figures and visuals support the telling and re-telling of the biblical stories. Objects, symbols, gestures, movements and words of the liturgy engage children in stories about the liturgy. Concrete and visual materials help the children to picture the story in their minds.

The storyteller is not an actor or entertainer and focuses on the materials and the story, so the focus for the children becomes the unfolding story, rather than the storyteller.

Children who experience the story told in this way not only remember the story but also learn from the teacher's presentation to reverence the story and materials.

Wondering

Following the story, 'I wonder' statements engage children with the story and invite reflection. A statement like '*I wonder what part of the story you liked best*' or '*I wonder what you think is the most important part of the story*' invites the children to ponder and share their understandings. There are no 'right' answers to wondering statements. They are not comprehension questions. As Nye points out, 'there is no attempt to manipulate responses to reach a premature "teaching point" or to explain what the story "really means"' (Nye, 2004).

In this way children learn by experience one of the most important lessons of all, 'that Scripture holds neverending layers of meaningfulness for each one of us, rather than collections of finite answers or recipes for Christian life' (Nye, 2004). The children will not only become familiar with the stories of Scripture but will also learn through experience that these stories give meaning, direction and hope to their lives. Above all, the teachers or catechists will 'avoid the risk of clouding God's Word with their own words' (Cavalletti, Coulter, Gobbi & Montanaro, 1996, p. 64). and will be able to apply to themselves, 'the mysterious words of Jesus: "My teaching is not mine, but his who sent me"' (John Paul II, 1979).

Wondering together also teaches the art of dialogue, of listening to others, accepting and learning from others' ideas and contributions. It lays the foundation for relating to others in Christian community. Wondering together allows for learning that comes from within each person. It recognises Scripture as the living Word of God, acknowledging the work of the Holy Spirit.

Response time

This element provides the opportunity for children to 'stay with' the story, reflecting on and exploring aspects which are personally meaningful for them. In most RE, there is an experiential element, which usually involves asking the child to identify a life experience and relate it to a religious message. However, in the approaches of Berryman and Cavalletti the story itself, told well, evokes meaningful connections with each person's experience. It is indeed the *living* Word of God.

Children explore these connections as they retell the story using the story materials, or respond to an aspect of the story through art work or other creative media. Young children find it easier to explore and express their feelings and ideas through art and drama. These activities differ from the usual art and craft work used in RE. They are not 'craft activities' with a set finished product. Rather the creative arts provide the 'tools' for children's own imagining, reflecting, and expression. The teacher's role is to respond to children's 'work' by engaging in dialogue with the child, asking open questions, describing what they see and not interpreting it.

Play

Research confirms the importance of play in children's development and early learning. The approaches to RE and spirituality discussed in this article are based on *play*, hence the term *Godly Play*.

Godly Play

Play is a natural way children explore their world and experiences. Through play and fantasy children investigate, create, role play and discover meaning. In imaginative play children are able to step out of the limits of their real situation to explore other worlds and experiences. In this case, they step into the world of the biblical and liturgical stories. They are invited to *play* through engagement with the story and materials, the symbols, actions and words.

Prayer & liturgy

Young children have a particular capacity for prayer. They often use few words and are comfortable with silence. They also enjoy ritual and repetition. In the approaches being discussed, the belief is that young children learn to pray through the experience of prayer. This respects young children's natural way of learning. Teachers help the children to pray by praying with them and providing regular opportunities for both traditional prayers and children's own prayers. Telling the stories of God's great love offers children a rich source and stimulus for prayer. In the liturgical stories, children engage with key symbols, ritual actions and words of the liturgy as a means of coming to know God through the language of symbol.

Moral formation

By this stage you may be wondering about when and how children are taught morality. Sofia Cavalletti believes that moral formation happens at two levels. The first level is the formation of the person, which is the foundation for moral behaviour. In this formation we gain our fundamental attitude towards life. Formation happens in relationship; we are formed by our relationships. This highlights the importance of the child's relationships with parents and others. It is why both the Catechesis of the Good Shepherd and Godly Play place such importance on the teacher's facilitation of communication and relationship within the community of children. But as Cavalletti points out, there is another relationship that is of paramount importance: the relationship with God. 'There is a Person who calls them by name, who creates the most steadfast and enduring relationship of love ...' (Cavalletti, Coulter, Gobbi & Montanaro, 1996, p. 84).

Catechists and teachers build the foundations for the moral life by helping children to know the God who is calling them by name and who loves them so deeply. In telling the stories and inviting children to wonder and respond, 'we are feeding that inner wellspring, the source from which the child's behaviour will flow forth in later childhood' (Cavalletti, Coulter, Gobbi & Montanaro, 1996, p. 84). In that later stage the focus shifts more naturally onto moral concerns and teachings. This is the second level of moral formation, that of doing.

In the Archdiocese of Sydney principles were developed, based on the research that had been done on the spirituality of the child and the learning needs of young children to guide the curriculum development and to ensure that the curriculum developed would reflect these beliefs.

K-2 Religious education principles

Kindergarten, year 1 and year 2 RE lays foundations that enable children to engage with, reflect upon and explore the mystery of God. It does this by introducing children to the stories, worship and life of the Catholic community.

RE (K-2) is based on the following guiding principles. Implications of these principles for the curriculum are identified in point form.

Young children have a natural capacity for curiosity, imagination and wonder

- The curriculum aims to nurture and engage these natural capacities.

Young children learn best in a safe and predictable environment

- Questions are open and children's ideas and attempts are accepted.

- Materials are suited to students' needs and available for their use.
- Routines are established so the environment is predictable.

Young children learn through story

- Scripture stories and stories of the Tradition are key elements of the curriculum.
- Open questions, reflection and opportunities for exploration engage students with the story.
- Children's literature is included in the curriculum.

Young children learn through play

- Play allows children to explore, imagine and create as a means of learning.
- Scaffolded 'play' is part of the curriculum.

Young children learn through symbols and rituals

- Symbols and rituals nurture the child's curiosity, imagination and sense of wonder.
- The curriculum engages children with the Church's signs, symbols and rituals as a means of learning.

Young children learn in kinaesthetic and visual ways

- Concrete materials, visual materials and the creative arts support the learning needs of K-2 students.
- Children are active participants in their learning.

Religious education is theocentric

- It is about God's activity in and with all creation. At the centre of RE is the mystery of God – Father, Son and Holy Spirit.

- Children are introduced to the mystery of God through both the Old and New Testaments.

'Story' is fundamental in the Christian Tradition

- Children are introduced to the faith and practices of the Church through stories from both Scripture and Tradition.

The Church's liturgy is part of religious education

- Children are introduced to the signs, symbols and rituals of the liturgical tradition both in lessons and daily routine.
- Children become familiar with short responses and parts of liturgy by experiencing and using them.

The experience of prayer is integral to religious education

- Children learn to pray through the experience of prayer.
- Children are introduced to various forms of prayer – including silence, movement, short liturgical responses, some formal prayers of the Tradition, spontaneous, verbal and non-verbal prayer.

Doctrine underpins religious education

- Children at this early stage are introduced to the source of doctrine in Scripture and Tradition.
- K-2 religious education lays the foundations for exploring the beliefs and practices of the Church more explicitly in later years.

The Emmaus Story inspires religious education

- Children begin to:
  - reflect on and find meaning in life-experience in light of Scripture and Tradition,

- celebrate the mystery of the Risen Christ,
- respond to the activity of God in their lives and in all creation.

In recent years, these principles have also been applied to the years 3-6 RE curriculum. Specifically, storytelling and its associated pedagogies have been incorporated into each unit to offer primary students the opportunity to continue to engage with the stories of faith through wondering, reflecting and exploring. Teachers have attested to the strengthening of children's engagement in RE through story.

Authentic learning and religious education

Education has long been regarded as the acquisition of knowledge. While acquiring knowledge is a significant part of education, promoting a love of learning, developing individual talents and social skills, and nurturing a person's critical capacity to make decisions on the basis of sound reasoning are all important underlying aspects of education.

Through education, but most explicitly through RE, young people can learn how to responsibly exercise personal freedom for the betterment of self and others, how to contribute to society and develop their capacity for critical thinking and moral reasoning. Religious education can not only stimulate learning and cognitive development, but also a young person's social, emotional and spiritual intelligence. For this to occur, students must be afforded high quality learning opportunities and experiences.

In recent years, Sydney Catholic Schools have engaged in a collaborative process of exploring the nature of authentic learning. The system's statement on authentic learning argues that it must be relevant, purposeful and engaging, rigorous and empowering, and enable young people to live lives of promise and meaning (Catholic Education Office, Sydney, 2015).

A review of the *Statement on Authentic Learning* showed a strong correlation between the guiding principles for authentic learning and those for the teaching of RE (K-2).

Students learn authentically when they:	K-2 Religious Education Story-telling approach
engage in work that is rigorous and challenging;	The work of the *Godly Play* approach always centres around a biblical, liturgical or faith tradition story. The stories used are those which have captured children's interest for over fifty years. Story by its nature invites one to engage with and seek meaning from it. In order to do this one brings one's own experience and process of meaning-making to the text. The subject matter here is what we are passing on, (in story form) about God, and God's relationship with God's people and how that is lived out. It is also about ourselves and exploring through story the existential issues that are part of all human life.
engage critically with the material being learned - both as individuals and in collaboration;	The use of 'wondering' and the particular wondering statements invite critical thinking and engagement with the material. Because there are no 'wrong' answers students are confident to offer their understandings. The collaboration in this part of the process is when students listen to others ideas and may adjust their own understanding in light of others' ideas. It is the community of children seeking meaning together.
make connections between the material being learned, and their own lives and experiences;	The whole approach is really about making meaning of the story/liturgical action. When a person hears or reads a story they relate to it in light of their experience. So too with children, they bring to the story their experiences and also hear others share different meanings based on different experiences. They can further their wondering in the exploring work.
share what they have learned with others;	Initially the students share their understanding of different aspects of the story through the 'wondering' together but later in the exploring stage (further work of their own choice on aspects of the story, of their own choice) they may develop or even change their understanding as they 'explore' the story more deeply.

exercise choice as they pursue their own passions and interests;	The exploring part is a time when students take up some aspect of the story they would like to explore further or immerse themselves in. This is not group 'rotation activities', but a chance for the child to choose what interests them or how they would like to 'stay with' the story. Often younger students choose to act out the story themselves. However older children may find they want to initiate projects or actions as a result of learning from the story.
believe that they are capable learners and have high expectations of themselves;	The whole approach focuses on the 'community of children' working together and individually to make meaning of the story and of their lives in light of the story. The teacher facilitates this process by listening to and accepting all attempts. The students are in control of their own learning and the meaning they make is never 'wrong' unless they themselves deem it to be and adjust or develop their understanding in light of others' responses. It requires teachers to listen to the students and accept their understanding or ask them, 'Can you tell me a bit more about that?' With this facilitation they see themselves as capable co-learners and are willing to back up their ideas. It is apparent that students who don't respond much in other KLAs are responding in this type of RE.
apply knowledge and skills creatively in a range of situations.	Students' work with a story may end up as a project of action, a play, a poem, a story, a prayer, a painting. Whatever form of response children choose, they are given appropriate time and support for meaningful reflection.

Conclusion

Catholic educators often ask how best to engage and nourish children's innate spirituality whilst 'handing on' the Catholic Tradition. Both the *Catechesis of the Good Shepherd* and *Godly Play* are two approaches which enable this. They bring together the essential components of knowledge, understanding, appreciation and celebration. Their incorporation into the religious education curriculum for the Archdiocese of Sydney has had a significant impact on the way young children learn. They engage children's natural curiosity, imagination and wonder as they hand on the greatest story of all in ways that meet the children's deepest needs. The content is drawn from the richness of our

Catholic Tradition: the Bible, the liturgy and the wisdom of the Church's teaching. As Cavalletti suggests, 'if we hold faithfully to these we will have a secure foundation' (Cavalletti, Coulter, Gobbi & Montanaro, 1996, p. 84).

REFERENCES

Archdiocese of Sydney (2003). *Religious education curriculum*. Sydney: Catholic Education Office.

Berryman, J. (2009). *Teaching godly play: How to mentor the spiritual development of children*. Denver: Morehouse Education Resources.

Bradford J (1995). *Caring for the whole child*. London: The Children's Society.

Catholic Education Office, Sydney (2015). *Statement on authentic learning in Sydney Catholic schools*. Sydney: Catholic Education Office.

Cavalletti, S. Coulter, P. Gobbi, G. & Montanaro, S. (1996). *The Good Shepherd and the child: A joyful journey*. Chicago: Catechesis of the Good Shepherd Publications.

Coles, R. (1989). *The Call of stories: Teaching and the moral imagination*. Boston: Houghton Mifflin.

Congregation for the Clergy (1971). *General Directory of Catechesis* http://www.vatican.va/roman_curia/congregations/cclergy/documents/rc_con_ccatheduc_doc_17041998_directory-for-catechesis_en.html,

Farmer, L. J. (1992). Religious experience in childhood: A study of adult perspectives on early spiritual awareness. *Religious Education, 87*(2), 259-268.

Hay, D & Nye, R. (1998). *The Spirit of the Child*. London: Fount Paperbacks.

Hide, K. (1991). Towards an Australian spirituality for children. *Word in Life,* August, 20.

Hyde, K. (1993). *Religion in childhood and adolescence*. Birmingham, Alabama: Religious Education Press.

John Paul II Catechesi Tradendae - On Catechesis In Our Time; http://w2.vatican.va/content/john-paul-ii/en/apost_exhortations/documents/hf_jp-ii_exh_16101979_catechesi-tradendae.html

Nye, R. (2004). *What is Godly Play?* accessed on: www.godlyplay.org.uk/

Plutarch, cited in Erricker , C & J. (1997). *The Education of the Whole Child*. London: Continuum International Publishing Group Ltd.

Robinson, D. (1977). *The original vision: A study of the religious experience of childhood*. Oxford: Machester College.

Robinson E. (1983). *The original vision: A study of the religious experience of childhood*. New York: Seabury Press

Sasso, S. *Children's spirituality: An Interview*, accessed on http://www.spiritualityandpractice.com/books/features.php?id=15228, 14 Oct 2007.

Simon, M. (1993). *Born Contemplative: Introducing Children to Christian Meditation*. London: Longman & Todd.

Westerhoff, J. (1985) in Edward Robinson *The Original vision: A study of religious eperience of childhood*. New York: The Seabury Press.

Anthony Cleary is the Director of Religious Education and Evangelisation for Sydney Catholic Schools, Archdiocese of Sydney. Prior to his appointment in 2006, Anthony was the Director of the Confraternity of Christian Doctrine (Sydney). Anthony holds a Bachelor of Education, Master of Religious Education, Master of Educational Leadership, and Master of Arts (Theological Studies).

Currently Anthony is completing his PhD, examining the impact of World Youth Day on young Australians. Anthony's engagement in the life of the Church is evident through his deep commitment to parish life (St Patrick's Church Hill).

Sue Moffat holds the degrees of Bachelor of Arts, Master of Educational Administration and Master of Education (RE). She worked in Sydney Catholic Schools from 1990, initially as principal for nine years at Blessed Sacrament, Clifton Gardens. She was then appointed to the Sydney Catholic Schools' Office RE and Curriculum team, followed by a long period in Religious Education Curriculum. She retired from full-time work in December 2015.

Sue took a leading role in the development of the Sydney Catholic Schools' revised Religious Education Curriculum K-6 (2002-2005). This project features a storytelling and wondering approach to specifically address the needs of early learners. Sue managed the implementation and ongoing development of this curriculum along with a number of other related projects. Prior to this, Sue served as a teacher, Curriculum Adviser and Principal in the Diocese of Armidale.

Chapter 16

Curriculum Focus

Fostering Social Justice in Catholic Schools in Bathurst Diocese

Paul Devitt

Introduction

Catholic educators hand on an authentic faith – a faith that 'always involves a deep desire to change the world, to transmit values, to leave this earth somehow better than we found it' (Pope Francis, 2013, p. 93). We have access to an incredible body of teaching and resources that give us a firm foundation on which to systematically bring about change for the better in all aspects of life – for everyone and everything on the planet.

We have as our model the perfect teacher - Jesus. He provides us with a vision and a methodology for bringing about change. His vision emanated from the unique understanding of God that he proclaimed in word and action. His followers came to realise that Jesus was revealing God as Love (1 John 4:8). Love changes how we live our lives and relationships with each other and creation. It gives deeper meaning to our lives. It gives us a vision of 'what can be'. It gives us the energy to transform 'what is now' into 'what can be'.

We take the vision of Jesus and make it real in our world by understanding and becoming intricately involved in the ways we structure our society and organise the relationships by which we live together in this world – the political, economic, social, legal, customary, religious, academic structures. These are the very things that we need to constantly transform in order to bring about change for the better. We not only have Jesus' vision, teaching and example, but we also have at our disposal the wisdom of the Jewish faith tradition that inspired him, and over 2000 years of continual reflection and development of his teaching as it has been applied in many different circumstances throughout the world in response to the needs of people and the earth.

The Catholic social justice tradition

This body of teaching mentioned is our Catholic Social Justice tradition. It gives us well-developed guiding principles on which to make sound decisions about transforming the complex social situations and structures that confront our daily lives as individuals, families, organisations, workplaces, societies, and nations.

The tradition is centred on Jesus. Jesus' vision was based on his unique interpretation of the Law of Judaism and his more profound understanding of the Prophetic teachings of his faith. Jesus interpreted the Torah through the lens of compassion, not legalism, thereby arriving at a different outcome in how to apply it. Jesus' teaching and actions show that he understood what the Prophets were calling people to, especially taking care of the vulnerable people in society - 'the orphan, the widow, and the alien in the land' – and trusting on God in living out the call to 'act justly, love tenderly, and walk humbly with God' (Micah 6:8).

St Paul described the Reign of God as 'Justice, Peace and Joy in the Holy Spirit' (Romans 14:17). By *'justice'* Paul meant Right Relationship – with God, self, others (neighbours), and creation. *'Peace'* (shalom) is that deep sense of being 'safe and sound', in harmony, the sense of wholeness and calmness that comes with life lived abundantly. *'Joy'* (chara) is having those essential things that enable us to become truly human - necessities like clean water, food, clothing, shelter, ability to participate in society, freedom - of expression, of travel, of religion, etc. We call these 'basic human rights.' *'In the Holy Spirit'* assures us that Jesus' Spirit is with us 'to the end of time' (Mt 28:20), guiding us and strengthening us to continue his work of bringing the Reign of God to completion. Jesus inaugurated this Reign. By his death on the cross, he taught us what perfect love is – total self-giving for the good of others. He calls us to spread the Good News of this reign – to be evangelisers who make the Kingdom present in our world (Pope Francis, 2013, p. 89).

The work of people at the grass roots of change has been encapsulated in the teachings of Church leaders at all levels. Since the 1890's Popes have attempted to summarise the major challenges facing our world and give a Christ-centred perspective on how these challenges can be met.

The major documents, and the issues that inspired their writing, can be summarised as follows:

1891 *The Condition of Labour* (Rerum Novarum) - encyclical, Leo XIII.
- Lays out rights and responsibilities of capital (owners) and labour (workers). Describes proper role of government. Condemns atheistic socialism.

1931 *The Reconstruction of the Social Order* (Quadragesimo Anno) - encyclical, Pius XI.
- Decries the effects of greed and concentrated economic power on working people and society. Proposes a society based on subsidiarity.

1941 *The Solemnity of Pentecost* (La Solennità della Pentecoste) – Radio message, Pius XII.
- Equitable distribution of whatever goods are available is more important than economic growth. The general right of all people to the use of the goods of the earth is more important than the right of individuals to a particular item of private property.

1961 *Christianity and Social Progress* (Mater et Magistra) - encyclical, John XXIII.
- Deplores widening gap between rich and poor nations, arms race and plight of farmers. Calls Christians to work for a more just world.

1963 *Peace on Earth* (Pacem in Terris) - encyclical, John XXIII.
- Affirms full range of human rights as the basis for peace. Calls for disarmament and a world-wide public authority to promote universal common good.

1965 *The Church in the Modern World* (Gaudium et Spes) – Bishops of the world at Vatican II.
- Laments growing world poverty and threat of nuclear war. Emphasises responsibility of Christians to work for structures to make a more just and peaceful world.

1967 *The Development of Peoples* (Populorum Progressio) - encyclical, Paul VI.
- Affirms right of poor nations to full human development. Decries economic structures promoting inequality. Calls for new international organisations and agreements.

1971 *A Call to Action* (Octogesima Adveniens) - Apostolic letter, Paul VI.
- Calls for political action for economic justice. Develops role of individual Christians and local churches in responding to unjust situations.

1971 Justice in the world - Synod of Bishops.
- Names action for justice as a constituent part of being Christian. Calls the church to model the justice she preaches.

1975 *Evangelisation in the Modern World* (Evangelii Nuntiandi) - Apostolic exhortation, Paul VI.
- Notes the dramatic societal changes and their challenge to the church. Calls evangelisation the transforming of all aspects of life from within.

1979 *Redeemer of Humanity* (Redemptor Hominis) - encyclical, John Paul II.
- Describes the threats to human dignity and freedom. States that current economic and political structures are

inadequate to remedy injustice. Human rights are essential to human dignity

1981 *On Human Work* (Laborem Exercens) - encyclical, John Paul II.
- Affirms the dignity of work based on dignity of the worker. Calls for workplace justice as responsibility of society, employer, worker.

1987 *The Social Concerns of the Church* (Sollicitudo Rei Socialis) - encyclical, John Paul II.
- East-West blocs and other 'structures of sin' hinder development of poor nations. Calls for solidarity and for an option for the poor by affluent nations.

1991 *The 100th Year* (Centesimus Annus) - encyclical, John Paul II.
- Reaffirms the principles of *Rerum Novarum*. Identifies failures of both socialist and market economies. Calls for society of freedom to choose work, and of enterprise and participation. Condemns consumerism.

1992 Catechism of the Catholic Church
- Part III, 'Life In Christ'.

1994 *Towards the 3rd Millennium* (Tertio Millennio Adveniente) – Apostolic Letter, John Paul II.
- A commitment to (i) justice and peace (ii) raising voices on behalf of the poor of the world (iii) substantially reducing or canceling outright International Debt (iv) reflecting on the difficulties of dialogue between cultures; and on problems connected with women's rights.

1995 *The Gospel of Life* (Evangelium Vitae) – encyclical, John Paul II.
- Recognition of the sacred value of human life from beginning to end. Names anti-life forces, and challenges us to find ways to promote life in all dimensions of society.

1998 *Faith and Reason* (Fides et Ratio) – encyclical, John Paul II.
- Examines the relationship between faith and reason in the search for answers to life's ultimate questions and the search for truth. Freedom to seek truth is foundational for human dignity.

2005 *God Is Love* (Deus Caritas Est) – encyclical, Benedict XVI.
- Love of God and neighbor is the centre of Christian life, the fruit of faith, and the mission of the Church. Lay faithful have the duty to work for a just ordering of society. The true meaning of love – Agape – reminds us that our work for justice must come from a place of love, and is impossible to accomplish without God's guidance.

2009 *In Love and Truth* (Caritas in Veritate) – encyclical, Benedict XVI.
- *Highlights* the relationship between human and environmental ecologies and links charity and truth in the pursuit of justice, the common good, and authentic human development. Points out the responsibilities and limitations of government and the private market, challenges traditional ideologies of right and left, and calls all people to think and act anew.

2013 *The Joy of the Gospel* (Evangelii Gaudium) – Apostolic Exhortation, Francis.
- Gives particular attention to the 'social dimension of Evangelisation'. Details current social problems, characterised as the 'crisis of communal commitment' and touches on the markets, the economy of exclusion, inner city life, spiritual worldliness and consumerism.

2015 *Praise Be to You* (Laudato Si') – Encyclical, Francis.
- Calls for 'swift and unified global action', particularly in relation to the destruction of the environment. We have

made incredible progress in science and technology, but this has not been matched with moral, ethical and spiritual growth. This imbalance is causing relationships with creation and with God to break down and our hearts to become hardened to the cry of the earth and the cry of the poor. Arrogantly neglecting creation we forget what God has entrusted to our care.

The teaching in these documents has given key principles that guide us in dealing with newly emerging challenges that we have to face. These principles can be summarised as follows:

1. **Dignity of the Human Person:** Belief in the inherent dignity of the human person is the foundation of all Catholic Social Teaching. Human life is sacred, and the dignity of the human person is the starting point for a moral vision for society. The person is made in the image of God and is the clearest reflection of God among us.

2. **Common Good and Community:** We are both sacred and social. Human beings grow and achieve fulfillment in community. Human dignity is realised and protected in the context of relationships with wider society. How we organise our society - in economics and politics, in law and policy - directly affects human dignity and the capacity of individuals to grow in community. The obligation to 'love our neighbour' has an individual dimension, but it also requires a broader social commitment. Everyone has a responsibility to contribute to the good of the whole society, the common good.

3. **Preferential Option for the Poor and Vulnerable:** The moral test of a society is how it treats its most vulnerable members. The poor have the most urgent moral claim

on the conscience of the nation. We are called to look at public policy decisions in terms of how they affect the poor. The 'option for the poor,' highlights that the deprivation and powerlessness of the poor wounds the whole community. It is an essential part of society's effort to achieve the common good.

4. **Rights and Responsibilities:** Human dignity can be protected and a healthy community achieved only if human rights are protected and responsibilities are met. Every person has a fundamental right to life and a right to those things required for human decency – food, shelter and clothing, employment, health care, and education. Corresponding to rights are duties and responsibilities - to one another, our families, and to the broader society.

5. **Role of Government and Subsidiarity:** The state has a positive moral function. It is an instrument to promote human dignity, protect human rights, and build the common good. All people have a right and a responsibility to participate in political institutions so that government can achieve its proper goals. The principle of subsidiarity (help) holds that the functions of government should be performed at the lowest level possible, as long as they can be performed adequately. When the needs in question cannot adequately be met at the lower level, then it is not only necessary, but imperative that higher levels of government intervene.

6. **Economic Justice:** The economy must serve people, not the other way around. Workers have a right to productive work, decent and fair wages, and safe working conditions. They have a fundamental right to organise and join unions. People have a right to economic initiative and private

property, but these rights have limits. No one should amass excessive wealth when others lack the basic necessities of life. Catholic teaching opposes collectivist and statist economic approaches. It rejects the notion that a free market automatically produces justice. Competition and free markets are useful elements of economic systems. However, markets must be kept within limits, because there are many needs and goods that cannot be satisfied by the market system. It is the task of the state to intervene and ensure that these needs are met.

7. **Stewardship of God's Creation:** The goods of the earth are gifts from God, and God has given them for the benefit of everyone. There is a 'social mortgage' that guides our use of the world's goods, and we have a responsibility to care for these goods as stewards and trustees, not consumers and users. How we treat the environment is a measure of our stewardship, a sign of our respect for the Creator.

8. **Promotion of Peace and Disarmament:** Peace is a positive concept. It is not just the absence of war. It involves mutual respect and confidence between peoples and nations through collaboration and binding agreements. Peace is the fruit of justice and is dependent upon right order in all relationships.

9. **Participation:** People have a right to participate in the economic, political, and cultural life of society. A fundamental demand of justice and requirement for human dignity is that all people be assured a minimum level of participation in the community. No person or group should be excluded unfairly and be unable to participate in society.

10. **Global Solidarity and Development:** We are one human family. Responsibilities to each other cross national, racial, economic and ideological differences. We are called to work globally for justice. Authentic development is full human development. It must respect and promote personal, social, economic, and political rights, including the rights of nations and of peoples. It must avoid the extremes of underdevelopment, and 'super development'. Accumulating material goods and technical resources will be unsatisfactory and debasing if there is no respect for the moral, cultural, and spiritual dimensions of the person.

Catholic schools and social justice

The function of Catholic schools as a faith community is teaching and learning within the values, traditions and contemporary mission and vision of the Church. A focus on social justice provides an appropriate context to re-examine commitment to the Church's mission. Social action and fundraising are opportunities for groups and individuals to show their concern and solidarity for social justice in our world.

What follows is an exploration is how social justice is nurtured and promoted in a Catholic School setting as enunciated in Catholic Social Teaching and the concept of wealth sharing. Acts of solidarity and opportunities for wealth sharing should be entwined to attitudinal formation that occurs within the curriculum and the co-curricular program of schools, as well as the various outreach programs of schools. Such acts of solidarity should be viewed as a core part of any Catholic community.

Curriculum

Social Justice is embedded in the RE curriculum in Catholic Schools, but can also be effectively brought into other curriculum areas. The RE Curriculum that I am most familiar with is that of the Bathurst Diocese (2011), which is a local contextualisation of the 2006 *Sydney RE Curriculum* and the *To Know Worship and Love* texts that accompany the curriculum. I will use the Bathurst curriculum as my reference point.

An effective curriculum for 'transformative education' aims at personal, institutional and systemic changes. The programme outlined by Robert Evans (1987) remains pertinent today. He emphasises that a curriculum must be based on the biblical understanding of justice and peace, stress the necessity for people to have access to sufficient resources to sustain life, emphasise solidarity with the poor, and aim to emancipate the 'non-poor' from their controlling ideologies. The process of transformation is raising awareness of social injustices, maintaining a 'restlessness' at the injustices uncovered, sustaining the biblical vision of justice outlined by Jesus, confronting the controlling ideologies held by those who are not poor, and redefining power in terms of trust in God and the Kingdom ideals. The pedagogical components are:

A. Encounter with the poor - through stories, film, case studies etc. but especially through direct and sustained meeting and dialoguing.
B. Immersion in the life situations of the poor that challenge 'non-poor' assumptions and ideology.
C. Taking the risk of going into vulnerable situations.
D. Building and maintaining a community of support and accountability.
E. Articulating and sustaining the Kingdom vision and values.

F. Maintaining a cycle of critical social, political and economic analysis so that isolation from the reality of the problems does not allow us to be overtaken by the controlling ideologies again.

G. Commitment to the process and constant involvement in it;

H. Use of symbol, ritual, and liturgy.

The RE curriculum systematically introduces students to the person of Jesus, his teaching and example, throughout their schooling. For instance, the year 9 unit on *Literary Forms in the Scriptures* includes the Parables – the principle way that Jesus taught about the Kingdom and presented the vision that guided his understanding of what could be in our world, and what he challenges us to build through our commitment to social justice. The year 9 unit on the *Ten Commandments and the Beatitudes* gives students an insight into how Jesus reinterpreted the law of Israel through the lens of mercy and compassion, and came to a radically different understanding to his own religious leaders of what God expects of those responding to God's faithful Love. More specifically, a unit in Year 8, *Living the Christian Life* focuses on:

- The relevance of Jesus' life and teachings to contemporary society and life experiences.
- Identifying ways Christians live out their discipleship in accordance with the ideals and values of Jesus.
- The principles of Catholic Social Teaching.
- Applying the teachings and values of Jesus to contemporary issues.

This unit includes the important elements of prayer and ritual, biblical and traditional justice teaching, and projects that enable students to learn how Jesus' teaching is not only relevant, but is practically lived out by many people and organisations in their own community. There is an abundance of print and web-based resources included for teachers' own information and background, and to aid the students learning. There are a variety of collaborative tasks included to assist students to understand justice teaching, and make in-depth studies of how individuals and organisations in the local community reflect the actions and teachings of Jesus.

More in-depth analysis of Australian society and the values that underpin it takes place in the year 10 unit *Working for Justice in Australia*. This unit challenges students to critique their own society and the value systems that influence people in that society – what Evans (1987) calls the 'controlling ideologies', that are often subconscious until brought to the attention of those who hold and are guided by them.

The content and tasks assist students to:

- Name the many dimensions of justice, and see how 'social justice' fits into that field.
- Name experiences of injustice they see in the world around them.
- Examine the causes and the consequences of injustice.
- Analyse injustice issues through the lens of Scripture and Catholic Social Teaching.
- Search out and analyse examples of individuals or organisations committed to fighting injustice.
- Work out what they as individuals or as a group can do to help right unjust situations.
- Ritually celebrate success stories in the fight against injustice, and also acknowledge and seek forgiveness for our own failures to stand up for justice or even unwittingly participate in unjust structures of systems.

This particular unit incorporates two established methodologies of social transformation that include:

- The See, Judge, Act method of Cardinal Joseph Cardijn (1882-1967).
- The Pastoral Circle Method of Social Analysis.

1. Starting Point
2. Social Analysis
3. Christian Reflection
4. Plan of Action
5. Evaluation

Resources

Students in our schools have access to an immense body of information on Catholic Social Justice teaching. A search of the web under 'Catholic Social Teaching' results in thousands of hits leading the searcher to the smallest social justice group in parish or school, the multifaceted websites of religious orders, university courses, parish groups, organisations that specialise in social justice teaching and work, the websites of bishops' conferences all over the world, the Vatican Justice and peace organisations, and all Papal teaching – to the last thing the Pope said a couple of hours ago!

Sometimes it can be too much. Some websites that give a good overview of Catholic Social Teaching, and links to find much more are:

http://www.socialjustice.catholic.org.au
http://www.catholicsocialteaching.org.uk
http://www.cctwincities.org/CatholicSocialTeaching - follow links under 'Advocacy'

There are excellent educational programs, resources and guides to well-established immersion experiences provided by Catholic agencies such as:

Caritas	www.caritas.org.au
Catholic Mission	www.catholicmission.org.au
Catholic Earthcare	catholicearthcare.org.au
Edmund Rice Centre	www.erc.org.au
Columban Mission Institute	www.columban.org.au

Social Justice in action in schools

Involving students in meaningful learning about service and justice is vital, but just as important is involvement in advocacy and action which seeks to bring about social change which is consistent with the principles of the Church's teaching (Catholic Education Office, 2014). What follows are a few examples of how schools in this diocese have developed opportunities for encounter by which students can learn and grow in understanding of others' plights, and serve in transforming unjust situations.

1. Mini Vinnies and Junior St Vincent de Paul groups as promoted by such schools as St Joseph's Primary School, Blayney, and Catherine McAuley Primary School, Orange, where school based groups introduce students

to the welfare and justice philosophy and action of the St Vincent de Paul Society.
2. Junior Joeys at St Columba's School, Yeoval, and Assumption School, Bathurst, where groups are inspired by one of the famous phrases of Saint Mary of the Cross MacKillop: 'Never see a need without doing something about it'.
3. Mercy and Justice Service Groups. For example:
    o Students working with those in need in their local community, deepening awareness of injustice issues relating to refugees and asylum seekers, and raising funds to help various causes combat poverty and injustice.
    o 'Green Teams' – groups of students who help older and/or less able-bodied people with practical things like gardening, lawn mowing, tidying yards, etc.
4. Refugee Support Groups such as those established at Catherine McAuley School, Orange, where student members assist refugees and asylum seekers through personal support, resettlement schemes, personal contact and communication with those still in detention.
5. One-off events that focus on particular issues. For example:
    o Teachers and students from St Stanislaus College and MacKillop College, Bathurst, along with members of the local Refugee Support Group, held a one day seminar/workshop about Refugee and Asylum issues. Lots of good accurate information was given on the day, but the highlight was hearing real life experiences from refugees and asylum seekers themselves. The personal contact on such an occasion energises students to search out what they can do to help.

6. Immersion Experiences - many secondary schools have developed immersion experiences by which students live with and experience the lives and struggles of people who are much less well-off than the students themselves. Schools often establish sister-school relationships with schools in poorer countries that share common founders and are guided by those founder's charisms. For example:
    - James Sheahan Catholic High School, Orange, has established a relationship with a La Sallian school in Sri Lanka. Students are markedly changed when they return from trips to Sri Lanka because they have come face-to-face with the stark differences between wealthy and poor communities;
    - St Matthews Catholic School, Mudgee, is establishing relationships with Indigenous communities in the Northern Territory so that Mudgee students can experience daily life in those communities;
    - MacKillop College, Bathurst, immersion experience with the Warmun Community in the Kimberley, where the Sisters of St Joseph have been working for many years.
7. Project Based Learning such as that experienced by year 8 students at James Sheahan Catholic High School. As part of the unit, Ministries and Christian Life, students are challenged to respond and research the driving questions of; *HOW does your group's support of Catholic Mission reflect Mercy and Lasallian values,* especially in *the Year of Mercy? Find links between these values and the Pope's call for Mercy in the Extraordinary Jubilee of Mercy.* As part of the Assessment task for this unit, students are asked to in groups create an expo stand

that raises money for Catholic Mission. (In 2016, students were able to raise $2700 in just under an hour.)
8. Students present research they have done into particular groups or organisations in a local community that exist to help others. Groups of students select an organisation and research:
   a. Who the group is and its history;
   b. What they do – who they are specifically trying to help;
   c. How they do that;
   d. Why they do it – what inspires them to do what they do;
   e. Each group presents their findings in as creative a way as they please in an 'expo' for the rest of the school as both an information and awareness raising exercise and a fundraiser for the groups or organisations that have been researched and presented.
9. Rahamim Ecological Centre, Bathurst – set up especially to educate people in the understanding of ecological justice and sustainability. It helps students understand and experience the ecological conversion needed by all of us, and explicitly placed at the heart of Catholic Social Teaching by the Popes of the late 20th century and comprehensively outlined by Pope Francis in Laudato Si' (2015).
10. Schools provide varied opportunities to use ritual, symbol and liturgy to focus on the plight of those in need, or events that require prayer, or to rejoice in those moments when there have been a real success story in helping change someone's life for the better. A significant example of this is the yearly Diocesan Launch of World Mission Month for Catholic Missions. Each year the Bishop selects one school of the diocese to plan and host the event where representatives from

all schools including principals, priests, teachers and students and other parishoners attend and participate. At each of these events Catholic Mission's Church appeal focus for year, such as Cambodia and Jamaica in recent years, is embodied in a prayerful, ritual rich liturgy that heightens the awareness of the most disadvantaged and poorest communities.

Conclusions

'To teach and to spread her social doctrine pertains to the Church's evangelising mission and is an essential part of the Christian message. The "new evangelization" ... must include among its elements a proclamation of the Church's social doctrine.' (Pope John Paul II, 1991).

Social Justice is a critical component of the Catholic School curriculum. In an era when the content of curricula is overwhelmed by demands for inclusion of ever more diverse subject areas, and social demands for inclusion of training that was once the domain of parents, this critical component of education must remain solidly embedded in every curriculum. Since 'action on behalf of justice and participation in the transformation of the world is a constitutive dimension of the preaching of the Gospel ... and of the Church's mission for the redemption of the human race and its liberation from every oppressive situation' (Synod of Bishops, 1971), it is vital that we give every generation of Catholic students the vision and essential teaching of Jesus, the wisdom of the Church's tradition, the key principles that underpin our actions, and the skills to enable them to engage in this transformative Kingdom work.

REFERENCES

Catholic Education Office (2011). *Religious education Curriculum: Kindergarten to Year 12.* Catholic Education Office, Bathurst.

Catholic Education Office (2014). *Advocacy, Fund Raising and Social Action Guidelines.* Catholic Education Office, Bathurst.

Evans, Robert A. (1987). Education for emancipation: Movement toward transformation. In Alice F. & Robert A. Evans (Eds.) *Pedagogies for the non-poor,* (pp. 257-284). Maryknoll: Orbis.

Pope Francis (2013). *Evangeli Gaudium: The Joy of the Gospel.* London: Catholic Truth Society.

Pope Francis (2015). *Laudato Si': On care for our common home.* Strathfield: St Paul's Publications.

Pope John Paul II (1991). *Centesimus Annus.* Città del Vaticano: Libreria Editrice Vaticana.

Synod of Bishops (1971). *Justice in the World.* Città del Vaticano: Libreria Editrice Vaticana.

Fr Paul Devitt is a priest of the Diocese of Bathurst and currently ministers as Dean of the Cathedral in Bathurst and Administrator of Blayney Parish. He has Degrees in Education, Philosophy, Theology and Social Science and also gained a significant education in his 'pre-priesthood' life as a steelworker with BHP at Port Kembla, a high school teacher at Farrer MAHS, Tamworth, and Cobar HS, and a council truck driver at Wagga Wagga.

He was a member of the Australian Catholic Social Justice Council for nine years and continues working in the field of Social Justice at local, state, and national levels.

Chapter 17

Curriculum Focus

Towards a New Integrated Approach to Religious Education: The Tasmanian Experience

Tony Brennan

Religious education needs a refresh

Religious education in Catholic Schools in Australia needs a refresh, just as the Australian Catholic Church does in the wake of the Royal Commission into Institutional responses to Child Sexual Abuse. As it faces these storms the Church may not recover if significant root and branch renewal does not occur. However, these existential threats ought not to be what motivates the renewal, as even such a decline may serve the Kingdom of God. Though there may be bushfires, storms and earthquakes, 'God's voice is not in them' (1 Kings 19:11-13). Rather the Church and Catholic schools need to enable a dialogue that can listen-in to God's 'still small voice'. Religious education or RE is a key expression of the mission of Catholic education so listening must be a vital element of its curriculum and pedagogy and the RE classroom will be a vital location for searching conversations that can hear the voices of young people.

Archbishop Mark Coleridge of Brisbane has invoked the example of Pope Francis in announcing a Synod of the Australian Church to be held in 2020. In this context, he has invited a 'new listening for a new language' (West, 2016). This statement has great relevance for a refreshed curriculum and pedagogy of religious education just as it has for the mission of the church more broadly. Archbishop Coleridge comments that the present moment is a time in which the global and local Church needs to listen-in to how its clerical and doctrinal language is heard by the wider culture. Pope Francis has listened, taught and led courageously, especially with difficult topics such as how the church itself treats people, the poor and the planet. He has invited the church to renew itself to become less clerical, less self-referential and more merciful to those it has excluded.

Inspired by the Holy Father's sentiments, several of Australia's church leaders are inviting a 'new language', deliberately reaching out to those feeling excluded by rigid scriptural interpretations and doctrinal formulations regarding questions of sexuality or marriage. This call for an inclusive church and language is exactly the point made by one of Australia's newest Episcopal leaders, Bishop Vincent Long OFM of Parramatta:

> For me, one of the greatest challenges the church faces today is to be inclusive, to be a big tent church. Pope Francis urges us to be a church where everyone can feel welcomed, loved, forgiven and encouraged to live according to the Gospel. You heard me say in my Installation Homily that there can be no future for the living church without this vital sense of ecclesial inclusiveness. By that I mean there must be space for everyone, especially those who have been hurt, excluded or alienated, be they abuse victims, survivors, divorcees, gays, lesbians, women, disaffected members. The Church will be less than what Christ intends it to be when issues of inclusion and equality are not fully addressed. That is why you heard me say that I am guided by the radical vision of Christ (Long, 2016).

This Kingdom vision of radical inclusiveness is attractive to younger people, and RE teachers and leaders need to hear that and embrace it wholeheartedly. If understood it will refresh the formation of RE teachers and leaders and the curriculum and pedagogy of RE teachers in the classroom.

A refreshing of Catholic school religious education is timely at this significant watershed moment but there are traps for leaders of RE that need to be avoided with contemplation and action:

1. Rather than the language of explicit doctrinal content or external secular standards, a new pedagogical process will listen to the language which speaks to the heart of young people and commence with their questions before progressing to curriculum content;
2. Rather than a self-referential language of 'Catholic identity', a refreshed theological method or 'wisdom pedagogy' – aligned with active-contemplative spirituality – will attune young people in the language that aids dialogue between a plausible Catholicity and modern culture.

This refreshed theological method and pedagogy will enable a greater engagement in the searching conversation which is invited in every RE classroom.

Of even greater urgency is the question of what is to be done to form the teachers who will offer this refreshed RE curriculum and pedagogy.

1. The formation of leaders and teachers is the most critical priority in Catholic education today as it is within all the church mission domains such as health, welfare and development.
2. There seems to be furious agreement with this priority but very little capacity or will to appropriately resource the work of formation at the grass roots level.

A national and diocesan collaboration to provide local, regular and accessible formation for teachers and leaders – rather than expensive excursions and diversions – will require significant creativity and dialogue, and it must be founded upon a rich and inclusive definition of Catholicity, on scripture and on the priority to 'teach them to pray' (Lk 11:1-13).

There is no one Catholic identity (Arbuckle, 2014) any more than there is one Catholic philosophy, Catholic curriculum or Catholic pedagogy. However, if Catholicity is defined richly and inclusively it can reconcile all tensions. *The Catechism of the Catholic Church* offers two clarifications of the meaning of 'catholic': firstly, and literally, as [kata-holou Gk] or 'according to the whole' [§830] and secondly, as universal in 'the mission to the whole of the human race' [§831]. Rather than accepting 'Catholic' as an exclusive cultural denominator, 'Catholicity' can be of great assistance for teachers to know their work, to address their students with a positive anthropology and to ground their teaching in an integrated or 'catholic' vision of the curriculum (D'Orsa & D'Orsa, 2012). It becomes the unifying and vitalizing foundation to a formation process which can clarify and inspire the work of RE teachers and leaders.

A Refreshed RE Curriculum

What will a refreshed RE Curriculum look and feel like for those who experience it as teachers and learners? Religious education lessons will be grounded in the freedom of religion of each learner, will listen in deeply to their story and to the questions learners have on their spiritual path, will draw authoritatively from scripture and tradition in a way that proclaims without proselytizing, will religiously educate learners in an inclusive Catholicity inspired by Jesus' Kingdom teachings and give learners every opportunity to engage their learning in real world circumstances. Refreshed RE teachers and their lessons will reveal increasing confidence to lead and sit in silence and stillness, to reverence the presence of God and listen deeply to the stories of others. With a strong sense that their intelligence and moral freedom are respected, many young people will experience renewed courage to ask and invite searching questions of faith, morality with their real implications for the way they will choose to live today.

A refreshed RE Curriculum will have clear learning intentions that are based in a hopeful anthropology. It will be integrated with the Australian Curriculum as a practical mechanism to ensure educational rigour. The learning outcomes will be that young people are schooled in a process of learning that they can continue themselves, free to be religiously observant or not. They will be faithful in Catholic identification and religious practice in larger numbers if the Catholic community in its parish life and public persona inspires them with its authenticity, the vitality of its religious expression and the coherent plausibility of its wisdom. Importantly they will be skilled in how to pray, to meditate, to reflect, to research, to navigate religious language and myth, to discern, decide and act ethically. They will be resilient, hopeful and merciful moral actors in very challenging times.

The RE Curriculum in each of the twenty-eight Australian dioceses needs to align pragmatically with the Australian Curriculum to give itself the best practical chance of being a 'subject with as much rigour as any other' (*General Directory of Catechesis,* 1997, §223). There are positive developments emerging from the Australian Institute for Teaching and School Leadership (AITSL) which is producing professional standards for teachers and school leaders. These are founded on the historic *Melbourne Declaration* (ACARA, 2008, p. 4) from which emerged a secular moral vision for the holistic development of young people, which included spiritual development. AITSL sees teaching as more than an individuated craft intended to career-assist students into the economy but rather to 'affect the life chances of students in terms of their intellectual, spiritual, physical, moral, social and cultural wellbeing' (Timperley, 2011, pp. 1-2). The National Catholic Education Commission endorses this holistic focus but goes further to assert that not only is spirituality important but so is the integration of faith, culture and life (National Catholic Education Commission, 2009). John Hattie, the chair of the AITSL Board since 2014, is perhaps the most prominent educational researcher in the English-speaking world, with breakthrough findings based on meta-data research quantifying measures of visible effects on educational outcomes. Hattie calls this 'visible learning' and proposes the most powerful instruction occurs 'when teachers see learning through the eyes of students and help them become their own teachers' (2008, p. 392). This establishes a dialogue between all those involved in the educational enterprise. Pope Francis on many occasions has emphasised the essential element of dialogue:

> You can't evangelise without dialogue. It's impossible. Because you must begin from where the person who is to be evangelised comes from (Rome Reports, 2014).

So 'dialogue' itself is an approach to evangelisation, which implicitly proposes an active and contemplative process and profound listening respectfulness of the freedom, dignity and flourishing of other. A refreshed RE Pedagogy would commence its phases and lessons with a genuine empathetic encounter by listening to young people and the culture from which they come, enabling a trusted space for profound thinking and questioning of the most important human issues for living, inviting responses that require pedagogies of contemplation, discernment and wisdom and ensuring the learning can be in 'real-time' transformative projects. There should be no romanticism about how difficult a task it is to skill Year 9 Australians to lean in to the respectful, other-focused, undistracted deep listening required for dialogue. Every teacher will have their own pedagogical gifts as was emphasised at the recent ACEL conference by the highly respected educator Frank Crowther (Crowther, 2016). So too, Every RE teacher must actualise their signature pedagogical gifts in their RE classroom and it is this which will perhaps be their greatest witnessing.

Refreshing religious education: An integrated approach

In first century Palestine, Nazareth was regarded as a bit of a backwater and some were discourteous enough to ask 'can anything good come from there?' (John 1:46). Some could perhaps ask the same question of Tasmania today with a stronger case. Nonetheless, in the Gospel account the disciple replies to the critic saying 'come and see'. Here are several projects which Catholic schools in Tasmania have been exploring, but which may have some wider significance for the challenge of an integrated RE approach:

1. Tasmanian Good News for Living *RE curriculum online in the Australian curriculum format embeds 'Catholicity' as a cross-curriculum priority*

The quality of religious education in Tasmanian Catholic schools has been strengthened by the development of the online RE Curriculum [curriculum.catholic.tas.edu.au] (2015). The Tasmanian *Good News for Living* RE Curriculum (2005) had its foundation in a curriculum writing partnership with several Victorian dioceses and developed upon *Sharing our Story* (1991) and the Canberra-Goulburn *Treasures New and Old* (2000). Adapting these strong foundations, the *Good News for Living* 2014 online iteration embeds 'Catholicity' as a 'cross-curriculum priority' and

'Wisdom' as a 'general capability' inviting an intriguing dialogue with the whole curriculum. In the Australian Curriculum, there are three cross-curriculum priorities which have national, regional or more global significance. Surely Catholicity is Catholic education's cross-curricular priority, and one that articulates well with the others given the vision and voice of Pope Francis on recognition of indigenous peoples, inter-faith dialogue and ecological conversion.

Aboriginal and Torres Strait Islander Histories and Cultures	national focus
Asia and Australia's engagement with Asia	regional focus
Sustainability	global focus
Catholicity	universal focus

As a curriculum planning tool, the refreshed online RE Curriculum in the Australian Curriculum format enables RE pedagogical planning, formative assessment in schools and fully aligned Religious Literacy Testing. In October 2015 at the National Gathering of Leaders of Religious Education and Faith Formation there was acknowledgement of the Tasmanian model of RE Curriculum online in the Australian Curriculum's format project as a model worthy of investigation.

At the level of explicit curriculum delivery, the Tasmanian RE curriculum provides an immediate and practical means to integrate RE with the wider Australian curriculum. As young people experience it in their timetables, the curriculum is compartmentalised into rarely connected parcels of information. student-directed inquiry and integrated studies tend more to be primary level approaches but can be very fruitful in secondary contexts. Though they are capable of synthesizing or interrelating knowledge, there are few opportunities to integrate the learning into their own worldview or search for enduring meaning. This surely impairs the retention and comprehension for learning. The

Australian Curriculum despite its worthy intentions for integration also struggles to do so in a substantial way that is not contrived by content (Gilbert, 2012).

I am currently teaching a year 9 History class focusing upon Australians in World War I (History ACDSEH096, 2013) and an RE class focusing on the Synoptic Gospels (Good News for Living-TCREK042, 2014). Without parachuting Jesus into Suvla Bay or the Somme, there are obvious opportunities for extending and deepening the learning of both the RE and History curricula for my classes by:

- Meditating on the horror of war and 'man's inhumanity to man' by reading Wilfred Owen's poem *Anthem for Doomed Youth* and counter-pointing the Stations of the Cross.
- Examining the image of Simpson and his donkey used on the 'Values for Australian Schooling' poster (2004), comparing it with the Good Samaritan story (Lk 10:25-37), and whether the poster glorifies war like WWI recruitment posters.
- Searching out similarities regard the changing social standing of women during WWI and provoked by Jesus' actions in provocative Gospel accounts (Jn 8:1-11; Lk 7:36-50).
- Debating if human beings tend to infighting and rivalry by researching how the Conscription debates in 1916-17 exacerbated deep sectarian divisions between Catholics and Protestants and how Jesus subverts such ethnic or cultural rivalries as between Israelites and Samaritans.

Any one of these cross-references will link to the deepest human reasons for schooling.

2. Wisdom Pedagogy and General Capability of Wisdom

Examining Judeo-Christian sources from scripture (Proverbs 8: 22-31; 1 Cor 12) and tradition can reveal a learning methodology relevant to unit planning, pedagogy choices and even the formation of leaders and teachers. Wisdom pedagogy is a formulation being experimented upon in Tasmania under the inspiration of Dr Drasko Dizdar, a theologian supporting educational projects and ministries at the Tasmanian Catholic Education Office. In Drasko's formulation of the gifts of the Holy Spirit there is an implied developmental sequence towards fuller transformation and maturity. Initially the learner experiences a sense of awe, which inevitably and logically inspires a reverent respect for whatever it was that had inspired the sense of awe, which builds a capacity for heartfelt commitment, strength and courage to receive one's very being and discover one's own human identity; which becomes the basis for the pursuit of knowledge, the development of understanding and the capacity for discernment. The process of formation within the dynamics of schooling is often contained in curriculum and syllabus statements that focus too narrowly on and detail the acquisition of knowledge and understanding. Yet a wider sense of these words is that they are integrally part of the 'sevenfold gift' of the Holy Spirit, the gift of wisdom, enabling the conversion, transformation and full flourishing of the whole person. Unless knowledge, understanding and discernment are held in creative and dynamic relationship with the Spirit's gifts of awe, reverence and courage, the learner will often not be personally engaged in the pursuit of knowledge, understanding and discernment, and will be impeded in their formation in wisdom as a human being fully alive (John 10:10). A Wisdom Pedagogy urges attention to both the ontological gifts (awe, reverence, courage) and the epistemological gifts (knowledge, understanding, discernment) – and RE classes, and indeed lessons in any learning area, will be more effective when both dimensions are attended to. The wise teacher, that hopefully all of us recall from our childhood, got this right: they acknowledged the whole person before them and modelled their own awe, reverence and courageous commitment for their subject before engaging the epistemological pursuit of knowledge, understanding and discernment.

Alongside the Australian Curriculum's seven General Capabilities (ACARA, 2015), the Tasmanian online RE curriculum (curriculum.catholic.tas.edu.au) includes a General Capability of Wisdom defined in terms of the gifts of the Holy Spirit [*Catechism of the Catholic Church,* §1831]:

> Wisdom capability begins with awe which forms a basis for respect, leading to personal courage and social commitment. This in turn grounds knowledge and understanding of ourselves, our world and to the degree we can ... the mysteries of life. This progressive process arrives in discernment of truth, beauty and goodness (Tasmanian Catholic Education Office, 2015).

While the Australian Curriculum's seven General Capabilities are well developed with key ideas, learning continuums and expansions for learning areas, a General Capability of Wisdom is still propositional and awaits work to do similar expansions.

To give an example of what I mean by Wisdom Pedagogy, I can mention a few strategies I have used this week while preparing Year 10 students for an exam on ethics in their last week of classes:

- **Awe:** contemplating embodiment, we sat in the sun in a prayer circle near the chapel, and slowed our breathing, attending to the way the sun played its light with colours on our closed eye-lids.

- **Reverence:** as the angelus bell rang though the school we interrupted our conversation on nuclear weapons to recall and reflect in silence on all those non-combatants who have fallen in war.
- **Courage:** explaining St Thomas Aquinas' Natural Law teleological premises I asked a confident class member to stand on a desk, and then asked the class 'what is Callan for?' leading to nervous laughter, increasingly brave questioning, and ultimately such purposes as 'life', 'love', 'work', 'worship' and 'reproduction'.
- **Knowledge:** I created a revision video introducing ethics and ethical approaches (Brennan, 2016) and encouraged them to depth their own knowledge by watching it on their devices in their own time. This is a pedagogical application called Flip Learning which sees the classroom as an unlikely place for imparting depth knowledge but a great space to engage, enable, differentiate and motivate learners to be active learners (Institute of Teaching and Learning Innovation, 2016).
- **Understanding:** the complex philosophical paradox of moral relativism (absolutist in defending non-absolutism) was explored by performing a short scripted role-play several times.
- **Discernment:** using a disciplined and respectful dialogue process in small groups I told them the true story of a man with a degenerative illness actively planning suicide, and in dialogue we weighed up the appropriateness of proportionalist, utilitarian and situationalist approaches.

Not just relevant to religious education but to all subject areas, and for that matter for the formation of teachers, a General Capability of Wisdom proposes a sequence which asserts learning commencing with the ontological elements of 'awe and wonder', 'reverence' and 'courage' before the epistemological learning of 'knowledge', 'understanding' and 'discernment' take hold of the imagination of learners. Here is the priority of listening-in and attending to the learner's experience but it is also the conclusion of the debates of past religious educationalists between a life experience or shared praxis approach or an educational outcome based approach (Ryan, 2007, p. 143). What will be the design of teacher training and formation that enables the next generation of teachers of all subjects, including RE, to open-up the awe, reverence and courage of inquiry in their students?

3. The Catholic curriculum project

The Tasmanian Catholic Education Office commenced an action research project in 2014 and brought seven schools into dialogue about 'the Catholic Curriculum'. The schools in the project were not seeking one prescription of what made a curriculum 'catholic' but were researching the impact of Catholicity as an integrating idea for both the implicit curriculum of their Catholic school's identity and culture and the explicit curriculum of learning areas. These school project reports describe innovations which include whole school and subject area approaches which explored how Catholicity 'permeates' (Ryan, 2005, pp. 136-8) the whole and the specific elements of their project. Acknowledging the D'Orsas' work (Catholic Curriculum: a Mission to the Heart of Young People, 2012) and efforts made in Queensland Catholic Education, the Tasmanian Catholic Curriculum project has become a means to engage schools in action-research exploring the implications of a rich and inclusive definition of Catholicity for their formal and informal curriculum. Religious educators and leaders who are interested to read these Action Research Project Reports can contact the Tasmanian Catholic Education Office in Hobart.

Some Tasmanian schools had chosen an ecological lens to their Catholic curriculum projects and were greatly encouraged by the publication of Pope Francis' encyclical *Laudato Si'* (in June 2015). They engaged with Catholic Earthcare and its ASSISI animation model (Catholic Earthcare, 2016) as a constructive and effective means of whole school integrated planning and creative development. For example, quite independently and at different ends of the island, two primary schools, Sacred Heart, Geeveston (Catholic Earthcare, 2014) and St Peter Chanel, Smithton, explored whole school ecological projects to engage their students within a range of curriculum areas and integrate them with Catholic faith and the traditions of the local aboriginal communities, their histories and cultures (ACARA, 2015).

4. The Make Jesus real (MJR) project

MJR is a values education project utilised in every primary school in Tasmania. Its purpose is to develop and nurture a student's imitation of Jesus, encouraging them to see Jesus in the everyday, in the way they 'greet, treat and speak to' others and in an 'attitude of gratitude' to life in the classroom, the yard and the home. The project, begun in the 1990s by Peter Mitchell, has spread in popularity throughout many Australian dioceses (Tasmanian Catholic Education Office, 2016). Mitch and the team worked closely with Garratt Publishing to develop a new *Make Jesus Real Student Journal* published early in 2016 and Garratt Publishing are delighted that it is attracting popular use and some international interest. The resource aimed at year 5-6s includes sayings of Jesus, statements of Pope Francis, catch-phrases and simple prayer forms all intended to be easy to remember.

Two schools quite independently developed 'Be-Attitudes' in response to MJR and its implications for integration of Catholicity throughout their school culture. A primary school in Launceston, Sacred Heart Catholic School and St Aloysius College (K-10) at Kingston, integrated MJR with their school behavioural and cultural goals. This meant for both schools that their affirmation of student happiness and wellbeing and positive school behaviours (e.g. be respectful) was promoted in a common language of gratitude and positive regard, in newsletters, posters and awards, all explicitly linked to Christ's beatitudes drawn from the Sermon on the Mount (Mt 5:1-12) of mercy, gentleness, peace-making and justice (Sacred Heart Catholic Primary School, Launceston, 2015).

Towards an integrated RE

If the church wants to engage today's young people, it must listen-in to the thoughts and passions they utter in their own words. For bishops, Catholic school principals and teachers and leaders of religious education, a critical moment has arrived. This moment invites them to refresh for plausibility a curriculum which is attractive to young minds and hearts and a wise pedagogy that engages young people, body and soul. Refreshed RE classes will be grounded in an integrated awe of God in creation, inspired by the Spirit to contemplation and conducted in the company of Jesus. This Jesus is not lost in history but is a mystery who loves us – a listening, merciful God incarnated into our human struggle to find peace and joy. Efforts to instill a wholistic definition of Catholicity and to utilise integrated and balanced pedagogies will enhance what has always been the best gift of RE in Catholic schools – the Risen Christ's Kingdom way of mercy, justice and peace. This integrated way imitates Jesus the teacher who always modelled the gift of 'listening-in' for the language of the people he met and taught.

REFERENCES

ACARA (2008, December 8). *Melbourne Declaration on educational goals for young Australians*. Retrieved December 30, 2015, from Australian Curriculum Assessment and Reporting Authority: http://www.curriculum.edu.au/verve/_resources/National_Declaration_on_the_Educational_Goals_for_Young_Australians.pdf

ACARA (2013). *History ACDSEH096*. Retrieved from Humanities and Social Sciences/7-10 History/Year 9/Historical Knowledge and Understanding/World War I (1914-1918). ACDSEH096: http://www.australiancurriculum.edu.au/humanities-and-social-sciences/history/curriculum/f-10?layout=1#cdcode=ACDSEH096&level=9

ACARA (2015). *Aboriginal and Torres Strait Islander histories and cultures*. Retrieved from The Australian Curriculum: http://www.australiancurriculum.edu.au/crosscurriculumpriorities/aboriginal-and-torres-strait-islander-histories-and-cultures/overview

ACARA (2015). *General Capabilities Overview*. Retrieved from Australian Curriculum: http://www.australiancurriculum.edu.au/generalcapabilities/overview/introduction

Arbuckle, G. (2014). *Catholic identity or identities*. Minnesotta: Liturgical Press.

Brennan, T. (2016, November 10). *Ethical approaches*. Retrieved from YouTube: https://youtu.be/Hn4wJ-yh_NE

Catholic Earthcare (2014). *Sacred Heart Geeveston participates in ASSISI Pilot School Project Tasmania*. Retrieved from Catholic Earthcare: http://catholicearthcare.org.au/2015/01/sacred-heart-geeveston-participates-assisi-pilot-school-project/

Catholic Earthcare (2016, October 25). *Catholic Earthcare ASSISI Project*. Retrieved from Catholic Earthcare: http://catholicearthcare.org.au/project/assisi-resources/

Crowther, F. (2016). Developing teachers' pedagogical gifts - the most important leadership challenge of our times. *Australian Educational Leader, 38*(3), 14-18.

Delio, I. (2005). *The humilty of God: a Franciscan perspective*. Cincinnati, Ohio: Franciscan Media.

Delio, I. (2014). *The unbearable wholeness of being* (2nd ed.). New York: Maryknoll, Orbis Books.

D'Orsa, J. & D'Orsa, T. (2012). *Catholic Curriculum: a Mission to the Heart of Young People*. Mulgrave, Victoria, Australia: Garratt Publishing, Broken Bay Institute Mission and Education Series.

Francis, P. (2014, May 8). *Rome Reports*. Retrieved May 31, 2014, from Pope's Mass: Sometimes the Church's bureaucracy distances people from God: http://www.romereports.com/pg156762-pope-s-mass-sometimes-the-church-s-bureaucracy-distances-people-from-god-en

Gilbert, R. (2012, August). *Curriculum Planning in a Context of Change:*. Retrieved from Victorian Curriculum and Assessment Authority: http://curriculumplanning.vcaa.vic.edu.au/docs/default-source/resources-page/curriculum-planning-literature-review.pdf?sfvrsn=6

Groome, T. (1998). *Educating for life: a spiritual vision for every teacher and parent*. Allen, Texas, USA: Thomas More.

Hattie, J. (2008). *Visible learning: A synthesis of over 800 meta-analyses relating to achievement*. New York: Routledge.

Institute of Teaching and Learning Innovation (2016). *What is the Flipped Classroom?* Retrieved from University of Queensland: http://www.uq.edu.au/teach/flipped-classroom/what-is-fc.html

Kelly, A. C. (2010, December 1). *The Exegete and the Theologian: is collaboration possible*. Retrieved October 24, 2014, from Australian eJournal of Theology: http://aejt.com.au/__data/assets/pdf_file/0014/301046/7.AEJT10.24_Kelly_ExegeteandTheologian_Formatted.pdf

Long, M. R. (2016, August 16). Retrieved from Catholic Outlook: http://catholicoutlook.org/bishop-vincent-long-ofm-conv-delivers-2016-ann-d-clark-lecture/

Martin, I. S. (2016, June 2). *Pope Francis tells priests mercy is a verb not a noun*. Retrieved from Crux Now: https://cruxnow.com/church/2016/06/02/pope-francis-tells-priests-mercy-is-a-verb-not-a-noun/

McBrien, R. (1994). *Catholicism*. New York: HarperCollins Publishers:.

National Catholic Education Commission (2009, February 12). *Accreditation Policy*. Retrieved December 18, 2015, from National Catholic Education Commission: http://www.ncec.catholic.edu.au/index.php?option=com_content&view=article&id=25:religious-education-accreditation-policy&catid=20&Itemid=120

Ryan, M. (2005). *Foundations of religious education in Catholic schools: an Australian perspective*. Thomson Social Science Press.

Ryan, M. (2007). *A Common search: the history and forms of religious education in Catholic schools*. Hamilton, Queensland: Lumino Press.

Ryan, M. (2014). *Religious education in Catholic schools*. Hamilton, Queensland: Lumino Press.

Sacred Heart Catholic Primary School, Launceston (2015, October 29). *Newsletter*. Retrieved from Sacred Heart Catholic Primary School, Launceston: http://sacredheartl.tas.edu.au/files/9114/4609/2525/29October2015.pdf

Tasmanian Catholic Education Office (2014). *Good News for Living- TCREK042*. Retrieved from Religious Education: Good News for Living / Year 9 and 10 / Knowledge and Understanding / TCREK042: http://curriculum.catholic.tas.edu.au/Browse?a=RE&a=E&a=M&a=S&a=H&a=G&a=ENB&a=CNC&a=da&a=dr&a=ma&a=mu&a=va&a=DI&a=DE&a=HPE&y=9&y=10&y=10A#page=2

Tasmanian Catholic Education Office (2015). Retrieved from Tasmanian RE Curriculum Good News for Living: http://curriculum.catholic.tas.edu.au

Tasmanian Catholic Education Office (2016). *Make Jesus Real*. Retrieved from Catholic Education Office: http://catholic.tas.edu.au/our-schools/curriculum/making-jesus-real

Timperley, H. (2011, October). *A background paper to inform the development of a national professional development framework for teachers and school leaders*. Retrieved December 29, 2015, from aitsl: http://www.aitsl.edu.au/docs/default-source/default-document-library/background_paper_inform_the_development_of_national_professional_development_framework_for_teachers_and_school_leaders

West, A. (2016, August 24). 'Historic Catholic synod to discuss married priests, women deacons slated for 2020' [Audio Podcast]. Retrieved from ttps://radio.abc.net.au/programitem/pgXK6Dp9J6?play=true

Tony Brennan has been a religious educator and RE curriculum leader for twenty-five years in Hobart, Tasmania. He served at the Tasmanian Catholic Education Office as Team Leader for Mission and Religious Education from 2012 to 2016. With his team in 2014, he relaunched the Tasmanian Religious Education *Good News for Living* RE Curriculum (2005) by creating an online version in the format of the Australian Curriculum (curriculum.catholic.tas.edu.au). Tony is married and has three young adult kids – he's a poet and songwriter. While writing this chapter, Tony has been teaching RE to Year 9s and 10s at Mackillop Catholic College on Hobart's eastern shore.

Correspondence to:
Email: tonybrennan2315@icloud.com
32 Wentworth Street, South Hobart 7004

Chapter 18

Curriculum Focus

Finding and Implementing Aboriginal and Torres Strait Islander Themes in Religious Education in Armidale Diocese: A Journey of Discovery and Reconciliation

Lee Herden

CHAPTER 18

In beginning this reflection on strategies to assist teachers of religious education identify ways that will help them integrate a genuine Aboriginal and Torres Strait Islander perspective in religious education, that is respectful of individual spiritualties and seeks to find intercultural dialogue, it is important to spend some time establishing three critical practices to ensure a good chance of success. These three practices have been identified by trial and error over nearly two decades of working in this area in the Armidale Diocese. There are, however, three practices that are transferable across Aboriginal and Torres Strait Islander nations, Australian states, dioceses, parishes and schools.

The first of these practices is to be able to answer the questions *'Who are you? Where are you from? and Who's your Mob?'* In any work that is trying to make meaningful connections to Aboriginal and Torres Strait Islander themes in RE you need to know the answer to those three questions.

- Who are the Aboriginal and Torres Strait Islander people in your community (school, parish, diocese)?
- What Aboriginal or Torres Strait Islander nations do their families come from?
- On which Country is your school, parish or diocese located?

These three questions are very important in identifying meaningful and sustainable themes and they become critical to developing a recurring theme in RE - that of relationships and the responsibilities within relationships. One of the greatest hurdles that RE teachers and those involved in the planning of RE at a school or systems level face is that of lack of knowledge. The identification of RE themes that will touch the hearts and minds of both Aboriginal and Torres Strait Islander students and those students who are of other backgrounds lies in each teacher knowing their own local story.

The second practice is to use the 'local, state, and national model' of selecting resources and approaches. There continues to be a misunderstanding that all Aboriginal and Torres Strait Islander peoples are the same. This could not be further from the truth. In the Armidale Diocese in which this reflection paper is written, the Diocese coexists on the traditional lands of the Aniawan, Kamilaroi, Ngoorabul, Banbai, Dungatti and Gumbaynggirr and Yukambil. Each of these countries has a unique language, culture and history. To make meaningful connections for students, schools and systems need to know this and begin to source local knowledge that will enable more effective intercultural dialogue. Any gaps in local resources should then be filled with resources from within the state in which the diocese is located and finally national resources should be sourced as a last resort.

The final, and in many ways most critical practice, is to establish meaningful relationships with the local Aboriginal and Torres Strait Islander community including those who belong to the Catholic community. This is often a real challenge as the Aboriginal and Torres Strait Islander people in your community may be strangers to the local worshiping community. However, experience tells us that developing meaningful connections does require effort and a commitment to deep engagement. This paper will explore three major themes that provide a sound basis for intercultural dialogue that will enrich students' understanding of the Christian message in our Australian context. These are reconciliation, relationship and stewardship. These themes have been interwoven in activities and practices developed in the Diocese of Armidale and have subsequently moved practice in all diocesan schools.

The underpinning process that the Catholic Schools Office has used to make connections with these themes is through the

CHAPTER 18

Emmaus Process. This is an action research and formation process that has its roots in the story of the journey to Emmaus on Easter Sunday (Luke 24:13-35). On this journey the followers of Jesus were faced with a problem and were trying to make sense of what they thought they knew about the events that had occurred to their movement and the leader of the movement. In a way they were pondering upon their failure to have seen things correctly. As they journeyed, they encountered a knowledge keeper, who listened to their story and as this knowledge keeper listened he guided them into a deeper understanding by inviting them into a deep relationship, one that was built on trust and journeying with, rather than one that just gave the answers. As the journey continued, the followers of Jesus, the knowledge keeper, began to recognise the gaps in their knowledge and sought understanding and meaning. This resulted in the great 'aha' moment when they realised that they had not been seeing things properly as they didn't have all the pieces of the story. All of a sudden it all made sense and was crystal clear. Once they understood the story they were filled with great energy and resolve and rushed back to the others in Jerusalem to put into practice all they had learnt.

This model of finding out what you don't know and understand is a beginning step in the process of identifying Aboriginal and Torres Strait Islander themes in RE. For Aboriginal and Torres Strait Islander people the sense of who they are and how they are connected is very important as are relationships they have with each other, the land and the creator. From our local journey, the CSO Armidale has identified the following practises as very effective in getting school communities to begin to raise awareness about the local Aboriginal and Torres Strait Islander communities:

- Provision of a memorial plaque for each school naming the local Aboriginal Country on which the school coexists.
- A practice of Welcome to or Acknowledgement of Country at all significant school events
- Provision of a comprehensive explanation of why Acknowledgement and Welcome are significant to Aboriginal and Torres Strait Islander people and why Country is so important.

These three things may seem insignificant but it is critical that teachers of RE have a good understanding of the meaning and significance of Country. For Aboriginal and Torres Strait Islander People the connection to land can be linked very closely to the Israelites connection to the Promised Land. For Aboriginal and Torres Strait Islander People, 'Country is a living entity with a yesterday, today and tomorrow, with a consciousness, and a will toward life. Because of this richness, Country is home, and peace; nourishment for body, mind, and spirit; It is heart's ease.'

This understanding of the significance of Country provides a springboard for teachers to develop the theme of stewardship, relationship and reconciliation at what could be called an entry level. This means that the teacher, once they have gained an awareness of who the local First Nations People are and have an understanding of why Country is important, can begin to make linkages to Scripture and the local RE curriculum. In Armidale diocesan schools the religious education coordinators have carriage of this in each of our diocesan Catholic Schools. As a collaborative project they examined each unit of our RE curriculum K-10 and identified each unit's major themes and then located Aboriginal and Torres Strait Islander resources to support that theme. This publication is reviewed annually and is published on the CSO Armidale website. This resource provides a platform for teachers not only of RE but of other KLAs to introduce meaningful connections to Aboriginal and Torres Strait Islander Spiritualties that meld seamlessly with our own Catholic world view. The RECs in each school take on the role of mentors to help teachers to link each RE theme with an appropriate resource or strategy within each unit of work. These resources and strategies range from the use of appropriate language, local stories that help explore a piece of Scripture or doctrinal point, to art works that lead students into the Christian story.

A cautionary tale

This process of introducing Welcome and Acknowledgement of Country as a first step in the process of introducing Aboriginal and Torres Strait Islander themes into the RE space was not without its challenges. When the global introduction of Welcome was introduced in our schools we realised, too late, a fatal flaw in our relational planning. We presumed that our clergy were on board with the whole Aboriginal and Torres Strait Islander reconciliation movement. After all, the Australian Bishops had released social justice statements and Pope John Paul II had been unequivocal in his support of Aboriginal spirituality. We had even produced a world first for the Eucharistic Congress in the development of a Catholic liturgy wholly in an indigenous language and not a direct translation, in 1973. It was with a shock that our beautifully prepared bookmarks with our words of acknowledgement were hurled back at us by an enraged senior cleric who let us know in no uncertain terms that he didn't believe in that sh*t and it would not be happening in his school or parish! We quickly learnt the hard lesson that not all our clergy were on side. It should be acknowledged at the same time that there were clergy who were extremely supportive of this work but even they acknowledged that some members of the clergy made progress at times slower than it need be.

The CSO has gently spent time building up the understanding of the clergy so that they are in a better position to support the work of schools in identifying and using appropriate Aboriginal and Torres Strait Islander resources to enrich all students' understandings. It is now normative for our significant events in the Cathedral to have an Acknowledgement or Welcome to Country and a growing practice in our diocesan parishes for school events.

In the Emmaus process two things occur that result in the deepening of understanding. Firstly, there is a journey. In the case of those journeying away from Jerusalem it was from the known to the unknown. The second is that of encounter and relationship. In the story the two followers of Jesus encountered an apparent stranger but they entered into a dialogue relationship with that stranger in a place that was not their own. They were 'off Country' as it were. In developing their relationship what changed? An obvious question but a deep one. For the followers of Jesus, they were able to see things from a different perspective and were able to process the current reality because they had the gaps in their understanding filled.

With process in mind the CSO Armidale has developed an immersion process that takes staff on an Emmaus journey. This journey explores for our staff the religious themes of reconciliation, relationship and stewardship on a deeply personal level. This process of immersion invites and at times cajoles staff to board a bus and leave their known world and understandings and journey into a different landscape. Our major program is called Let's Talk Dahwunda. Which means let's talk on country. The immersion program uses the Emmaus story as its cornerstone but then adds relevant scripture as the journey unfolds. The journey begins in the white world with a reflection on the Emmaus story and the notion of travel, pilgrimage and change. This section is led by a white male. The journey then leaves the built up world and the participants are taken into the landscape visiting an ancient art site and reflecting on the ingenuity and skills of the local people. The idea of Aboriginal people as skilled agronomists, engineers, botanists, builders, and farmers is explored and the notion of the wandering nomad is challenged and the skilfulness of stewardship of the landscape and relationship with the land is introduced and explored.

The journey then moves to the Myall Creek Massacre site. This site is on the national heritage register and is the heart and soul of the Reconciliation movement in Australia. At this site participants hear the story of how 28 innocent Aboriginal people were murdered on 10 June 1838 by a group of white men intent on claiming land for a wealthy squatter. As the tale is told the participants view of the frontier wars begins to change and the facilitators encounter a range of emotions from the participants, the most common of which is anger that they did not know the story. The group then walks the memorial pathway where stone plaques recount the tale until they arrive at the memorial rock which overlooks the distant massacre site. It is in this silence that the Catholic notion of reconciliation and healing is explored and the knowledge sharers begin to transition from a white male to two Aboriginal women.

The journey continues onto Moree and the participants hear firsthand from Aboriginal people the stories of living in the camps, of being registered under the noxious weeds act until 1967. They hear how Aboriginal people were restricted in movement and every step of their lives controlled by officials. They hear the stories of hope in the Freedom Rides and the stories of courage by Aboriginal and non-Aboriginal people who stood up for the rights of Aboriginal people. Again the participants gain a sense of knowledge gaps and begin to yearn for knowledge.

The bus moves on to Lightning Ridge and Goodooga. Where the participants are now instructed by Aboriginal knowledge sharers. Here the participants are taken to ancient sites thousands of years old and hear stories of creation and are taught the message of these stories and instructed on how these moral tales are like the ones in the Bible. They are shown how the Aboriginal people of that land knew the land intimately and how and why they care for it. Depending on the group the participants are given the opportunity to share in men's or women's business. Each night as in the Emmaus story the knowledge givers share a meal and chat and talk about the meaning of relationship, stewardship and reconciliation from their perspective. The participants are taken care of by the community of Goodooga which is a mostly Aboriginal community with no services other than a school, post office and hotel. For the first time many of the participants are welcomed into an Aboriginal person's home. Often the host will give up their beds so the participants have a bed rather than having to sleep on the floor.

The most challenging day lies in Brewarrina where the participants hear about the Mission System and the Brewarrina Mission. At this mission terrible things took place, the people from many nations were brought to a new land on the Mission away from their countries. They were forbidden to speak their own languages, or sing their own songs, or engage in their practices or their own customs. Our key scripture passage here reflects on

Psalm 137, By the Rivers of Babylon. The Mission is on the banks of the Barwon River, so the scripture comes alive for the participants out of lived experience.

Let's Talk Dahwunda uses its facilitators to walk alongside each participant and help fill in missing pieces in their understanding and for each person that is different. The process challenges people but it builds a deeper understanding of how the Aboriginal and Torres Strait Islander people of our area view the world through Aboriginal and Christian eyes. They experience what relationship and reconciliation look like from an Aboriginal and Torres Strait Islander perspective. The three key questions of *'Who are you? Where are you from? and Who's your Mob?'* gain a new clarity. For Aboriginal and Torres Strait Islander peoples, relationship to Country and Family is the heart of reconciliation and stewardship. No book can tell you this with the same integrity and insight as listening to the 'heart stories' from an Elder sitting by a camp fire under the Milky Way.

Cautionary tale two

Now this may seem to be a wonderful week long journey and you think this would be great let's do it! Our learnings are that for any immersion program to be successful the organisers of it need to follow a few simple but critical steps.

- Build a relationship with your local Aboriginal and Torres Strait Islander Elders. This takes time. Talk to them about their story.
- Start small. With the help of your local Elders find out about the local places of significance to the people in your community. This might be an art site, a mining site, a meeting place, a scar tree, a massacre site or a burial

ground. By working with the Elders and building up trust they will guide you in finding the right places.
- Go with the Elders to plan the journey which may only be a day trip and reflect on where the Scriptures can be introduced.
- As the trust grows you may find that the local community will share some more with you especially if they can see that it is helping the Spiritual lives of their children.

Two diocesan schools have used this model to develop a one-day program for staff and a three day program for students. Both programs relate to developing the themes of reconciliation, stewardship and relationships.

It is not always possible to go on immersion for a range of reasons and it could be argued strongly that a local immersion is always a first preference, then another in your state and then nationally. With this in mind the CSO has developed four multimedia resources to provide a platform to explore the three themes being focused on in this paper. The resources have been developed in conjunction with our local communities and are gifted to the country so that the story of reconciliation, relationship and stewardship can be told from a Catholic perspective. The resources are known as Soundtrails and use GPS to allow students and staff to walk around the sites to hear the sounds and voices of people telling the stories from their perspective again based on the Emmaus Process but on location through the use of smart devices. The beauty of the system is that it allows a class teacher anywhere in the country to download the Soundtrail via an app so that students can hear the story and see the graphics, photographs and maps without having to be physically present at the site. The work of exploring the religious themes of reconciliation, stewardship and relationship is then left to individual teachers. In this way the reality of a lived suffering and a practical voice for reconciliation and social justice can be enhanced at all grade levels.

The Soundtrail project

The Soundtrail project is free for use by anyone. The four developed by the CSO Armidale are:

The Moree Bore Baths (https://soundtrails.com.au/moree-freedom-rides/). This resource explores how many country towns routinely banned Aboriginal people from a range of places – pubs and clubs, certain areas of town, shops, restaurants and swimming pools. In Moree this legal discrimination provided the perfect target for the Freedom Riders from Sydney University who were travelling around NSW to highlight the injustice being meted out to Aboriginal people. They won a famous victory; entry into the pool. That day showed Aboriginal people that colour didn't have to hold them back.[1] This resource helps to explore the themes of inequality and the harm that not respecting the dignity of the human person can have on our relationships with those in our communities. The Moree Aboriginal Cemetery (https://soundtrails.com.au/diggers-moree-aboriginal-cemetery/). This resource explores some of the stories of the remains of 220 Aboriginal people. Most here were buried between the years of 1940 and 1968. This was at the height of segregation, opportunities for Aboriginal people were few and lives were carefully controlled by the white authorities. Beneath the plinths, the plaques and headstones stories from this time are revealed: the Archdeacon who determined Aboriginal people ought to have their own burial section; the young Aboriginal men who signed up to fight for king and country, who these extraordinary men were and the life to which they returned and the treatment they received as second class citizens.[2] This resource can provide a means to explore the importance of relationships and the corporal work of mercy to bury the dead.

The Walgett Freedom Rides (https://soundtrails.com.au/freedom-rides-walgett/). Walgett was where the Freedom Ride exploded onto the national stage. It was the place, as Charlie Perkins said, which was the first big test of moral courage. 'Are you with it? Or are you against it? Are you fair dinkum? Or are you not?' It was the place where the Freedom Rides students found the discrimination they were looking for and an Aboriginal population who were prepared to stand up and fight. It provides an opportunity to explore the themes of standing up for beliefs when you could get seriously hurt if not killed. It was here in Walgett that Australia's unfair treatment of its First Peoples hit the national press. The refusal by the Walgett RSL to admit Aboriginal Diggers to its membership provides a wonderful opportunity to explore the Gospel story of you who are without sin throw the first stone (John 8:7). As one Freedom Rider would later say, 'As city dwellers, we just had no idea of this hostility. It was palpable. You could feel it.'[3]

The Tenterfield Story (http://soundtrails.com.au/web-app/new-england-and-north-west-nsw-region/uralla/tenterfield-soundtrail/). This is a gentler Soundtrail that explores the history of a town. It looks at the contribution of the local Aboriginal people and to the role of the Church in that community. It looks at the role the town played in Federation and of course the famous Tenterfield Saddler for Peter Allen fans. But it allows teachers to lead students on a journey to reflect on the continuity of God's presence in the landscape and to reflect on how good relationships help to build community.

Added to this list is a poignant Soundtrail that was not developed by the CSO but the Bingara community of NSW. It tells the story of the Myall Creek Massacre, which was referred to earlier in the paper (http://soundtrails.com.au/web-app/new-england-and-north-west-nsw-region/gwydir/myall-creek/) 'The path to the future passes through the past. In 1838 at Myall Creek, shed blood went into the ground and cried out for justice. Just this once, justice was done. Just this once there was a linking of hearts, from the Governor of the day to the convict who refused to participate: a shaft of light powerful enough to penetrate the deep darkness of our national denial. The Myall Creek story did not finish then. The story is still being written and we are all part of it. In 2000 at Myall Creek, hundreds witnessed a descendant of the massacred embrace a descendant of the perpetrators, watched by a descendant of those who had brought them to justice. In that embrace, we who were condemned by our actions to be restless wanderers in this land, were welcomed home to country at last.'[4] This is a powerful resource to explore healing and reconciliation and the themes of courage for standing up for the rights and dignity of each human person.

The resources above have been designed to connect a strong RE theme with other curriculum areas, and to also provide teachers of RE and other subjects the opportunity to bring a truly Catholic focus to the curriculum, rather than leaving it just to the RE world. They help explore who we are, where we come from and where our country is. By now you will have begun to pick up the strong theme of story and in developing any Aboriginal and Torres Strait Islander RE themes it is about the story and not 'stuff'. It has taken the CSO a number of years to build up relationships and understandings to move us to where we are currently. However, we did also explore other avenues to open up Aboriginal and Torres Strait

Islander themes in RE. And the paper will now explore two of these. The first is through art and the second is through dedicated Aboriginal and Torres Strait Islander retreats.

Who do you say I am?

When we began the journey of exploring themes the first major theme was that of 'Who do you say I am?'. Sadly, in 2000, when we started this journey very few of us could answer the question. Our research and conversations led us to discover the lands that made up our diocese and the CSO commissioned the artist Richard Campbell to create an Aboriginal map depicting the diocese. This map now forms a pivotal feature in the CSO and helps us tell the story of who we are, who our mobs are and where our country is. This single art work stimulated diocesan schools to explore how art can pick up and enhance RE themes. St Joseph's Warialda commissioned a piece to tell the story of St Mary MacKillop and their school. While St Joseph's Walgett has commissioned a local artist to paint a mural throughout the school which focuses on the theme of reconciliation and forms a visible connection to the story of that place as does the memorial garden to deceased members from the Aboriginal community within the school which is done in a style which honours the dead in stark contrast to the story of the Moree cemetery.

Finally, the CSO conducts an annual retreat for all our Year 8 to Year 12 Aboriginal and Torres Strait Islander students. This program is called Warramalya, and is held off country and it explores with the students their own Aboriginal and Torres Strait Islander spiritualties in a Catholic context. This is done with the help of local Catholic Elders. The program seeks to develop their understanding of who they are and how they can be both Christian and

Aboriginal or Torres Strait Islander and that the Gospel message is for them as well as non-Aboriginal people. The CSO has been working very closely with the Missionary of God's Love Sisters and Brothers to provide the Catholic spiritual formation for this retreat program. The students, as teenagers, explore traditional views of morality and become aware that in many cases they are similar to Catholic morality.

The retreat allows the students to explore the things that erode who they are and their relationships with family. This program has been running successfully for almost a decade and we have been able to track the levels of engagement in faith and education of the students over time. Many of the students who have finished schooling have entered university or TAFE and are pursuing rich career paths that allow them to express their Aboriginal and Torres Strait Islander heritage as well as their Catholic/Christian heritage with pride.

In looking back at almost two decades of trying to make real links between Aboriginal and Torres Strait Islander themes in RE, we have sought to make these links living and transformative. Are we there yet? Most certainly not! Are all the staff and schools on board most certainly not! But what has changed is a growing cultural competence in being able to incorporate such themes not only in RE but across the whole curriculum. We now have all our schools able to name the Country on which they are located and to include Welcome or Acknowledgement of Country. We have staffs who can now talk to Aboriginal and Torres Strait Islander people as equals and we are continuing to grow our knowledge of the past so that we can understand the problems of today. It is through this understanding that we are able to confidently move forward to close the gap of spiritual ignorance. We have a greater understanding of the importance of relationships as a system, we have a growing understanding of what true reconciliation is and we are better able to articulate it. As a system of schools we want to share our learnings and our mistakes so that all Australians can share in the Spirit that has always dwelt in this land.

Bird, Deborah Rose, 'Nourishing Terrains: Aboriginal views of landscapes and wilderness'. Australian Heritage Commission, 1996, https://www.environment.gov.au/system/files/resources/62db1069-b7ec-4d63-b9a9-991f4b931a60/files/nourishing-terrains.pdf

NOTES

1. CF https://soundtrails.com.au/moree-freedom-rides/
2. CF https://soundtrails.com.au/diggers-moree-aboriginal-cemetery/
3. CF https://soundtrails.com.au/freedom-rides-walgett/
4. CF http://soundtrails.com.au/web-app/new-england-and-north-west-nsw-region/gwydir/myall-creek/

CHAPTER 18

Lee Herden is Head of Mission and Evangelisation for the Catholic Schools Office in Armidale. He has held positions of principal, assistant principal and religious education coordinator in schools in the Diocese of Armidale as well as being a member of the CEC NSW Education Policy Committee and Chair of the Mission and Identity Working Party for the CECNSW.

Lee has qualifications in education, religious education, TESOL, Indonesian and holds the Croce Pro Eccelsia for services to the Church. Lee works in collaboration with Aboriginal and Torres Strait Islander communities in the diocese to build reconciliation and understanding. Lee has presented papers on this work internationally.

Correspondence to:
Email: lherden@arm.catholic.edu.au

www.ingramcontent.com/pod-product-compliance
Lightning Source LLC
Chambersburg PA
CBHW070933230426
43666CB00011B/2422